MR BALFOUR'S
POODLE

MR BALFOUR'S POODLE

An account of the Struggle between the House of Lords and the Government of Mr Asquith

ROY JENKINS

BLOOMSBURY READER

LONDON · NEW DELHI · NEW YORK · SYDNEY

This electronic edition published in 2012 by Bloomsbury Reader

Bloomsbury Reader is a division of Bloomsbury Publishing Plc,

50 Bedford Square, London WC1B 3DP

Visit www.bloomsburyreader.com to find out more about our authors and their books
You will find extracts, author interviews, author events and you can sign up for
newsletters to be the first to hear about our latest releases and special offers

First published by Heinemann 1954
Second edition published by William Collins 1968
This paperback edition first published in 1989

ISBN: 978 1 4482 0320 8
eISBN: 978 1 4482 0287 4

'The House of Lords is not the watchdog of the constitution; it is Mr Balfour's poodle.'

David Lloyd George, 1908

Contents

Author's Foreword

The primary purpose of this book is not to draw parallels or to prove a thesis. It is merely to describe a short period of parliamentary history which is sufficiently near to be within the memory of many, although not of the author, but sufficiently far away for many of its political habits and subjects of controversy to be unfamiliar and worth recalling.

The author is particularly indebted to Mr. P. M. Williams, Fellow of Nuffield College, and Mr. Anthony Elliott, both of whom read the manuscript, and made suggestions upon it, and to Mr. Michael Alison, who gave much help in compiling the reference and biographical footnotes.

R. H. J.

London, October, 1953

I

The Liberal Triumph

A rthur Balfour resigned on December 4, 1905. He was the
last Prime Minister to surrender office to his opponents
without a previous defeat at the polls. But there was nothing
quixotic about his action. No election was necessary to confirm
the belief, held alike by himself, his supporters and the Liberal
Party, that his Government had lost the confidence of the electorate; and the growing insubordination of a large section of his
own party provided an added incentive to lay down the cares of
office.

So persistent, however, was Balfour's reputation for political
subtlety that his resignation before an election was widely
regarded as a move of surpassing dexterity. 'The Liberal Press,'
in the words of Campbell-Bannerman's biographer,ⁿ 'was
almost unanimous that Mr. Balfour's resignation was the last of
the tricks in the long game of skill, and earnestly exhorted the
leader to beware.' And there can be no doubt that Balfour,
apart from his other pressing reasons for resignation, was

1

influenced by the hope that office before the election might prove an embarrassment to the Liberal Party. With a conceit not unusual in those whose party had been long in office, he believed that the country might recoil from the reality of a Liberal Government, headed by Campbell-Bannerman, who was reputed to be unpopular, and made up of the inexperienced men who surrounded him. At the same time Balfour hoped that the rifts in the Liberal Party, particularly that between the 'Liberal Imperialists' and the radical wing, might prove to be as deep as, or deeper than, those which reft his own party. Might not Asquith and Grey and Haldane make great difficulties about serving under the Campbell-Bannerman who had talked of 'methods of barbarism'?

The first point proved to be quite invalid, or at any rate to be submerged beyond recognition in the great wave of revulsion against the Unionist Party which swept the country. The second was more substantial, but not quite sufficiently so for any of Balfour's hopes to be fulfilled. There were unusual difficulties in Cabinet-making, which arose, nominally at least, from questions of persons rather than of policy. Campbell-Bannerman arrived from Scotland on the morning of Balfour's resignation, and immediately saw Asquith and Grey. He found them 'very amiable and reasonable on the subject of Ireland and ... there was no difference worth thinking of between him and them'.[b] But later that day Sir Edward Grey again called to see Campbell-Bannerman and informed him that, unless he took a peerage and left the leadership in the Commons to Asquith, he (Grey) would not feel able to serve. Grey's attitude was that he felt in any event unhappy about joining a Government of which Lord Rosebery was not a member, and that his doubts could only be allayed if one of his own close associates were to be the principal spokesman in the House of Commons; and he had a quite genuine reluctance for office at any time.

This was a heavy problem for Campbell-Bannerman. He wished Grey to have the Foreign Office, and the latter's defection would leave the Government weak in that field in which it was thought most likely to be distrusted. On the following day, that on which he kissed hands as Prime Minister (in the event he left the King's presence having forgotten to perform the actual ceremony), his difficulties were eased by Asquith's unconditional acceptance of the Exchequer; the new Chancellor was clearly not a full party to the ultimatum. But the crisis was not over. On Wednesday, December 6, Asquith came up from Hatfield where, most surprisingly as it now seems, he was the guest of Lord Salisbury, and made a personal appeal to the Prime Minister to solve the difficulty by going to the Lords. Later on the same day Lady Campbell-Bannerman also arrived in London, and more decisively advised 'no surrender'. After that the Prime Minister was in no doubt that he would not give way.

Grey remained adamant for another twenty-four hours, but Haldane was already wavering, and by midnight on the Thursday they had both decided to come in. After this the filling of offices proceeded normally. The lists were ready for the King on the Sunday, and Ministers received their seals on Monday, December 11. It was a day of very thick fog, and the members of the new Government began their periods of office, inauspiciously if not symbolically, by losing their way and groping for up to an hour around the Mall and the incomplete Victoria statue in front of the Palace.

It is now a platitude to say that it was a strong and unusually able Government. On the one hand were men of the outstanding intellectual ability of Asquith, Haldane, Morley, Bryce,[1] Birrell,[2] and Samuel. On the other, at least equally outstanding, but possessed of gifts differing very widely, not only from those of the 'intellectuals', but from those of each other, were Grey, Lloyd George, Mr. Churchill, and the Prime Minister himself. In many quarters the new Ministry was greeted with enthusiasm, and nowhere with derision. On the day after the publication of the lists *The Times* succeeded in confining its general remarks on the subject to a sullenly non-committal: 'Sir Henry Campbell-Bannerman has succeeded in forming his Ministry';[c] but in its immediately previous issue it had remarked: 'In some respects the Cabinet as it now seems likely to be composed is the best that could be made with the available material, but the Irish appointments[3] ... inspire the profoundest distrust, and the position in the House of Lords is excessively weak.'[d] As, however, *The Times* clearly regarded a record of never having made a partisan speech (in which respect, apparently, only Lord Elgin,[4] the Colonial Secretary, was without blemish) and a promise never to

---

[1] 1838–1922. Later 1st Viscount Bryce of Dechmont. Liberal member for Tower Hamlets, 1880–85, and for Aberdeen, South, 1885–1907. Chancellor of the Duchy of Lancaster, 1892–94. President of the Board of Trade, 1894–95. Chief Secretary for Ireland, 1905–7. H.M. Ambassador in Washington, 1907–13. Historian and Constitutionalist.

[2] 1850–1933. Liberal member for Fifeshire, West, 1889–1900, and Bristol, North, 1906–18. President of the Board of Education, 1905–7, and Chief Secretary for Ireland, 1907–16. Author and literary critic.

[3] James Bryce as Chief Secretary and the Earl of Aberdeen as Lord Lieutenant.

[4] 1849–1917. Victor Alexander Bruce, 9th Earl of Elgin and Kincardine. Succeeded to title, 1863. Viceroy of India, 1884–89. Secretary of State for the Colonies, 1905–8.

4

implement Liberal legislation as the best qualifications for Liberal Ministers, its strictures need not be taken too seriously.

The Cabinet certainly had no excessive radical bias. Campbell-Bannerman, like Gladstone, had moved to the left as he had grown older but, the more so perhaps because he had a possibly difficult election to face, he had not allowed his personal predilections unduly to influence his choice of a Government. Sir Robert Reid,[5] who, as Lord Loreburn, went to the Woolsack, and Sinclair,[6] the new Secretary of State for Scotland, closely represented his own point of view. Ripon,[7] Morley, Herbert Gladstone,[8] and Bryce all represented the Gladstonian tradition, which, in so far as it associated them with Home Rule, was thought to make them left-wingers. And there was Lloyd George, together with, as it transpired, that pillar of conservatism, John Burns.[9] On the

---

[5] 1846–1923. Liberal member for Hereford, 1880–6, and for Dumfries, 1886 1905. Solicitor-General, 1894. Attorney-General, 1894 95. Lord Chancellor, 1905–12. Created a baron, 1906, and an earl, 1911.

[6] 1860–1925. Liberal member for Forfarshire, 1897–1909. Created 1st Lord Pentland, 1909.

[7] 1827–1909. Son of Lord Goderich, later 1st Earl of Ripon, sometime Prime Minister. Member for Hull, 1852–59, when he succeeded to title. Secretary of State for War, 1863, and for India, 1866. Lord President of the Council, 1868 73. Viceroy of India, 1880 84. First Lord of the Admiralty, 1886. Secretary of State for the Colonies, 1892–95. Lord Privy Seal, 1905–8. Created 1st Marquess of Ripon, 1871. Converted to Roman Catholicism, 1873.

[8] 1854–1930. Created 1st Viscount Gladstone, 1910. Youngest son of W. E. Gladstone. Liberal member for Leeds, West, 1880–1910. First Commissioner of Works, 1894–95. Chief Liberal Whip, 1899–1905. Home Secretary, 1905–10. Governor-General of South Africa, 1910–14.

[9] 1858 1943. President of the Local Government Board from 1905 until February, 1914. President of the Board of Trade from February, 1914,

other hand there was the triumvirate of Asquith, Haldane and Grey, two of whom were placed in dominating positions, old Sir Henry Fowler,[10] and a number of essentially 'moderate' men like Crewe,[11] Tweedmouth,[12] Elgin (whose moderation, as we have seen, was beyond reproach), and Carrington.[13] Compared with its Conservative predecessor, the new Cabinet was of course inexperienced, but a party cannot reasonably hold power for seventeen out of twenty years and then attack its rival for the gross fault of appointing men unversed in the ways of office.

The election campaign itself did not begin until after Christmas, but the overture was given at the Albert Hall on December 21, when Campbell-Bannerman deployed his party's line

---

utbreak of wauntil his resignation at the or in August, 1914.

[10] 1830–1911. Created 1st Viscount Wolverhampton, 1908. Liberal member for Wolverhampton, East, 1880–1908. President of the Local Government Board, 1892–94. Secretary of State for India, 1894–95. Chancellor of the Duchy of Lancaster, 1905–8.

[11] 1858–1945. Robert Ottley Ashburton Crewe-Milnes, 1st Earl of Crewe. Created 1st Marquess, 1911. Lord Lieutenant of Ireland, 1892–95. Lord President of the Council, 1905–8 and 1915–16. Lord Privy Seal, 1908 and 1912–15. Secretary of State for the Colonies, 1908–10. Secretary of State for India, 1910–12. President of the Board of Education, 1916. H.M. Ambassador in Paris, 1922–28.

[12] 1849–1909. Edward Marjoribanks, 2nd Lord Tweedmouth. Liberal member for Berwick, 1880, until he succeeded to the peerage in 1894. Chief Liberal Whip, 1892–94. Lord Privy Seal, 1894–95. First Lord of the Admiralty, 1905–8. Lord President of the Council, 1908.

[13] 1843–1928. 2nd Lord Carrington. Succeeded to title, 1868. Created 1st Earl of Carrington, 1895, and 1st Marquess of Lincolnshire, 1912. Liberal member for Wycombe, 1865–68. President of the Board of Agriculture, 1905–11. Lord Privy Seal, 1911–12.

of argument. The main stress was on free trade, but there was a careful reference to Ireland—'those domestic questions which concern the Irish people only and not ourselves should, as and when opportunity offers, be left in their hands'—some strong but vague phrases about the land, which was to be 'less of a pleasure-ground for the rich and more of a treasure-house for the nation', an announcement that instructions had already been given to stop the importation of Chinese coolies into South Africa, a promise to deal with trade union law, and suggestions of reform of the poor law and of the rating system, and of measures to deal with unemployment. There were varied reactions to the speech, from Liberal enthusiasm to the distaste of the City, which summed up the programme, 'in its practical way', as *The Times* said, 'as robbery of everyone who has anything to be robbed of'.[e]

Early in the New Year the election addresses were appearing. Balfour told the electors of East Manchester that 'there are many things still obscure in the long catalogue of revolutionary changes advocated by new Ministers, but some things are plain enough—Home Rule, disestablishment, the destruction of voluntary schools, and the spoliation of the licence-holder have lost none of their ancient charm in the eyes of Radical law-makers'. He then spoke oracularly of tariff reform, dealt patronisingly with the Government's foreign policy, regarding it as a weak imitation of his own, and ended with a few gibes on the subject of Cabinet splits. Joseph Chamberlain, in his appeal to the electors of West Birmingham, described the new Administration as 'essentially a Home Rule and Little Englander Government'. He then turned to a forthright statement of the case for tariff reform, and devoted the remainder of his address to this.

Asquith, in East Fife, wrote an address almost exactly complementary to that of Chamberlain. He berated the late Government for incompetence and then passed to a close-knit argument of the case against tariff reform. He concluded with a reference to 'the measures of social and domestic reform' which ought to occupy the new Parliament, and his attitude to which he promised to develop elsewhere during the campaign. Sir Edward Grey, in Berwick-on-Tweed, was more specific. He opened with a statement of his belief in the virtues of free trade, but devoted much less space to the issue than did Asquith. Next came a reference to Chinese labour in South Africa—rather surprisingly from the least partisan of the new Government's principal Ministers—and then a promise of Irish reform accompanied by a specific statement that no measure such as those attempted in 1886 or 1893 would be introduced without another appeal to the electorate.

The Prime Minister, at Stirling, after a passing reference to the Chinese labour issue, attacked the late Government for its partisan legislation, designed to propitiate those interests which supported it rather than to benefit the country, for its refusal to deal seriously with the social problem, and for its gross extravagance. This last point, on which he laid great stress, is a strong reminder of how different, on budgetary matters, was the old Gladstonian radical tradition, which Campbell-Bannerman represented, from the new one which Lloyd George was soon to develop. He then turned to what he called the positive side of his case, by far the greater part of which was occupied by a long restatement of the argument for free trade. His conclusion was more general, and suggested, although it did not specify, a heavy programme of legislative measures: 'Should we be confirmed in office it will be our duty, whilst holding fast to the time-honoured principles of Liberalism—the principles of peace, economy, self-government, and civil and religious liberty—and whilst resisting with all our strength the attack upon free trade, to repair so far as lies in our power the mischief wrought in recent years, and, by a course of strenuous legislation and administration, to secure those social and economic reforms which have been too long delayed.'

It is clear from these addresses and from the spate of oratory which accompanied them that, apart from the fiscal controversy, which was outstandingly predominant, and apart also from purely ephemeral issues, attention was most concentrated on the legislation which would follow from a Liberal victory, which both sides discussed in terms of measures dealing with education, licensing, the land, and possibly Home Rule.

The extent of the Government's victory became known only gradually, for polling in the different constituencies was then spread over a period of nearly three weeks. But from January 12, which brought the news of the first gain at Ipswich, and January 13, when Arthur Balfour lost his seat in a spate of Government successes in Manchester and the North-West, right through to the end, the story was always the same. Supposedly safe Conservative seats crumbled, and Government victories in the most unlikely places brought into the House of Commons a flood of new Liberals who had been fighting almost without hope. There were in all 377 Liberal members. And with them, in some ways an even greater sensation, came fifty-three Labour members, twenty-four of whom were closely allied to the Liberal Party, with the other twenty-nine elected under the auspices of the Labour Representation Committee; but even these twenty-nine had in most cases escaped Liberal opposition in the constituencies. The Irish produced their usual contingent of eighty-three, which, added to the Liberal and Labour strengths, gave a total of 514 members who, in a straight clash with the

Tories, might be expected to support the Government. The Opposition numbered 132 Conservatives and twenty-five Liberal Unionists, or, by an alternative method of classification, 109 Tariff Reformers, thirty-two upholders of Balfour's tortuous view, eleven 'Free Fooders' and five who were uncertain. The Government's normal majority was 357—a preponderance unequalled since the Parliament of 1832—and the Liberal Party's majority over all other parties was 129.

The election brought into the House of Commons more than 300 men who had not been members before, and many of these came from a social background which had not previously supplied more than a handful of members of Parliament. Obviously this applied with especial force to the new Labour members, but the Liberal Party itself was more widely based socially than had ever before been the case. Of its 377 members, which excludes the 'Lib-Labs', sixty-four were practising barristers, twenty-two were service officers, and sixty-nine were in the category attracting the label of 'gentlemen'; all these followed ways of life which had been well represented in previous Parliaments. There were eighty businessmen who had started life in well-to-do circumstances, and another seventy-four who had started from humble conditions. Both these categories had, of course, been represented in previous Liberal parties and in the Unionist Party, but never to this extent. Of the remaining sixty-eight Liberal members, twenty-one were solicitors, twenty-five were writers and journalists, nine were teachers, mostly university teachers, eight were trade unionists, and five were doctors of medicine.[14] In the Conservative and Liberal Unionist parties

---

[14] These are exclusive categories, although many members were, for example, both barristers and Fellows of Colleges, or solicitors and businessmen. In

there were forty-eight 'gentlemen', thirty-two service officers,[15] twenty-six businessmen who had started life in easy circumstances, and thirteen who were self-made (the majority of these were Liberal Unionists); in addition there were six journalists and writers, five solicitors, three dons, two doctors of medicine, and one accountant. So far as the main categories are concerned, it is clear that the relative strength of barristers, solicitors, journalists and writers, and businessmen was greater on the Government side of the House, although only in the case of self-made businessmen was the preponderance overwhelming; officers and country gentlemen were much more heavily represented on the Opposition side.

In so far as their occupations are a guide, the Liberal members of this Parliament had clearly not become a true cross-section of the nation (no parliamentary party is ever likely to be quite this), but they had for the first time become a real cross-section of the middle and upper classes; and as such they were much more broadly based than their opponents.

This analysis of the social composition of the Parliament may be pushed a little further by a consideration of educational background. One hundred and twenty-five—a third—of the Liberal members had been to a public school, thirty-two of them to Eton; and 135 to Oxford or Cambridge. Of the Conservatives,

---

these cases they have been classified under what appeared to be their principal occupation.

[15] A great number of Conservative members had one foot in each of these two categories. They held a commission for a few years, and then retired to live as country gentlemen. In these cases, a member is not categorised as a 'service officer' unless he had held a regular commission for ten years or more.

eighty-two—nearly two-thirds—had been to a public school, and forty-five of them to Eton; fifty-six had been to Oxford or Cambridge. The Liberal Unionists had ten (out of twenty-five) who had been to a public school (five to Eton), and twelve who had been to Oxford or Cambridge.

Another question which may be asked about the members of this Parliament is the extent to which they were men of great wealth. In the case of many individuals this is, for obvious reasons, a difficult question to which to reply accurately, but the answer appears to be (the degree of error which may exist should at least be constant for the different parties) that 102 Liberals (27%), forty-six Conservatives (35%), and ten Liberal Unionists (40%) fell within this category. The variation between parties was surprisingly small.

The geographical spread of the Liberal strength also requires analysis, and here it is of interest to make a comparison with the distribution of Labour strength in 1945—the only occasion since 1906 on which a great left-wing majority was elected to the House of Commons. It is a commonly held view that these two majorities were geographically almost identical. Mr. Churchill, for example, expressed in 1949 his belief that 'the House returned in 1906 represented ... more or less the same slice of the population, the people who elected it coming very largely from the same homes and from the same areas, as does this majority today'./ This view contained a great deal of truth although there were certain striking exceptions to the general proposition. The Liberals of 1906 were very strong in Scotland, Wales, East Anglia, the West Country and most of the industrial areas. They were fairly strong in London and most of the mixed agricultural and residential counties of England. They were weak only in the Universities, in Northern Ireland, and in Birmingham, Liverpool

12

and Sheffield. Labour strength in 1945 was less evenly spread. It was greater in London and most of the industrial areas than that of the Liberals had been, but overwhelmingly low in the Highlands, rural Wales and the West Country, and substantially low in most English agricultural and residential districts. Conservative successes in industrial seats were somewhat more frequent in 1906 than in 1945, but in the small country town, the mixed county division, or the seaside resort the Liberal candidate of 1906 was a much stronger contestant than his Labour counterpart of thirty-nine years later.[16]

---

[16] A detailed comparison between the results of 1906 and those of 1945 is given in appendix A.

II

The New Government
and the Lords

S ir Henry Campbell-Bannerman had taken office with a big
majority against him in both Houses of Parliament. He had
been able, quickly and sensationally, to rectify the position in the
Commons, but in the Lords the strength of the Opposition
remained unimpaired. At the beginning of the first session of
the new Parliament there were 602 peers, including twenty-five
bishops, who were entitled to take part in the proceedings of the
House of Lords. Of these only eighty-eight described themselves
as Liberals—and this number included a few who were as uncertain in their support of the Government as was Lord Rosebery.
One hundred and twenty-four were Liberal Unionists and 355
were Conservatives, leaving only thirty-five, including fourteen
bishops and a number of Princes of the Blood, who gave themselves no political label. The nominal Unionist majority was 391,
a preponderance still more decisive than that of the Government

in the new House of Commons.

This degree of Tory dominance in the Upper House was of comparatively recent growth. At the beginning of the eighteenth century, in a House of about 150 members, there had been a small Whig majority, which Queen Anne, in the year 1711 and on the advice of the 1st Earl of Oxford of the Second Creation,[1] had turned into a still smaller Tory majority by the simultaneous creation of twelve peers for the specific purpose of securing a Government majority for the ratification of the Treaty of Utrecht. A few years later, after the death of the Queen, this change was reversed by a more gradual programme of creations, and the Whigs resumed control. And they continued to hold it until the accession of the younger Pitt to the premiership. Thereafter, creations proceeded on a hitherto unknown scale. During Pitt's seventeen years as Prime Minister, 140 ennoble-ments took place. The Tories were not merely given a majority in the House of Lords, as had happened to themselves and the Whigs on previous occasions. They were built up into a position of ascendancy from which they could not be dislodged save by a policy of creation on an almost revolutionary scale.

It has been suggested that Pitt's creations brought a new social and occupational element into the House of Lords. In a passage in *Sybil*, Disraeli tells of his having 'created a plebeian aristocracy and blended it with the patrician oligarchy. He made peers of second-rate squires and fat graziers. He caught them in the alleys of Lombard Street and clutched them from the counting-houses of Cornhill.'[a] But this view is hardly borne out by a consider-ation of the individuals concerned; for the most part they were

---

[1] Six years later this was made one of the counts for his impeachment, a still worse fate than that suffered by the 1st Earl of Oxford of the third Creation.

Tory country gentlemen, and very reactionary ones. They and their first heirs provided the greater part of the vote against the Reform Bill in 1831.

The next important change in the party balance in the Lords occurred with the secession of the Peelites from the Conservative Party and their gradual move towards alliance with the Whigs. Then, for the first time since the French Revolution, the Tories were almost balanced by a combination of Whigs and Peelites. This did not last long. The natural tendency of an hereditary House to move to the right soon came into play, and by the closing stages of the Crimean War the Lords were in opposition to the Aberdeen Coalition. A few years later, in 1860, there was a majority of eighty-nine against the second reading of Gladstone's Paper Duty Bill. But this measure, which was supported only very lukewarmly by the Prime Minister, probably attracted more than the normal anti-Government vote into the 'not-content' lobby.[2]

This vote did much to foster the growing radicalism of Gladstone, and this in turn, with its effect upon the development of the Liberal Party, still further increased the Tory bias of the House of Lords. An evenly-balanced Upper Chamber, recruited mainly by the inheritance of titles and partly by the ennoblement of men of great wealth, was possible only so long as the differences between the two parties were more superficial than real or, in so far as they had reality, corresponded only to the difference between one form of wealth and another. The growth of radicalism and of the Liberal hold on the working class inevitably meant the decline of Liberal strength in the House of Lords.

It was quite a rapid decline. In 1868 Lord Granville informed

---

[2] Its rejection had been moved by the normally Whig Lord Monteagle.

the Queen that, excluding the bishops and nominal Liberals who preferred to vote Tory, the anti-Government majority in the Upper House was between sixty and seventy.[b] A few Liberal creations then followed, but they did little more than compensate for defections which were simultaneously taking place. When Gladstone came in again, in 1880, he assembled a Cabinet which with one duke, one marquess,[3] and five earls (of a total of twelve members) should have personally, if not politically, recommended itself to their lordships. But this did not avail. The rate of defection became greater rather than less. Three great magnates who were members of the Government itself—the Duke of Argyll, the Duke of Bedford and the Marquess of Lansdowne—were impelled by the Government's attitude to the Irish land question to join the move to the right. They were followed by others of lesser note during the lifetime of this Government.

These changes were as nothing to the shifting of allegiance which followed the events of 1886, when Home Rule, in Rosebery's words, 'threw the great mass of Liberal Peers into the arms of the Conservative majority'.[c] This marked both a social and a political upheaval. Lord John Manners wrote that 'Gladstone can't find a duke who will allow his wife to become Mistress of the Robes',[d] and the Government vote in the Upper House was reputed to have fallen to thirty. It was seven years before there came a test vote on a major issue, the Home Rule Bill of 1893, and that showed a majority of nearly four hundred— 419 to 41—against the Government. The Liberal Party had taken a decisive turn towards radicalism and it had paid the price of creating a Conservative predominance in the House of

---

[3] Hartington, whose marquessate was a courtesy title and not a peerage.

Lords of a degree never approached before, not even after the creations of the younger Pitt, and which has persisted ever since.

In 1906 it was therefore a House of Lords of which the political shape had been largely formed by the events of 1886 and 1893 that confronted the new Liberal Government. The eighty-eight nominal Liberals, had they been allied with the 124 Liberal Unionists,[4] the sons of men who had followed Hartington and Chamberlain in 1886 or, in many cases, the men themselves, would have been a respectable minority. On their own their only strength was that they were allied to political forces which, in the House of Commons, had just won nearly three-quarters of the seats.

To what extent this was to be recognised by the majority of their lordships as a legitimate source of strength and as a reason why they should exercise their own power with circumspection was a question to which an answer was eagerly awaited. It had not been held for many years that the Lords should be indifferent to the opinion of the constituencies as expressed through the House of Commons. Even such a high Tory as Lord Lyndhurst[5]

---

[4] The extent to which Liberal Unionism was a revolt of the Whig magnates in defence of the position of the landlord in Ireland and elsewhere (as well as of Birmingham businessmen against Little Englandism) is indicated by the fact that these 124 included no less than seven dukes (as against sixteen Tory dukes and a solitary, but not very inspiring, Liberal representative in the shape of the Duke of Manchester). Liberal Unionism was also popular amongst the episcopate; of eleven bishops who chose to wear party labels, four, including the Archbishop of Canterbury, called themselves Liberal Unionists.

[5] 1772–1853. Lord Chancellor in Tory Governments between 1827 and 1846.

had declared, in 1858, that 'I never understood, nor could such a principle be acted upon, that we (the House of Lords) were to make a firm, determined and persevering stand against the opinion of the other House of Parliament, when that opinion is backed by the opinion of the people.'ᵉ This statement begged the vital question of who was to decide when the opinion of the House of Commons coincided with the opinion of the people, but it would be difficult to argue that the period immediately following a great electoral victory should not be so regarded; certainly this had been the view immediately after 1832, when the removal of the rotten boroughs—of Croker's 'certain elasticity which acted like springs, and ... prevented violent collision'—gave the problem for the first time a modern form.

In the first session of the 1832 Parliament the Lords had behaved with great restraint. Confronted with the huge Government majority in the House of Commons and chastened by their recent humiliation, they had allowed such controversial measures as the abolition of slavery, Scottish burgh reform and the Irish Church Bill to pass. In Peel's words: 'The business was got through, but only because that which we prophesied took place; namely that the popular assembly exercised tacitly supreme power; that the House of Lords, to avoid the consequences of collision, declined acting upon that which was notoriously the deliberate judgment and conviction of a majority.'ᶠ But as soon as the Government's 'honeymoon' period was over and there were indications that it might be losing some support in the country, the Tory peers began to regain their courage. In the 1834 session an Irish Tithes Bill was rejected and a measure for the prevention of bribery at elections was so amended as to cause its withdrawal by the Government. After the interlude of the Peel Government of 1834–35, the Lords proceeded to deal in a still more brutal fashion with bills sent up from the Commons. Both the English and the Irish Corporation Bills were smothered in amendments, and the Irish Tithes Bill went down for a third time. So sweeping, indeed, was their policy of rejection or wholesale amendment that when, in 1836, they allowed the passage of a bill permitting persons accused of felony to be defended by counsel (which had already been passed on three occasions by the Commons) it was regarded as a triumph of moderation and a vindication of the liberal sentiments of Lord Lyndhurst, who had at the last moment changed his mind on the issue. And all this occurred when the Tory peers were under what was subsequently regarded as the unusually restraining influence of Wellington's leadership. At times, however, as in the case of the English Corporations Bill, the degree of restraint exercised was so little that even the Tory Opposition in the House of Commons could not subscribe to the demands of the peers; but at least this meant that the Upper House was acting as something more than the servant of the leader of the Opposition in the Commons.

Strong interference by the Lords with Government measures continued so long as the Whig Administration lasted, although the decline in the reforming zeal of the latter naturally tended to lessen the force of the conflict. During the greater part of the life of Peel's 1841-46 Government there was no conflict. It was a Tory Government, and trouble showed signs of arising only when the Prime Minister had quarrelled with his less enlightened supporters on the issue of the Corn Laws. On this occasion Wellington fully acted up to his reputation. He wrote individually to each of the Tory peers, urging them not to oppose the bill, and they accepted his advice.

Between 1846 and 1868 the Tory majority in the House of Lords was smaller than at any other time between 1789 and the present day, and the country was governed by a series of weak Administrations, none of which commanded the support of a straight party majority in the House of Commons. As a result, conflicts between the two Houses were comparatively rare, and most of those which arose were not on matters of major importance. In the case of the principal exception to this rule, that of the Paper Duty Bill of 1860, the effect of rejection on Gladstone may have been great, but that on most people was modified by the limited support which the measure enjoyed in the Cabinet, and the even more limited support which the Cabinet enjoyed in the country. And in the following year, by reverting to the earlier practice of taking all the major financial measures as one, the Chancellor was able to get his Paper Duty provisions through as part of the Finance Bill.

The Reform Bill of 1867 passed the Upper House with little difficulty. Lord Derby had anticipated some trouble, but, except for a few rumblings from such high Tories as Salisbury[6] and Rutland, none developed. The colour of the Government was more important than the content of the bill.

In 1868 the colour of the Government changed, and the Liberals came back with a majority of 112—the strongest party Government for a quarter of a century. Its first major measure was the Irish Church Bill of 1869, which the majority of their lordships vehemently disliked, but to which they gave a second reading by a majority of thirty-three. Thirty-six Conservative peers, led by Lord Salisbury,[7] voted for the bill. Salisbury was no

---

[6] The 2nd Marquess, 1789–1868.

[7] The newly succeeded 3rd Marquess, 1830–1903, who was later three times Prime Minister.

doubt giving effect to a view which he expressed three years later that it was the duty of the Lords to give way 'only when the judgment of the nation has been challenged at the polls and decidedly expressed'.[g] This principle, he thought, was 'so rarely applicable as practically to place little fetter upon our independence'. Certainly he applied the principle very sparingly, and his moderation towards the Irish Church Bill was not repeated for any of the Government's other major measures. The bill to abolish the purchase of army commissions, which had met with bitter Tory opposition in the Commons, was summarily rejected by the Lords; but in this case the Government was able to obtain its objective by administrative action. The Ballot Bill twice failed in the Upper House, and would probably have done so a third time had not Disraeli's caution proved stronger than Lord Salisbury's pugnacity.

This was not the only occasion during this Parliament on which the leader of the Opposition in the Commons tried to exercise a moderating influence on his followers in the Lords. In 1870 a private member's bill to abolish religious tests at the universities, which had received Government support, failed to get a second reading in the Upper House.[8] But a year later Disraeli's influence was strong enough to get a similar measure accepted.

In 1874 Disraeli's second Government came in, and six years of almost complete peace between the two Houses began. But the peace was not quite complete. Even with a Conservative

---

[8] 'Avowedly to regulate that assembly (the House of Lords),' Disraeli wrote to Lord Stanhope, 'by the prejudices, or convictions, of the University of Oxford, cannot be wise.' (Moneypenny & Buckle, *Disraeli*, vol. v, pp. 124–5.)

Government in office the House of Lords retained a touchiness on any question affecting the ownership of land, which led to its refusal to accept one or two measures or parts of measures.

The return of the Liberals in 1880 provoked more serious differences between the two Houses, although until the Reform Bill of 1884 these were not on the scale which had marked the life of Gladstone's previous Administration. Both the Irish Land Bill of 1881 and the amending Arrears Bill of the following year were seriously altered in the Upper House, but when the Government remained firm, the peers' amendments were mostly not pressed. The big dispute of this Parliament arose over the Reform Bill of 1884. On second reading the Conservative Opposition in the Commons divided in favour of a reasoned amendment that an extension of the franchise should be accompanied by redistribution, but on third reading there was no division. In the Lords an amendment to the motion for second reading in similar terms to the one which had been defeated in the Commons was carried against the Government by 205 to 146. The Prime Minister announced that the bill would be re-introduced in the autumn, and, the Lords having defended their action not so much in relation to the merits of the bill as to their right to force a dissolution on an issue of such importance, the summer saw a bitter Liberal campaign against the composition and powers (but more particularly the former) of the Upper House. Joseph Chamberlain attacked the peers as the representatives of a class 'who toil not, neither do they spin', and John Morley announced that their House must be either 'mended or ended'. By the autumn both sides were more disposed to compromise, and an arrangement was arrived at by which the Lords passed the Franchise Bill and the Government followed it up with a redistribution measure.

The events of 1886, despite the great change in the allegiance of peers to which they led, gave the Upper House no work to do. The Whigs and the Chamberlainites who destroyed Gladstone's majority in the House of Commons and threw out the first Home Rule Bill did its job for it. And the six years of Conservative Government which followed were, as always, a period of rest for their lordships. But the formation of the Liberal Government of 1892 brought them back to the centre of the stage. Their first task was to dispose of the second Home Rule Bill, and they did this with alacrity, and by the biggest anti-Government majority ever recorded. The Government was fresh from a victory (although not a great one) at the polls, and Home Rule had certainly figured prominently in the electioneering of both major parties; but the Lords excused themselves from the influence of these considerations by saying that there was no majority in Great Britain for the bill, and that full weight must be given to the wishes of the 'predominant partner'. The Prime Minister was for dissolving, but he was apparently unable to carry his Cabinet with him.

In the view of Lord Rosebery it was not so much by the rejection of the Home Rule Bill (he was influenced by the absence of an 'English' majority in the House of Commons) as by the destruction of Asquith's Employers' Liability Bill in the following session that the House of Lords showed its extreme partisanship. The loss of this bill, combined with the drastic alteration of the Parish Councils Bill, which gave Gladstone the subject for his last speech in the House of Commons, provoked Lord Rosebery, when he became Prime Minister, to devote most of his public speeches to the subject of the relations between the two Houses, and to address urgent memoranda to the Queen on the same point.

'When the Conservative Party is in power,' he wrote in April, 1894, 'there is practically no House of Lords: it takes whatever the Conservative Government brings it from the House of Commons without question or dispute; but the moment a Liberal Government is formed, this harmless body assumes an active life, and its activity is entirely exercised in opposition to the Government.... I cannot suggest any remedy,' he rather helplessly continued, 'for any remedy which would be agreeable to the House of Commons would be revolting to the House of Lords, and any remedy which would please the House of Lords would be spurned by the House of Commons'.[h]

Seven months later he was writing again on the subject and announcing: 'Nearly if not quite half of the Cabinet is in favour of a Single Chamber. The more prominent people in the Liberal Party appear to be of the same opinion'.[i] But the defeat and resignation of the Government occurred before even a declaratory resolution against the Lords which had been proposed was carried. Indeed both Morley and Harcourt (whose controversial Finance Bill of 1894 had passed the Commons by a majority of only twenty, and escaped unscathed) thought that the Lords had not exposed themselves sufficiently to make an attack practicable.

During the ten years of Unionist Government which followed Rosebery's resignation in 1895, the Upper House was more than usually quiescent. The tendency for the peers to be more active against a Liberal Government, which we have seen growing and which reached its culmination after 1906, was accompanied by an equally strong tendency for their repose to be more complete when a Government of the right held office.

The most controversial legislative proposal of these ten years was the Education Bill of 1902. It marked a sharp departure of policy on an issue which aroused very strong sectarian feeling; it was bitterly opposed by the Liberal Party (although supported by the Irish Nationalists); it was introduced against the known wishes of an important section of the Government; and it was passed by a House of Commons in the election of which a discussion of the issue had played no important part. Yet the only reaction of the House of Lords was to insert into it an amendment, moved by the Bishop of Manchester, which made it a still more extreme and partisan measure. Many of the same considerations applied to the Licensing Bill of 1904; and the Government had by then begun to lose very heavily in the bye-elections. But the Lords passed it with alacrity.

It was therefore difficult to predict with any degree of certainty the treatment which the new Liberal Government would get from the Upper House. Obviously there could be no doubt of the power of the Lords to wreck a Liberal legislative programme; and equally obviously there could be no hope that throughout the whole life of the Government this power would remain entirely unused. But on the basis of what had been said and what had been done in the past there was good room for hope that at least the earlier and electorally more discussed measures of this enormously popular Government would be allowed to pass. If the electorate were not held to have spoken with a clear voice in 1906, the test of audibility must have been an unusually severe one.

Nevertheless, too much reliance could not be placed on precedent. The growing partisanship of the House of Lords made a more extreme course of action a possibility. This view was strengthened by Balfour's ominous remark, made in an election speech at Nottingham on January 15, 1906, that it was the duty of everyone to see that 'the great Unionist Party should still control, whether in power or whether in Opposition, the destinies of this great Empire'. Asquith interpreted this as a direct call to the House of Lords to redress the balance of the constituencies. To what extent this was so could not be determined at the time, but the unfolding of events quickly provided the answer.

III

Ploughing the Sands

The king's speech at the opening of the 1906 session forecast a great crop of legislation. Twenty-two bills in all were promised, but pride of place was clearly to be given to the Education Bill. This was the only measure which achieved a paragraph of its own in the Gracious Speech. 'A Bill will be laid before you at the earliest possible moment,' it ran, 'for amending the existing law with regard to Education in England and Wales.' A Trades Disputes Bill, to rectify the position created by the Taff Vale and *Quinn* v. *Leathens* decisions, and a Plural Voting Bill, to prevent the owners of numerous property qualifications from exercising more than one vote, were the other contentious measures. The remainder could be described, at least for the purpose of reassuring the King, as 'uncontroversial' or 'departmental'.[a]

The Education Bill, which, while leaving intact the administrative structure created by the Act of 1902, sought to remedy some of the more keenly-felt grievances of the Noncom-formists,[1] was introduced into the House of Commons by Augustine Birrell on April 9. It was greeted with a storm of protest, not only from the Unionist Party but also from the Anglican and Roman Churches. The Bishop of London took the Albert Hall for a demonstration of opposition.

In the meantime, with the two Houses in recess, Balfour and Lansdowne were using the interval to discuss the general strategy of dealing with Liberal legislation. Lansdowne had prepared a memorandum a few days before Parliament rose in which he set forth a proposal for closer liaison between the leaders of the Opposition in both Houses.

'The Opposition is lamentably weak in the House of Commons and enormously powerful in the House of Lords. It is essential that the two wings of the army should work together, and that neither House should take up a line of its own without carefully considering the effects which the adoption of such a line might have upon the other House. In dealing with such Bills as the Trades Disputes Bill or the

---

[1] Its objects have been described more fully by Asquith as 'to put an end to the dual system created by the Act of 1902; to secure that every school maintained out of rates and taxes should be under the exclusive management and control of the representative local Authority; to abolish religious tests and the obligation to give denominational teaching, in the case of all teachers appointed by the Authority, and paid out of public funds; to permit "Cowper-Temple" teaching in the "provided" schools; and in the "transferred" schools to give facilities for special denominational instruction, but not by the regular teachers'. (Earl of Oxford: *Fifty Years of Parliament*, vol. II, p. 43.)

Robartes Bill, I cannot help thinking that the leaders in the House of Commons should have before them at the very outset a definite idea of the treatment which the question might receive in the event of either of those Bills coming before the House of Lords later in the session. Similarly, there are very important questions which will from time to time be debated in the House of Lords and which should be discussed with an eye to the effect of the discussion upon the temper of the House of Commons. At this moment no such machinery as I have suggested is in existence.

'Mr. Balfour might like to call a few of us together after the holidays in order to consider the procedure which might be adopted.

'I should myself be inclined to propose that he should institute a not too numerous Committee, including, say, four or five members of each House, who might meet in his room at the House of Commons, once a week at least, for an exchange of ideas....

'As a House of Lords' delegation I would suggest Lord Halsbury, Lord Cawdor, Lord Salisbury, and myself.'[2b]

Balfour replied on April 13, hedging on Lansdowne's specific proposal, but going on to a general analysis of the position.

'The real point is, as you truly say, to secure that the party in the two Houses shall not work as two separate armies, but shall co-operate in a common plan of campaign. This is all-important. There has certainly never been a period in

---

[2] Not a markedly moderate selection.

our history in which the House of Lords will be called upon to play a part at once so important, so delicate, and so difficult.... I conjecture that the Government methods of carrying on their legislative work will be this: they will bring in Bills in a much more extreme form than the moderate members of their Cabinet probably approve: the moderate members will trust to the House of Lords cutting out or modifying the most outrageous provisions: the Left Wing of the Cabinet, on the other hand, while looking forward to the same result, will be consoled for the anticipated mutilation of their measures by the reflection that they will be gradually accumulating a case against the Upper House, and that they will be able to appeal at the next election for a mandate to modify its constitution.

'This scheme is an ingenious one, and it will be our business to defeat it as far as we can.

'I do not think the House of Lords will be able to escape the duty of making serious modifications in important Government measures, but, if this is done with caution and tact, I do not believe that they will do themselves any harm. On the contrary, as the rejection of the Home Rule Bill undoubtedly strengthened their position, I think it is quite possible that your House may come out of the ordeal strengthened rather than weakened by the inevitable difficulties of the next few years.

'It is, of course, impossible to foresee how each particular case is to be dealt with, but I incline to advise that we should fight all points of importance very stiffly in the Commons, and should make the House of Lords the theatre of compromise. It is evident that *you* can never fight for a position which *we* have surrendered; while, on the other hand, the fact that we have strenuously fought for the position and been severely beaten may afford adequate ground for your making a graceful concession to the Representative Chamber.'[c]

Lord Lansdowne's biographer comments that the 'only flaw' in this exposition was the view that the Upper House might emerge from the struggle with its position strengthened; but others may take the view that Balfour's calm assumption that half the Liberal Cabinet did not believe in the measures which he himself found distasteful—a not untypical Tory illusion—was equally dangerous.

The Education Bill, after its second reading on May 10, was bogged down in committee for twenty parliamentary days and its emergence at the end of this period was only secured by an extensive use of the guillotine. It was given a third reading on July 30 by 369 to 177, but the shadow of the House of Lords lay heavily upon the debate on this occasion. J. A. Spender, in his life of Campbell-Bannerman, has told us that 'Liberals, seeing their overwhelming preponderance in the House of Commons, found it difficult to believe that the Peers would venture even the one stroke (the attack on the Education Bill)....'[d] This may have been the view at the beginning of the session, but it had certainly changed by the time that the bill reached its final stage in the Commons. Balfour, in a famous passage of his speech, expressed his view that 'the real discussion of this question is not now in this House and has not been for some time; the real discussion must be elsewhere; and everybody is perfectly reconciled to the fact that another place is going to deal with large tracts of the Bill which we have not found time even to touch upon … it is in the highest degree improbable that the Bill will come back in the shape in which it leaves us. The honourable Gentleman who has just sat down controverted a prophecy of mine that the Bill will never pass. Does he think the Bill will ever pass? I do not think he or anybody else does.'ᵉ Birrell was naturally more cautious, but his words implied no great confidence in the future of the bill, while a Liberal backbencher, the radical and Anglo-Catholic Charles Masterman,³ said that 'they were sending the Bill to another place knowing that large changes would be made there and were prepared to accept at least a certain number of those changes.... It was sad to think that this great democratic movement ... should have as one of its first results the fact that 2,500,000 Catholics and a more indefinite number of Liberals were saying: "Thank God for the institution of the House of Lords." 'ᶠ

If in fact this was the position (which is very doubtful), it was for Arthur Balfour and not only for their lordships that God should have been thanked; for it was his views rather than those of the peers themselves which determined the future course of the bill's progress. He advised them to let it through on second reading, which they did without a division. He drew up and presented a detailed memorandum setting forth a whole table of amendments, which they accepted, so that the bill returned to the Commons in a quite unrecognisable form. What had been intended as a measure of relief for the grievances of

³ Member for West Ham (North). Later Parliamentary Secretary, Local Government Board, 1908–9. Under-Secretary, Home Office, 1909–12. Financial Secretary to the Treasury, 1912–14, and Chancellor of the Duchy of Lancaster (and a member of the Cabinet), 1914–15. His High Anglican views made him unhappy about the Bill, but, unlike his Roman Catholic colleague Hilaire Belloc, not to the extent of causing him to with hold his vote.

Nonconformists became a bill which would place the upholders of denominational teaching in the schools in a position still more favourable than that which they enjoyed under the 1902 Act. The behaviour of the House of Lords in regard to this bill, even more perhaps than on any other occasion, fully justified the taunt of Lloyd George from which this book's title is taken.

When the bill came back to the Commons, early in December, two courses were open to the Government. They could either attempt to recover their original measure by the long and laborious process of stripping off layer after layer of destructive amendment; or they could take the unprecedented but effective and time-saving course of moving to disagree with the Lords' amendments *en bloc*. The latter alternative was chosen, and despite Opposition protests at the new departure (to which the Government retorted with at least equal force that the extent of the Lords' amendments was also without precedent), the motion was carried by the enormous majority of 416 to 107, the Irish voting with the Government.[4]

A week later the matter again came before the Lords, and Lansdowne moved, and carried by 132 to 52, a motion 'that this House do insist on its amendments to which the Commons have disagreed'. There was a small revolt of the 'moderates' against the official Unionist attitude which led the Duke of Devonshire[5] and Lord Ritchie of Dundee[6] into the Government lobby, but it

---

[4] Their interest in the primacy of the Commons was greater than their dislike of the bill.

[5] The 8th Duke, who achieved his political fame as Lord Hartington.

[6] 1838–1906. Formerly C. T. Ritchie, Conservative member for Croydon. President of the Board of Trade, 1895–1900. Home Secretary, 1900–2. Chancellor of the Exchequer, 1902–3.

did not extend to men such as Lord St. Aldwyn[7] and Lord James of Hereford,[8] who were later to be included in this category. The Archbishop of Canterbury[9] and seven other bishops voted with Lansdowne; with the exception of Dr. Percival of Hereford, who voted with the Government, the remainder abstained.

The deadlock was now complete, the more so because private negotiations had already taken place and failed. There had been several conversations between the Primate and the Prime Minister and a conference attended by Asquith, Crewe, Birrell, Balfour, Lansdowne, Cawdor[10] and the Archbishop had been held on the day before the final vote in the Lords. Both sides had been willing to retreat a little from their public position, but even very substantial Liberal concessions failed to meet the minimum Tory demands. The King had used considerable personal influence to try to bring about a settlement, but it was compromise from both sides, rather than a recognition by the Lords of the relevance of the recent Liberal electoral victory, that he urged.

There was nothing further for the Government to do but to move to discharge the order and abandon the bill. This

---

[7] 1837–1916. Formerly Sir Michael Hicks-Beach. Conservative member for Gloucestershire, East, 1864–85, and Bristol, West, 1885–1905. Chancellor of the Exchequer, 1885–86 and 1895–1902.

[8] 1828–1911. Formerly Sir Henry James. Solicitor-General, 1873. Attorney-General, 1873–74 and 1880–85. Chancellor of the Duchy of Lancaster, 1895–1902.

[9] Randall Thomas Davidson, 1848–1930. Bishop of Rochester, 1891–95, and of Winchester, 1895–1903, Archbishop of Canterbury, 1903–28. Created 1st Lord Davidson, 1928.

[10] 1847–1911. Frederick Archibald Vaughan Campbell, 3rd Earl of Cawdor. Conservative member for Carmarthenshire, 1874–85. First Lord of the Admiralty, 1905. Chairman of the Great Western Railway.

Campbell-Bannerman did in the House of Commons on the day following the vote in the Lords. The enormity of the action of the Upper House in rejecting the much-canvassed, first major measure of a Government elected by a huge majority, whereas four years previously it had let through without a whimper a far more revolutionary and less discussed bill on the same subject, introduced by an old and weak administration, was plain for all to see.

'It is plainly intolerable, Sir,' said the Prime Minister, 'that a Second Chamber should, while one party in the State is in power, be its willing servant, and when that party has received an unmistakable and emphatic condemnation by the country, the House of Lords should then be able to neutralize, thwart, and distort the policy which the electors have approved.... But, Sir, the resources of the British Constitution are not wholly exhausted, the resources of the House of Commons are not exhausted, and I say with conviction that a way must be found, a way will be found, by which the will of the people expressed through their elected representatives in this House will be made to prevail.'[g]

One method by which a way might have been sought was by an immediate dissolution, with a proposal to curb the power of the Lords in the forefront of the Liberal programme. Campbell-Bannerman's biographer tells us that 'a few, a very few, voices' were raised for this, but that 'the great majority' thought that the education issue was not big enough to afford favourable ground from which to force the issue.[h] Another consideration working against dissolution was the comparative poverty of many Government members. They did not want the expense of a second general election, unless it were quite unavoidable, within eleven months. The writer[i] of a contemporary statement of the Liberal case gives considerable importance to this point, and suggests that Balfour depended on it in calculating his risks.

There would have been much to be said for an immediate dissolution. The result would certainly have shown a Liberal majority almost as great as a year previously, and the constitutional issue might well have been resolved before it was allowed to waste away so much of the Liberal strength. Mr. Spender tells us that 'more than once during the subsequent months he (Campbell-Bannerman) was heard to express a doubt whether he had been right in not taking up the challenge and going to the country again in December 1906'.[j]

Had the Lords treated all the major measures of the session in the same way as the Education Bill, the Prime Minister's decision might have been different. But their behaviour towards the Trades Disputes Bill, the loss of which would have caused more popular indignation than the loss of the Education Bill, was more circumspect, although the constitutional case for damage or delay would here have been much stronger.

When the Liberal Government came in there was common agreement amongst its members that a measure was to be introduced to undo the effect of certain recent decisions in the Courts and to restore the presumptive meanings of the Act of 1871. The law of conspiracy was to be relaxed, peaceful picketing was to be legalised, and trade union funds were to be given special protection. So much was agreed; but there was sharp disagreement in the Cabinet as to the method by which the last objective was to be attained. The lawyers, who were very strong both in numbers and in ability, wished to proceed indirectly by restricting the law of agency, while some others wished to give a direct exemption. At this stage the lawyers won, and a bill along their lines was introduced.

This was coldly received by the powerful new Labour group, and one of its members, Walter Hudson, introduced a private member's bill embracing the principle of direct exemption. The Prime Minister listened to the arguments deployed in favour of this bill, and proceeded, without consultation, to accept it on behalf of the Government. The protagonists of the original measure accepted the change with a bad grace, and so (if anything, with a somewhat better grace) did Arthur Balfour. The Opposition divided against neither the second nor the third reading of the bill.

This left Lord Lansdowne with little room for manoeuvre if he was to act in accordance with the principle laid down by Balfour in his memorandum of the previous April: 'It is evident,' Balfour had then written, 'that *you* can never fight for a position which *we* have surrendered.' Lansdowne agreed, and neither a motion of rejection nor an amendment to the bill was put forward in the Upper House, although several peers spoke strongly against its provisions. Lansdowne tried to justify his own position, which even his biographer, Lord Newton, clearly regarded as quite unjustifiable, in the following terms:

'We are passing through a period when it is necessary for this House to move with very great caution,' he said on December 4. 'Conflicts, controversies, may be inevitable, but let us, at any rate so far as we are able, be sure that if we join issue we do so upon ground which is as favourable as possible to ourselves. In this case I believe the ground would be unfavourable to this House, and I believe the juncture is one when, even if we were to win for the moment, our victory would be fruitless in the end. I say then that, so far as I am concerned, I shall not vote against the Bill. I regard it as conferring excessive privileges upon the Trade Unions, as conferring dangerous privileges upon one class and on one class only—privileges in excess of what the most trusted exponents of their views have formerly asked for, privileges fraught with danger to the community and likely to embitter the industrial life of this country; but I hold also that it is useless for us, situated as we are, to oppose this measure.'[k]

There was no suggestion here that it was the duty of the Upper House to hold up the hasty and the ill-considered proposals, and to allow to pass the well-matured, nor even that it was to attempt to judge measures on their merits. The distinction to be made was to be one purely of expediency. If it suited the tactics of the Tory Party for the 'calm judgment' of the House of Lords to be exercised in favour of the worst measure in the world, through it would go, without any delay or hindrance at all. But even from the point of view of the purest expediency Lansdowne was laying down rules of discreet behaviour which it would have been difficult for him to pretend, in subsequent years, that he and his followers were observing.

The Plural Voting Bill, on the other hand, which had been opposed by the Tories in the House of Commons, was treated by the Lords with even less respect than the Education Bill. After a debate lasting little more than an hour and a half it was thrown out on second reading by 143 to 43. Both the mover of the reasoned amendment[11] and Lansdowne himself rested their case

---

[11] Lord St. Aldwyn, whose moderation deserted him on this occasion.

less on the advantages of plural voting, which were difficult to put in a popular form, than on the more sophistical argument that there were a number of anomalies attached to our (or indeed any) system of representation, and that unless they could all be removed it was futile and unfair to try to remove one. Lansdowne was even seized with that sudden interest in votes cast, as opposed to seats won, which is sometimes a characteristic of Tory leaders in Opposition, and told the House of the plight of the under-represented Unionists of Wales. Against such dialectics the crude argument of the mandate was naturally powerless.

The next session opened in February, 1907, with a King's Speech which noted that 'serious questions affecting the working of our parliamentary system had arisen from unfortunate differences between the two Houses' and announced that 'His Majesty's Ministers have this important subject under consideration with a view to a solution of the difficulty'. A very substantial programme of legislation, including a Licensing Bill, was also announced.

To what extent the Unionist Party was alarmed by this vague threat of constitutional reform is difficult to judge. F. E. Smith in the debate on the Address declared confidently—but not very accurately—that the Liberal Party had been attempting for 250 years to quell the House of Lords by resolution, and that their latest attempt was likely to be no more successful than previous ones had been. But the actions of Lord Newton[12] and of the Unionist Peers who supported him were more significant than the words of the Tory Party's principal *frondeur*. Lansdowne's biographer, then an active but independent member of the

[12] 1857–1942. Thomas Wodehouse Leigh. 2nd Lord Newton. Conservative member for Newton division of Lancashire, 1880–86. Paymaster-General, 1915–16.

Opposition in the Upper House, took advantage of the easy days in the early part of the session when there were no Government bills to mutilate and introduced a measure for the reform of the House of Lords. This was an issue which had been raised on a number of occasions previously, notably by Rosebery in 1884 and 1888. But neither of these attempts nor any of the others had prevented the Upper House emerging from the 'century of reform' in exactly the same mould, save only that bankrupt peers could no longer sit and vote, in which it had entered it.

Nor was Lord Newton's bill any more effective than the efforts of Rosebery and the others had been. Its significance lay not in its practical result, but in the fact that it emanated from the Unionist side, in the sweeping departure from the hereditary principle which its acceptance would have involved, and in the support which it received. It provided that hereditary peers not possessed of certain qualifications were to elect only one fourth of their number to represent them in the Upper House, and that the places so vacated were to be filled by life peers appointed by the Government of the day; and its supporters included the Duke of Devonshire, the Archbishop of Canterbury and the Duke of Northumberland. Lansdowne and Cawdor, speaking officially for the Opposition, expressed no direct hostility to the proposals and contented themselves with postponing the issue by having it referred to a Select Committee, which was impressively strong in its composition, but which took eighteen months to report.

The direct opposition to the bill had come from the unusual combination of Lord Halsbury,[13] the die-hard ex-Lord

---

[13] 1823–1921. Formerly Sir Hardinge Gifford. Lord Chancellor, 1895–1905. A man who must surely hold the record for rapid changes of electoral

Chancellor, and the supporters of the Government. Crewe, the Lord President, saw the issue with great clarity. Newton's proposals, while they might make the House of Lords less of an anachronism, would do nothing to make it less partisan; his idea that there existed 'a sort of reservoir of eminent men who were not partisans and who might profitably be added to the House' was 'pure fallacy'. In any event, it was 'not expedient to proceed with the discussion of various proposals for reforming the constitution of this House until provision has been made for an effective method of settling differences which may arise between this House and the other House of Parliament'.[l]

In this view Crewe had the full support of the Prime Minister, who, as his biographer has informed us, 'from the beginning, was clear in his mind on one point: a Liberal Government would be extremely ill-advised to touch the composition of the Second Chamber until it had settled its powers. To set up a nominated Second Chamber composed of grave and reverend but necessarily conservative-minded individuals would, if such a Chamber succeeded to the powers of the present House, both increase the evil and abolish the remedy which the present system provided in the last resort through the creation of peers. On the other hand, to set up an elective Second Chamber would be to destroy the unique character of the House of Commons, and to introduce a new dissension into the heart of the Constitution'.[m]

This was the soundest of radical doctrine, and a great advance on most Liberal thought on the subject during the 'eighties and 'nineties. The pursuit of these principles alone was to prevent the

fortune. In 1874 he stood for Launceston and received one vote. In 1877 he was elected unopposed for the same constituency.

Liberal Party from becoming hopelessly lost amongst the quick-sands of the constitutional conference of 1910; and temporary deviations from them were to lead to needless dangers and difficulties.

Campbell-Bannerman had his own opportunity to stand by the simple principle of the supremacy of the Commons and to show his distaste for attempts to solve the problem by institutional innovation. This came in the late spring of 1907, when the Cabinet committee which had been set up early in the year to consider means of adjusting the relationship of the two Houses reported in favour of joint sittings between the Commons and a delegation of a hundred peers, which would take place in the event of disagreement, and the decisions of which would be final. The Prime Minister greatly disliked this scheme, and he attacked it strongly in a memorandum dated May 31," alternating effectively between high constitutional arguments and practical objections. Where would the joint assembly meet? Who would preside over it? What would its rules of procedure be? And would the House of Commons continue to meet during its sittings? As an alternative he revived the proposals for a suspensory veto which John Bright had put forward in a speech at Leeds in 1883. In the event of disagreement a conference of perhaps five or ten members of each House should be set up. If this body produced a scheme which the Government could accept, no further special procedure was likely to be needed. If it failed to do so, the bill in question, after passing twice more through the Commons, could become law over the heads of the peers. No minimum period of time for this process was laid down; theoretically it could all have been done with a lapse of no more than six months from the first rejection by the peers. Between the bill's first and second passage through the Commons the Government could make whatever changes it thought fit; but on the third occasion the bill would be required to maintain the form in which it had most recently passed.

Decisive action from the Government was now urgently necessary. The session had not so far been marked by any fresh conflicts between the two Houses, but the shadow of the Lords lay heavily upon everything which the Government tried to do. A short Education Bill, a poor substitute for the lost measure of the previous session, had been introduced, but it so disappointed the Government's friends, without propitiating their enemies, that it had been withdrawn after a few weeks. An attempt to legislate for Ireland failed equally dismally, and for much the same reasons. A 'Home Rule' Chief Secretary, serving under a 'Home Rule' Prime Minister, was forced by circumstance to introduce a petty little devolution bill.[14] It was attacked by Arthur Balfour and rejected by an Irish National Convention. It made enemies, but no friends, and, like the second Education Bill, had ignominiously to be withdrawn. The Licensing Bill, which had been announced in the Speech from the Throne as the chief business of the session, had not even been introduced. It was clear to the Cabinet that any measure which would command the support of the Liberal Party would be heavily assailed in the Lords, that the Government could hardly sustain a second major legislative defeat within eighteen months without dissolution, and that the cause of temperance reform, dear though it was to Liberal hearts, was not the most popular of election issues.

At Whitsuntide, therefore, the outlook for the Government was not bright. There was a general desire to avoid an autumn

---

[14] Augustine Birrell himself described it as a 'little, modest, shy, humble effort to give administrative powers to the Irish people'.

session, and if this was to be met,[15] the Prime Minister was left with only ten weeks in which to achieve something to show for a year's work. The bye-elections, at that stage, had indicated no substantial falling-off in support for the Government—only Brigg had changed hands to the Unionists—but it was feared that this would not continue if more achievement could not be shown.

There were four land bills to be brought forward—an Evicted Tenants Bill for Ireland, a Small Holdings Bill for England, and a Small Landowners and a Land Values Bill for Scotland; but it was doubtful whether there was sufficient time to get all these through the Commons, and, even if this were achieved, four Liberal measures, although not of the first importance, on their lordships' favourite subject, could hardly be regarded as a certain harvest for the Government.[16] What was required, and required urgently, was some indication of how the Liberal leaders proposed to deal with the Lords.

Campbell-Bannerman had first to secure agreement in the Cabinet to his proposals as opposed to the plan of the Cabinet committee. In this task he succeeded, although not without difficulty. Asquith, at this stage, was a seeker after solutions less drastic than that of the suspensory veto. This is clear from his speech in the House delivered a few weeks later. It was not only his explicit statement: 'personally I have been a slow and, to some degree, even a reluctant convert to the necessity of this particular method of dealing with the problem';[a] nor his

---

[15] It was met, and the achievement has only once since been repeated.

[16] In the event the English bill escaped largely unscathed, the Irish bill was substantially amended and weakened, and the two Scottish bills were wrecked.

confession that he had 'coquetted with the referendum'; but the whole tenor of his speech which indicated that his natural approach to the question differed widely from the robust radicalism of the Prime Minister.

Against this opposition Campbell-Bannerman did well to carry the day at all, and doubly well to be ready by June 24 to lay his plan before Parliament. He proceeded by the innocuous, but then usual, method of a Government resolution in the House of Commons. By a vote of 432 to 147 the Lower House resolved 'that, in order to give effect to the will of the people as expressed by their elected representatives, it is necessary that the power of the other House should be so restricted by law as to secure that within the limits of a single Parliament the final decision of the Commons must prevail'. An amendment to abolish the House of Lords, moved by Arthur Henderson, had previously been rejected by 315 to 100, the Irish and a few radicals voting with the Labour Party. The resolution as carried was given more specific meaning by the speech of the Prime Minister, which also contained a notable attack on Balfour's disloyalty to the House to which he belonged and to the tradition of moderate statesmanship which he should have inherited from his predecessors. 'I cannot conceive of Sir Robert Peel or Mr. Disraeli,' Campbell-Bannerman said, 'treating the House of Commons as the rt. hon. gentleman has treated it. Nor do I think there is any instance in which, as leaders of the Opposition, they committed what I can only call the treachery of openly calling in the other House to override this House. These great states men were House of Commons men. I venture to say that if Bills were mutilated and rejected elsewhere when Sir Robert Peel sat upon that bench, it was not done at his instance'.[p]

The remainder of an often stormy three days' debate was

chiefly notable for Balfour's wonderfully arrogant charge that the Prime Minister, who was in fact at his wits' end to show the country a few worth-while Acts, framed his legislative proposals for the express purpose of getting them rejected,[17] and for a sustained piece of invective from Lloyd George, in which he showed that he had not taken too seriously previous royal warnings about the violence of his language on the subject.[18] Mr. Churchill[19] added his conviction that the House of Lords was 'a one-sided, hereditary, unprized, unrepresentative, irresponsible absentee'.

---

[17] Balfour's attitude was well reflected by his biographer, who summed up this debate with the blandly condescending statement that 'the Liberal Party were by this time suffering from a sort of "persecution mania" on the subject of the House of Lords'. (*See* Blanche E. C. Dugdale: *Arthur James Balfour*, vol. ii, p. 28.)

[18] After a speech at Oxford in December, 1906, in which Lloyd George had demanded to know whether the country 'was to be governed by the King and the peers or by the King and the people' a remonstrance from Buckingham Palace against the use of the Sovereign's name provoked the pleasantly ingenious, if unconvincing, excuse from Lloyd George that 'he would have considered it would be disrespectful to speak of either the "the peers" or "the people" alone, omitting the reference to the supreme Head of the State'. (*See* Spender's *Life of Campbell-Bannerman*, vol. II, pp. 313–15.) The Chancellor of the Exchequer might have considered referring His Majesty to the precedent set by Lord Grey when, on May 17, 1832, he spoke of the dangers of 'a majority of this House (the House of Lords) ... opposing the declared and decided wishes both of the Crown and the people'.

[19] The ability of the Under-Secretary of State for the Colonies to secure for himself a place as a Government spokesman in a debate on a major constitutional issue is both a tribute to his own confident energy and an indication of the less rigid 'departmentalism' of those days.

This was all very good in its way and may well have given some satisfaction to angry Liberal supporters in the country; but no such debate and no resolution would of itself do anything to bring the ending of the veto a day nearer. Was it the intention of the Prime Minister to press on with an attempt to place his plan on the statute book, if need be (and need there certainly would have been) dissolving on the issue? Nothing could have been expected in the session of 1907, but 1908 would have brought new opportunities. Why were they not taken? Mr. Spender has told us that in the autumn of 1907 the Prime Minister saw only two courses before the Government, 'either to accept these conditions (a veto on all major aspects of Liberal policy) and be content with the minor legislation and administrative changes which were within the boundaries imposed by the House of Lords, or to go boldly forward and challenge that House. Campbell-Bannerman,' Spender added, 'was never in doubt about the choice between those alternatives. Submission, he believed would be death to Liberalism; and a long term of inglorious office on the sufferance of the House of Lords was the last thing that he contemplated either for himself or his Government.'[q]

Professor Emily Allyn also assumes that the Prime Minister was all for immediate and decisive action, and writes: 'The failure to take further action ... was due in part, doubtless, to differences within the Cabinet; but the decisive factor was the illness and death of Campbell-Bannerman, and succession of Asquith to the premiership in the spring of 1908.'[r]

But the chronology of this argument is unconvincing. The Speech from the Throne at the opening of the 1908 session, which contained no hint of a Parliament Bill, was delivered on January 29, at the end of a week of preparatory Cabinets presided over by the Prime Minister himself, who had just returned from a convalescence at Biarritz. Although he had only another two or three weeks of active life ahead of him, his illness involved no period of gradual decline. During this crucial week, according to the testimony of Spender, 'He seemed to have recovered all his old buoyancy and energy ... he was ready for the fray and confident that the session was going to be a great one'[^*] There seems no reason why, had he intended a Parliament Bill for this session, he should have lacked the enthusiasm to put it forward or the vigour to commend it to his colleagues. It is difficult to accept any conclusion other than that the Prime Minister intended to give the peers another year's trial before attempting to proceed any further; and it follows from this that the retirement and death of Campbell-Bannerman and the accession of Asquith made no practical difference to the date on which the issue between the two Houses was finally joined.[20]

Nor did the change in the premiership make as much difference to the balance of political forces within the Government as, two years previously, would have been expected. Lloyd George may not have been in the true Gladstonian tradition of Campbell-Bannerman, Morley, Bryce, or Ripon, but he was certainly not a Liberal Leaguer, and his promotion to the Exchequer did much to counter any impression of a swing to the right which the change at 10 Downing Street may have given. For the rest, there were no sensational appointments. No attempt was made by Asquith to retrieve for Haldane the Woolsack which the ineffective Relugas Compact[21] had failed to give him, and all

---

[20] Except, perhaps, for the indirect effect of creating a vacancy at the Exchequer and a new Chancellor to introduce the Budget of 1909.

[21] In September, 1905, Asquith, Grey, and Haldane, who were all staying in Scotland, met at Relugas, where Grey had a fishing cottage, and agreed

Campbell-Bannerman's Cabinet appointments, with the exception of Elgin at the Colonial Office (who was replaced by Crewe) and Tweedmouth at the Admiralty (who was replaced by McKenna[22]), were left intact. There were viscountcies, without change of office, for Morley[23] and Fowler, and of the new appointments, that of Mr. Churchill to Lloyd George's old post at the Board of Trade probably excited the most interest. His promotion to the Cabinet strengthened what can best be called the radical opportunist wing of the Liberal Party.

These changes occurred at the beginning of April. Campbell-Bannerman resigned on the fifth, and on the following night

---

that, when a Liberal Government was formed, they would only serve if Campbell-Bannerman left the leadership in the Commons to Asquith and gave Haldane the Woolsack. What happened in the event has already been related.

[22] 1863–1943. Liberal member for Monmouthshire, North, 1895–1918. Financial Secretary to the Treasury, 1905–7. President of the Board of Education, 1907–8. First Lord of the Admiralty, 1908–11. Home Secretary, 1911–15. Chancellor of the Exchequer, 1915–16.

[23] Morley, shortly before the Government changes, had told Asquith that 'I suppose ... I have a claim from seniority of service for your place at the Exchequer, but I don't know that I have any special aptitude for it under present prospects....' (Morley: *Recollections*, vol. II, p. 251.) It is interesting to speculate what would have transpired had he pressed the claim, for Asquith comments on the incident in his own *Fifty Years of Parliament* (vol. 11, pp. 52–3) without indicating that he regarded it as in any way outrageous. Morley by this time, as he made clear in many conversations with his Clerk at the Privy Council Office (*see* Sir Almeric Fitzroy: *Memoirs*, vol. III, *passim*), was anxious to be thought of as a little above the battle and too intelligent not to see all sides of a case. It is consequently difficult to believe that much in the way of adventurous Budgets would have emanated from his Chancellorship, particularly as he was never a social reform radical.

Asquith left for Biarritz, where he had been summoned to kiss hands against the unusually exotic background of the Hôtel du Palais.[24] He was back in London on the tenth, and he drove from Charing Cross station on a fine spring evening, through the cheers of the crowd (which Mrs. Asquith hoped would not reach the ears of the dying ex-Prime Minister), to call upon Campbell-Bannerman at Downing Street. He had reached the highest post at the age of fifty-five, after twenty-two years in the House of Commons and a career of unbroken, almost inevitable ascent. His constructive intellectual equipment was certainly more massive than that of any Prime Minister since Gladstone, he was in the fullness of his great powers of physical resilience, and he was to hold his high office for a longer continuous period than any of his predecessors since Lord Liverpool. Nevertheless, perhaps for the very reason that his rise had been so inevitable, his formation of a Government marked no new point of political departure. He had been brought to office by no great victory at the polls—there were only a few bye-election defeats to welcome him—such as had heralded Gladstone in 1868 and 1880, or Campbell-Bannerman in 1906, or Attlee in 1945; nor by a great shifting of parliamentary forces, as with Lloyd George in 1916 and Churchill in 1940. There was nothing of political cataclysm in the air, nothing which could sweep away old barriers and give him new opportunities. He was circumscribed by the limitations which had beset his predecessor, and was prevented, partly by these and partly, perhaps, by his own temperament, from that feeling of impatience to put his hand to the plough and to strike out in new

---

[24] A Royal suggestion that the subsequent surrendering and receiving of Seals of Office by the whole Cabinet should be carried out at the halfway house of the Hotel Crillon in Paris was tactfully overruled.

directions which was to be experienced most strongly by Lloyd George and by Churchill when they, in turn, ascended to the central control of affairs. The programme for the session was laid down. There was the Licensing Bill, there was yet another attempt at an Education Bill, there was his own Budget, already prepared, and which he himself was to introduce a fortnight later, and there was the Old Age Pensions Bill which sprang from it. And, most important of all, there was still the House of Lords. Whether it was to be in the sand or in a more fruitful soil, he could only, for a time at any rate, plough in clearly-marked furrows.

The Licensing Bill, a somewhat delayed *riposte* to Balfour's Act of 1904, received its second reading in the Commons at the end of April. Its object was a compulsory reduction in the number of public-houses, so that they should not in any area exceed a fixed ratio to the population.[25] The money for compensation was to be raised by a levy on the liquor trade, but payments to the holders of extinguished licences were to cease at the end of fourteen years. The measure was denounced by the Unionists as confiscatory and vindictive.[26] Arthur Balfour is recorded by his biographer as being 'furious about it', and as

---

[25] Lord Salisbury expressed his scepticism that the measure was a remedy for intemperance by remarking that he felt no more inclined to sleepiness at Hatfield, where there were more than fifty bedrooms, that at a seaside villa with perhaps a dozen. (*See* Lord Oxford's *Fifty Years of Parliament*, vol. II, p. 59n.)

[26] Lord Lansdowne at this time saw little but vindictiveness in the Government's policy, not only on licensing, but with regard to education, land, the House of Lords and almost everything else. (*See* Newton, *op. cit.*, pp. 366–7.) But those who wish to make omelettes can always be accused of being vindictive to the eggs.

holding the belief that its effects were 'against every interest of public decency and morality'.[1] The Bill was opposed most bitterly at every stage of its passage through the Commons and did not secure its third reading until November 20.

In view of the experience with other bills, there was naturally a widespread expectation that the Lords would not allow the measure to pass. Indeed, as Lord Newton has recorded without comment, the brewers had already threatened to withdraw their support from the Unionist Party if this did not happen.[a] The King, with the approval of the Prime Minister, had also attempted to exercise influence—but in the other direction, and less effectively. He had summoned Lansdowne to see him on October 12, and had told him of his fear that 'if the attitude of the Peers was such as to suggest that they were obstructing an attempt to deal with the evils of intemperance, the House of Lords would suffer seriously in popularity'. He assured Lansdowne that the Government was likely to accept an extension of the time limit to twenty or twenty-one years, and urged him to secure for the bill a second reading and to amend it, if necessary, in committee.

Lansdowne told the King that he had not discussed the matter since the summer 'either with the front bench peers or with Mr. Balfour and those who act with him in the House of Commons', and added that it was impossible for him to decide what advice he would give to the Unionist peers until he had seen how 'the Bill fared in the House of Commons'. He agreed however (it would have been a little shameless for him to have done otherwise) that 'it was not desirable that the peers and the brewers should be *represented* (my italics) as in too close alliance'.[b] For the rest, he warned the King that he saw danger in accepting the principle of the bill, and spoke of the 'bitter experience' which the peers had undergone with the Old Age Pensions Bill.

This last measure, providing for non-contributory pensions at the age of seventy, which had been taken earlier in the session, had not been warmly received in the Upper House. One peer had talked of it as 'so prodigal of expenditure as likely to undermine the whole fabric of the Empire', and another had regarded it as 'destructive of all thrift'. But the policy of amending it in committee rather than of rejecting it on second reading had been adopted. The resultant amendments, however, had been treated by the Commons as inadmissible, because the measure was a money bill. Under protest, the Lords had accepted this, but they adopted the incident as an excuse for a more intransigent attitude on licensing.

This intransigence was decided upon at a meeting of Unionist peers held in Lansdowne House on November 24. Here a small but distinguished body of peers was opposed to rejection. They numbered about ten, and included St. Aldwyn, Cromer,[27] Milner,[28] Balfour of Burleigh[29] and Lytton.[30] Their motives were varied, but Milner, for example, was in favour of moderation both because he believed the bill to possess intrinsic merits and because he thought its rejection by the Lords would stem the

---

[27] 1841–1917. Evelyn Baring. Created 1st Earl of Cromer, 1901. Agent and Consul-General in Egypt, 1883–1907.

[28] 1854–1925. Alfred Milner. Created 1st Viscount Milner, 1902. Chairman, Board of Inland Revenue, 1892–97. High Commissioner for South Africa, 1897–1905. Member of War Cabinet, 1916–18. Secretary of State for War, 1918–19. Secretary of State for Colonies, 1919–21.

[29] 1849–1921. Alexander Hugh Bruce. 6th Lord Balfour of Burleigh. Secretary for Scotland, 1895–1903.

[30] 1876–1947. 2nd Earl. Succeeded, 1891. Governor of Bengal, 1922–27. Acting Viceroy, 1925.

Unionist tide which he saw flowing very strongly in the country. But the majority were probably more afraid of checking the brewers than of stemming the tide, and thought that in any event a clash between the two Houses had become inevitable, and that there was little point in attempting to postpone it.

Their policy was adopted. After a three-day debate, the House of Lords declined, on November 27, to give the bill a second reading by a vote of 272 to 96. It was a big attendance of peers, and Lord Fitzmaurice,[31] for the Government, remarked that the Upper House was at least giving the bill 'a first-class funeral. A great number of noble Lords have arrived who have not often honoured us with their presence.' Yet a third Education Bill had also perished at the hands of the Lords during the year.

In this way the third session of the 1906 Parliament came to an end. As in the two previous sessions, no measure, other than a money bill, had passed on to the statute book in anything like its original form unless, on third reading in the Commons, it had secured the acquiescence of Arthur Balfour. For three years the smallest Opposition within living memory had effectively decided what could, and what could not, be passed through Parliament. In the language of the day, the cup was full, and the sands were exhaustively ploughed.

---

[31] 1846–1935. Under-Secretary of State for Foreign Affairs, 1882–85 and 1905–8. Chancellor of the Duchy of Lancaster, 1908–9. Second son of the 4th Marquess of Lansdowne, a brother of the Unionist leader in the Lords, and one of the few Whigs still in the Liberal Party.

IV

The People's Budget

At the beginning of 1909 three points must have been clear to the Prime Minister, the Chancellor of the Exchequer, or any other informed person who was considering the prospects of the Liberal Party. The first was that the Government was losing support in the country. Its bye-election record, which had been good during its first and second years in office, had worsened sharply. During 1908 it had been little short of disastrous. Mr. Churchill, standing for re-election on his appointment to the Board of Trade, had been defeated at North-West Manchester and had sought refuge at Dundee. And there had been other Unionist gains from the Government at Ashburton, Peckham, Ross-on-Wye, Shoreditch, Newcastle-on-Tyne, and Pudsey. The Conservative leaders and organisers who predicted after the Christmas recess that a general election would give them a majority of at least twenty were not indulging in baseless optimism.

The second consideration was that no useful purpose could be served by passing through the House of Commons controversial measures of social or political advance in a normal legislative form. Unless they could be incorporated in money bills they were certain to meet their death at the hands of the House of Lords. There were only two ways in which the Government could hope to regain the initiative, to satisfy its adherents, and to rally its erstwhile supporters: by a full use of the Finance Bill, so that it achieved much more than the mere raising of a given amount of revenue; or by the destruction of the absolute veto of the Upper House.

The third factor was the Chancellor's need in the forthcoming financial year for substantially more revenue than Asquith had raised by the previous Budget. This arose partly from the cost of the new old age pensions and partly from increased expenditure on the Navy. Of the need for this latter increase a large section of the Liberal Party (including some members of the Cabinet)[1] and all the Labour and Nationalist members were quite unconvinced. It was therefore necessary that the revenue to meet this unpopular outlay should be raised in a form acceptable to most of these normal supporters of the Government.

All these considerations added up to one conclusion, and to one only. The Government's next major move had obviously to be the introduction of a highly controversial Budget. But how

---

[1] Asquith wrote to his wife on February 20, saying: 'The economists are in a state of wild alarm, and Winston and Ll. G. by their combined machinations have got the bulk of the Liberal press into the same camp.... They (the two) go about darkly hinting at resignation (which is bluff) and there will in any case be a lot of steam let off, and at any rate a temporary revival of the old pro-Boer animus. I am able to keep a fairly cool head amidst it all, but there are moments when I am disposed summarily to cashier them both.' (J. A Spender and Cyril Asquith: *Life of Herbert Henry Asquith, Lord Oxford an Asquith*, vol. I, p. 254.)

much was such a Budget to be designed to accomplish? Was it to be based on the assumption that as a money bill it would be immune from the attacks of the peers, and would thus serve for the Government as an alternative to a 'battle of the veto'? Or was it intended to provoke the peers to rejection, and thus act as a prelude to the 'battle of the veto'? Lloyd George's biographer, Mr. Malcolm Thomson, who is always sparing in his documentation, is at once confusing and dogmatic on the point.

> 'To Lloyd George it was clear that there must be a fight to curb the Lords' power of veto,' he tells us. 'But he was not prone to the dangerous miscalculation of wishful thinking, and he did not deceive himself into thinking that rates for Church Schools or reduction of public-house licences, however hotly he and some of his friends thought about them, were issues that would rouse the mass of the nation to a constitutional revolution. "Resign and appeal to the electorate!" taunted the Tories when successive Education Bills were thrown out by the Lords. "If a dissolution comes," retorted L.G., "it will be a much larger measure than the Education Bill that will come up for consideration, if the House of Lords persists in its present policy!" He was restlessly devising how to shape that larger measure.'[a]

The implication of this seems clear enough, but the same cannot be said of a later passage on the same point. Here Mr. Thomson tells how, after the rejection of the Licensing Bill, Lloyd George

> 'had settled his strategical plan of attack on them (the peers) and won Asquith's approval of it. When the Old Age

Pensions Bill was before the Lords, Lansdowne had dissuaded them from throwing it out on the ground that, though not strictly a Money Bill, it was essentially a Bill of a financial complexion and was linked with provisions in the Budget allotting funds for it. Finance, he admitted, was by constitutional principle the exclusive concern of the Commons, with which the Lords should not meddle. Very well: Lloyd George planned to link further measures of social reform with Finance—measures which would be acutely disliked by the Peers—and if the Upper Chamber grew exasperated enough to throw them out, it and not the Liberal Government would be violating the Constitution and making a change in the powers of the Lords inevitable!

'Accordingly he proceeded to frame his Budget for 1909 with the threefold purpose of raising the extra funds needed for old age pensions and other intended reforms; of making provision for these reforms in the Finance Bill; *and of adopting tax-raising devices which would be particularly distasteful to the Peers and might rouse them to throw out the Budget* (my italics).'[b]

But why, if Lloyd George's desire was to produce a peer-rousing Finance Bill, should Lansdowne's statements on the Old Age Pensions Bill have stimulated him to action? Surely the Unionist leader's reiteration of the principle of the Commons' exclusive control of finance should have made him sceptical of the possibility of this outcome. The argument only makes sense if his primary object was to circumvent the veto rather than to destroy it.

Nor does the speech which the Chancellor of the Exchequer delivered to the Law Society on January 30, on the occasion of the presentation of a portrait of himself, bear out his biographer's theory. In July of the previous year he had threateningly announced: 'Next year I shall have to rob somebody's hen-roost, and I must consider where I can get most eggs, and where I can get them easiest, and where I shall be least punished.' But at the Law Society he went out of his way to undo the effects of this statement. He referred to this 'bad jest' on the subject of hen-roosts, and, in the words of the *Annual Register*, 'emphatically disclaimed any vindictive spirit in his financial plans. The single purpose of the Chancellor of the Exchequer (he said) should be the protection and confirmation of the national interests; and in that spirit he approached his task.' Vague conciliatory statements, delivered in this way, do not perhaps mean very much, but there is no conceivable reason why a Minister intent on stirring up the maximum of opposition should trouble to make them at all. This was not an isolated case. Lloyd George continued to be *suaviter in modo* until well into the summer.

The view that Asquith was from the first a party to the Chancellor's supposed tactic of shaping a Budget for the peers to reject is still less convincing. Such a device would have been alien to his character, and in direct contradiction to his clearly expressed belief, repeated at many stages in the controversy, that the House of Lords would never dare to throw out a Finance Bill. In the debate on the Address at the beginning of the 1909 session he was confronted with a direct challenge to the Government's inactivity on the House of Lords issue in the form of an amendment, moved by Campbell-Banner-man's successor[2] in the Stirling Burghs, which called for legislation in the

2 1871–1946. Arthur Ponsonby, later 1st Lord Ponsonby of Shulbrede subsequently joined the Labour Party and became Under-Secretary of State for

current session to implement the 1907 resolution. This was pressed to a division[3] and gave serious embarrassment to the Government. But Asquith in his reply, while he stressed (as had been done in the King's Speech) the heavy calls upon the time of the session which the Finance Bill would make, gave no shadow of a hint that it might also precipitate constitutional action.

This approach was characteristic of the Prime Minister's public utterances at the time. At Glasgow, where only a fortnight before the introduction of the Budget he spoke of 'unprecedented financial strains', he was at pains to prepare the country for a controversial Budget and concentrate attention on financial issues. But there is every indication that he, and the Government, regarded the Budget as an alternative to the struggle with the House of Lords rather than as a method of prosecuting this struggle.

Lloyd George therefore proceeded with the framing of his proposals in the knowledge that the stage had been cleared for their reception. It has been suggested that he had grave difficulty in securing Cabinet approval for his more controversial imposts. To quote Mr. Thomson again:

'He (Lloyd George) said that by far the most difficult fight he had was in the Cabinet, not in the country. Harcourt was the most inveterate in obstructing his proposals, while

---

Foreign Affairs, Chancellor of the Duchy of Lancaster, leader of the Opposition in the House of Lords, etc.

[3] This, together with other back-bench Liberal revolts which were carried as far as the division lobby, as, for instance, on the Army Estimates, is a good indication of the low state of morale of the Government's supporters at the time.

posing all the time as an ardent Radical. Crewe, while not liking them, said very little. Grey said nothing. But at heart they were all against him. Sir Robert Chalmers, then the head of the Treasury, walked up to the door of the Cabinet room with L.G. one day when he was going to a meeting to discuss his Budget proposals, and when L.G. had gone in Chalmers turned to the man at his side and said, "That little man goes into the fight absolutely alone." When L.G. came out, Chalmers said to him apprehensively, "Well? ..." "Oh, I carried them all right," was L.G.'s cheerful reply.'*d*

This story, even if *vero*, is certainly not *ben trovato*. Even under Lloyd George's regime, it can hardly have been the practice for the Permanent Secretary of the Treasury to wait outside the door of the Cabinet Room in 10 Downing Street, presumably chatting to the messengers, throughout the length of Cabinet meetings.

'Asquith alone was helpful when it came to a vote,' Mr. Thomson continues, 'although he never supported the proposals actively. Once, when nearly everyone around the table had raised objections to a certain proposal, Asquith summed up with the words, "Well, I think there is substantial agreement on this point." 'It appears from the example cited that the Prime Minister was more helpful in avoiding a vote than 'when it came to' one, and indeed, if Mr. Thomson's account of Cabinet divisions is true, Lloyd George's own proposals would hardly have seen the light of day had continual votes been the method of procedure.

Asquith himself has since expressed a certain lukewarmness towards some of the more controversial of the Budget proposals.

'Being supposed myself to be a financier of a respectable and more or less conservative type,' he wrote in 1926, 'I was, in the course of the debates, frequently challenged by Mr. Balfour and others to defend the new imposts, and especially the Undeveloped Land and the Increment Duties. I have undertaken in my time many more intractable dialectical tasks, and though I was fully alive to the mechanical difficulties involved, and perhaps not so sanguine as some of my colleagues as to the progressive productiveness of the taxes, I had never any doubt as to their equity in principle.'[e]

But by the time these words were written a Government presided over by Lloyd George himself had long since repealed the taxes in question. It may therefore be thought that they constitute no irrefutable proof of the half-heartedness of the head of the Government, as against the full-blooded enthusiasm of his Chancellor, in 1909. And the Prime Minister was probably much more prepared for financial adventure (for which, over a period of three months, he had sedulously been preparing Parliament and the country) in the heat of the day than he was anxious to admit in the cool aftermath of the 'twenties.

Grey, once described by Arthur Balfour as 'a curious combination of the old-fashioned Whig and the Socialist', indicated by his subsequent statements that he might have reacted somewhat equivocally to the Budget proposals. If his 'socialism' impelled him to welcome them, and his 'whiggery' to abhor them, he resolved the conflict by saying that he approved of the proposals themselves but disliked the way in which they were advocated. When a correspondent wrote to him abusing the Chancellor of the Exchequer, he replied sternly: 'I cannot agree with what you say. Mr. Lloyd George is a colleague with whom I have always

63

been on the best of terms personally, and the Budget raises the money required in a way which presses much less, I believe, upon the poorer classes than any alternative that could be devised.'[f] And in June he went out of his way, at a dinner given in his honour by the National Liberal Club, to reply to statements made by his old Chief, Rosebery, and to defend the Budget. It 'was good', he said, 'by whatever general principle it was tried; it took taxes from superfluities, and taxed people in proportion to their ability to pay'.[g] But in private conversation he expressed the view that the Chancellor's speeches were unfair, and later in the year he wrote to Mrs. Asquith: 'I am no optimist: X— (whose identity is not difficult to guess) has made too much running, I fear, to carry the electors with us: in this country they move slowly and distrust rhetoric.'[h] All this was no doubt compatible with a somewhat uneasy acquiescence in Cabinet, although not, it may be thought, with any definite opposition.

Haldane, the third member of the Liberal League triumvirate, was not very well disposed towards Lloyd George at this (or any other) time. A remark of his on Budget Day is quoted by Austen Chamberlain's biographer: '"It seems to me," remarked Austen's friend, Leverton Harris,[4] speaking of the Chancellor of the Exchequer to Mr. Haldane in the smoke-room of the House of Commons that night, "that he read that speech like a man who does not understand what he is reading." "Of course he doesn't," replied the other. "Why, we have been trying for weeks to make him understand clauses of the Bill, and he can't."'[i]

[4] 1864–1926. Unionist Member for Tynemouth, 1900–6, Stepney, 1907–10, and East Worcestershire, 1914–18.

This malicious story,[5] while it certainly shows that Haldane had no desire to enhance the Chancellor's reputation, is quite incompatible with the theory that the Budget proposals, believed in only by Lloyd George himself, were forced down the throats of a reluctant Cabinet.[6]

The ultimate test, however, of whether or not Lloyd George had to face and overcome the united opposition of the rest of the Cabinet lies less in any attempt to reconstruct from their subsequent statements and writings the attitude of various Ministers at the time than in the hard facts of the support which they gave to the Chancellor throughout the long struggle to put the Budget through. If the other members of the Government were as hostile to the Budget as some would have us believe, their loyalty in the ensuing months, both to Lloyd George himself and to the measures which they disliked, was one of the most remarkable things in the history of British politics. Asquith himself, in the Chancellor's own words, 'was firm as a rock'. For the rest, there were no deliberate indiscretions, no attempts by Ministers to let it be widely known that they stood a little above the conflict, and no resignations. In the House of Commons too, while there was a little cross-voting on individual points, the Liberal back-benchers supported the Government in the key divisions with great solidarity. Mrs. Asquith recorded after the third reading that 'the remarkable thing about the passing of this Budget was the unanimity with which people of different views backed it. Even

---

[5] The substance of which is completely denied by Lloyd George's subsequent conduct of the bill.

[6] On the assumption that the clause was one of some importance; if it were not, then the story loses all point, as the Chancellor would certainly not have dealt with the matter to which it referred in opening his Budget.

the men who act according to their humour … voted for the Bill.²ʲ The shedding of its right wing had for so long been a habit with the Liberal Party that it would indeed be remarkable, even without the suggestion of a reluctant Cabinet, that so controversial a measure as Lloyd George's first Budget should have produced not a single defection of note.

What were the proposals which this famous Budget contained? Today they inevitably seem unexciting, as do the sums of money involved, for financial issues survive the passage of time even less well than do most other subjects of political controversy. The Chancellor wanted £164m., against the £151m. which he had received in the preceding year, and the £148m. which he calculated existing taxes would give him in the year that was then beginning.[7] This left him with a prospective deficit of £16m., and as the increased expenditure on battleships and social services was likely to be cumulative, it was important that he should close this gap by taxes of which the yield would increase as time went on.

His first proposal was for a reduction of £3m. in the sinking fund payment. Death duties, and the associated legacy, succession and settled estate duties, were to bring in another £4m. in the current year, and another £6½m. in subsequent years. This

---

[7] This anticipated decline was due to a fall-off in industrial activity, and it is a striking indication of the limited role which a Budget and a Chancellor of the Exchequer played in those days that Lloyd George was able to refer to this circumstance—'a year of exceptionally bad trade'—as one of the *objective* factors in the situation, for which he had no direct responsibility. There was no attempt to explain it away, or to suggest how its recurrence might be prevented. He might have been talking of the effect of a wet season upon the harvest.

involved increases in scale to the extent of making estates of £1m. and over liable to a total duty of approximately 25%. The income tax was adjusted to yield another £3m. The rate of tax on the former remained at IS. (9d. under £2,000); on the latter it was increased to IS. 2d. A £10 children's allowance, to apply only to incomes under £500, was another innovation. A much more important one, however, was the introduction of the super-tax. This was to be charged, at a rate of 6d. in the £, on the amount by which all incomes of £5,000 or more exceeded £3,000. It was to bring in £500,000 in the current year and £2,300,000 in the following year. Of all the Chancellor's proposals, this was much the most pregnant with social change; but this was not appreciated at the time, and it was not the proposal which aroused the most controversy.

This distinction was reserved for the land taxes. There were three of these. The first provided for a tax of 20% on the unearned increment in land values, which was to be paid either when the land was sold or when it passed at death. The second provided for a capital tax of ½d. in the £ on the value of undeveloped land and minerals;[8] and the third for a 10% reversion duty on any benefit which came to a lessor at the end of a lease. These taxes were to bring in only £500,000 in the current year, but their yield was expected to increase considerably in subsequent years.

The next important group of new taxes related to alcohol and tobacco. The licence duties were to be increased so as to bring in another £2,600,000. Spirits were to pay another 3s. 9d. a gallon, which would have the effect of increasing the price of whisky by ½d. a glass, and the tobacco duty was raised by 8d. a pound.

---

[8]   On the first two points concessions were made at the committee stage.

The combined yield of these two taxes was to be £3½m. in the current year.

The taxation of the road-user became for the first time of moderate importance. For motor-car licences a graduated scale, varying from two to forty guineas according to horsepower, was introduced. Motor bicycles were to pay a flat rate of £1. In addition, a tax of 3d. a gallon was imposed on petrol, but there was to be a rebate for taxicabs and buses. The yield of this group of taxes was put at £750,000, but this sum was to be paid into a Road Fund and not used to meet general expenditure. In the same way the proceeds of a mineral rights duty of a shilling in the £ on mining royalties and wayleaves were to be used to finance a Miners' Welfare Fund.

These, with a few other miscellaneous changes, were the provisions of the 'People's Budget'. Lloyd George introduced them to the House of Commons on April 29, and despite the fact that he had lightened his task by the innovation of circulating beforehand a printed statement of the financial results of the past year, he took four and a half hours to do it. As a speech, it excited mixed comment. '(The Chancellor) was fagged before he began,' Austen Chamberlain wrote to his stepmother. 'Halfway through he was dead-beat, and had to ask for a half-hour adjournment. He recovered somewhat after this, but much of the speech was read, and badly read. He stumbled over the sentences, rushed past the full stops, paused at the commas, and altogether gave the impression that at these points he did not himself understand what he was saying.'[k] But Austen, more than most men, had the gift of believing that the speeches of his opponents were as bad as those of his friends were good. The half-hour adjournment had been very willingly granted by the House. According to *The Times*, it was suggested by the leader of the Opposition, who leant across the table to speak to the Prime Minister, and was taken up with sympathetic shouts of 'Half an hour' and 'Give him an hour.' And the same newspaper wrote of the speech as a whole as 'a wonderful effort'.

So far as the substance of the proposals was concerned, they were favoured with a greater weight of pejorative comment than has been the lot of any other Budget, either before or since. Arthur Balfour denounced it as 'vindictive, inequitable, based on no principle, and injurious to the productive capacity of the country'. It 'means the beginning of the end of all rights of property', said Sir Edward Carson. 'It is a monument of reckless and improvident finance,' said Lord Lansdowne. 'It is inquisitorial, tyrannical and Socialistic,' said Lord Rosebery.

In these and many other ways the Budget was strongly denounced by all the opponents and by some of the erstwhile supporters of the Government. But the denunciation did not begin as soon as the Chancellor had announced his proposals. His four-and-a-half-hour speech had enabled him to elaborate them in some detail, and his peroration, in which he spoke of a 'war Budget—for raising money to wage implacable warfare against poverty and squalidness', gave a clear indication of what he was about. But the Opposition were at first more bemused than exasperated. It was then customary, as it is not now, to carry on a full-scale debate immediately after the Chancellor's speech and to divide on certain of the Budget Resolutions at the end of the day. Austen Chamberlain therefore followed Lloyd George, and although, in his own words he 'only skimmed the surface of (the) proposals', he took over an hour to do so. But there was no hint in his speech of resistance *à outrance*. One of his main points was to suggest that the Liberal Party might now have a better understanding of the reasons why the previous

69

Administration had not reduced expenditure. *The Times*, on the following day, apprehended that 'the huge deficit ... is to be raised almost exclusively at the cost of the wealthy and the fairly well-to-do', but it accompanied this by the strange statement that it was an un-adventurous Budget in the sense that it broke no fresh taxation ground.

This was very much the lull before the storm. By May 1, *The Times* was very worried, not so much by the detailed proposals of the Budget as by its political implications. 'The Chancellor of the Exchequer,' it noted somewhat turgidly, 'discussed various matters not relevant to the matter in hand, deliberately with the intention of raising questions the discussion of which might lead to controversies likely, in his judgment, to be useful to his Party in the future.' In the debate on the general principles of the Budget which arose out of the Tea Resolution on May 3, 4, and 5, Balfour was strangely mild in his condemnation,[9] but this hesitancy had disappeared by the time of his Albert Hall speech to the Primrose League on May 7. Thereafter the campaign against the Budget rapidly gained momentum. City opinion quickly mobilised itself, and the leading financial houses sent a letter to the Prime Minister on May 15, which was phrased in familiar terms.

'... while prepared to bear their full share of increased taxation, which they recognised as necessary, (they) expressed alarm at the increasing disproportion of the burden placed on a small class. They held that the increase of the death duties ... and of the income tax coupled with

---

[9] One of his principal objections to the land taxes was that they might injure market gardening.

the super-tax, would injure commerce and industry; that the prosperity of all classes had been greatly due to the indisputable safety for capital afforded by Great Britain, and that the taxes in question would discourage private enterprise and thrift, thus eventually diminishing employment and reducing wages.'[1]

A few weeks later the Budget Protest League was formed, under the presidency of Walter Long,[10] and the Unionist Party committed itself at all points to the most resolute resistance to the Chancellor's proposals.

In the Liberal camp the Budget was on the whole enthusiastically received. Some of the old Whigs were unhappy about the land taxes, and at a later stage thirty of them formed themselves into a deputation to the Prime Minister on these points. But they never carried their doubts to the extent of provoking a serious split in the party. On the majority of Liberal members the effect was quite the reverse. They approved of the detailed proposals, but even more strongly, as is always the case with a party from which support has been slipping away, did they approve of their leaders' recovering the initiative. They hailed 'the first democratic Budget', and they felt that they might recover something of the spirit of the 'glad, confident morning' of 1906.

---

[10] 1854–1924. Created 1st Viscount Long of Wraxall, 1921. Conservative member for Wiltshire, North, 1880–85, Devizes, 1885–92, Liverpool, West Derby, 1892–1900, Bristol, South, 1900–6, Dublin, South, 1906–10, Strand, 1910–18, and Westminster, St. George's, 1918–21. President of the Board of Agriculture, 1895–1900. President of the Local Government Board, 1900–5 and 1915–16. Chief Secretary for Ireland, 1905. Secretary of State for the Colonies, 1916–18. First Lord of the Admiralty, 1918–21.

On some of the allies of the Government the effect was less encouraging. The Labour Party was well enough pleased,[11] although its members had their reservations and found a number of occasions, starting with the vote on the Tea Resolution, for dividing against the Government. But the numerically more important Nationalist Party was far from content. Redmond[12] spoke on Budget night and condemned the increased whisky tax and the excise duty on tobacco as unfair to Ireland; his party divided against them. A few days later he was seeing the issue in better perspective to the extent of describing the Budget as 'admirable and courageous from the British point of view', and saying that he would gladly see issue taken with the Lords on questions of social reform; but he remained adamant on his detailed criticisms, and neither on the second nor the third reading of the Finance Bill were the Nationalists able to support the Government.[13] With the huge Liberal majority this was of no immediate parliamentary importance, but it was to become an issue of some significance in the next Parliament.

So the long battle began. Every stage from the Chancellor's opening of his Budget to the end of the Finance Bill's passage through the Commons was contested by the Opposition with the utmost vigour and at the greatest possible length. Anyone who wishes to believe that pre-1914 Parliaments were always leisured

---

[11] Philip Snowden had previously advocated a Budget very much on Lloyd George's lines. (*See* R. C. K. Ensor: *England, 1870–1914,* p. 415.)

[12] 1851–1918. Nationalist member for Wexford, North, 1885–91, and for Waterford, 1891–1918. Chairman of Irish Parliamentary Party, 1900–18.

[13] On second reading they voted with the Opposition, and on third reading they abstained, a curious proceeding in view of their agreement in principle and their strong objection in detail.

and gentlemanly affairs, membership of which conflicted little with the life of a country squire, must keep his eyes firmly averted from the session of 1909. The parliamentary exertions of that year have not since been equalled.

The Budget, as we have seen, was introduced on April 29. The debate on the various stages of the Resolution required fourteen days, and they were finally obtained only on May 26. Then came a long week-end, which was all that was possible in the way of a Whitsun recess.

The House came back on Thursday, June 3, and on the following Monday the debate on the second reading of the Finance Bill was begun. This lasted for four full days, at the end of which Austen Chamberlain's amendment to reject was defeated by 366 votes to 209. There was no cross-voting amongst the main parties. The House then occupied itself with other business until June 21, when the long marathon of the committee stage started. For four weeks the pattern was quite regular. Each Monday, Tuesday, and Wednesday was devoted to the bill, and such other business of the session as could not be postponed was fitted in on the Thursdays and the short Friday sittings.

At first the Government did not allow the committee days to continue too late. In the first week motions to 'report progress and ask leave to sit again' were moved from the Treasury bench on successive nights at 11.30pm, midnight, and 2.45am respectively. By the second week there was a deterioration, and the corresponding times were 2.45am, midnight, and 4.0am. The third week was worse still, with the House at work on the bill until 4.0am on the first day's sitting, 1.30am on the second, and 3.45am on the third. And in the fourth week it was a case of 2.45am, 1.45am, and 9.0am. The principle of an 'early night' on the

Tuesday was preserved, but its 'earliness' became less absolute.

The fifth week began in a crescendo of lateness, with the Monday sitting lasting until 6.0am and the Tuesday sitting until 7.15am. But this pace of activity could not be continued. The next four full parliamentary days had to be devoted to Supply, and during this period of comparative relaxation the Government was able to consider the progress which it had so far made, and what were the future prospects for the bill. It was after July 20, and within two or three weeks of the date at which Parliament would normally expect to reach the end of the session. Fourteen days had already been devoted to the committee stage of the bill; largely as a result, the rest of the Government's legislative programme for the year was in chaos. And, to show for this, the Government had obtained nine clauses of a bill which had started with seventy-four clauses and which was showing every sign of expansion.

No one could have accused the Opposition of lack of tenacity. They talked about everything that could be talked about, and they divided against everything that could be divided against. For such progress as they were able to make, the Government had to rely upon a very free use of the closure. Whenever the House sat late the Opposition ensured that as much as possible of the time so gained was devoted, not to dealing with the bill, but to discussing whether or not it was proper to continue the debate at that hour. At 1.0am Arthur Balfour or Austen Chamberlain would move to report progress. This motion would not be used, as is now generally the case, merely to obtain from the Government a statement of their intentions for the night, but would be debated at length, usually until the closure was moved from the Government front bench. This would be divided against by the Opposition, who, when it was carried, would force the Government into the lobby again to defeat the motion to adjourn the debate. At three o'clock, and probably again at five o'clock, if the House were still sitting, Balfour or Chamberlain or one of their lieutenants would be on their feet once more to move the same motion, and the same tedious procedure would again be gone through. The maximum amount of sleep was lost, and the minimum of Government business was transacted.

In these circumstances the Government made three decisions. They and their supporters would have to reconcile themselves to a long summer at Westminster; a part even of the exiguous legislative programme of the session must be jettisoned; and there must be some change in the Standing Orders of the House so as to facilitate the passage of Government business. The two proposals under this last head were introduced by the Prime Minister on July 28. The first was certainly not very drastic. It provided that, when the House was in committee, the Deputy Chairman, and not merely the Chairman as had hitherto been the case, should have the right to accept a motion for the closure. The effect of this was both to relieve the burden on the Chairman during long sittings, and to make sure that whoever was leading for the Government[14] should not be prevented from moving to bring the debate to an end at the earliest possible moment. The second introduced a device which came to be known as the 'kangaroo', and which permitted the Chairman or Deputy Chairman to call amendments, by leave of the House, from among those for which he had accepted the

---

[14] It was then customary for the Prime Minister or the Chancellor of the Exchequer or whoever was the principal Minister on the Treasury bench to 'rise in his place and claim to move that the question be now put', and not leave this to the Government Chief Whip, as is now the practice.

closure. This, in effect, enabled the Government to exclude discussion on amendments of no importance or over which discussion had already ranged, without the consequence of excluding certain others in the same group with which it would clearly be improper not to deal. These changes were only carried against strong Unionist opposition. Arthur Balfour described them as instituting 'martial law in the House', and the impartiality of the Chairman and his deputy was challenged. After divisions and a sitting which lasted until nearly one o'clock, the proposals were carried.

The House returned to the Finance Bill on Monday, August 9, and devoted the whole of that week to it. There were two all-night sittings and instead of the normal short day on the Friday the House sat until dinner time. On the following Tuesday there was another all-night sitting,[15] and this, together with a day lasting only until midnight on the Wednesday, brought another stage in the battle to an end. By this time Clause 27 had been reached, and the first part of the bill, dealing with the land taxes, was almost completed.

For the next fortnight the House was occupied with the Irish Land Bill and the Housing Bill. The former, particularly, was moderately controversial,[16] but as it guaranteed the presence and support of the Nationalists, the time devoted to it enabled

[15] It was on this occasion that an Opposition member raised objection to the presence 'in his pyjamas' of Mr. Churchill, who was wearing these garments, apparently beneath some other clothing, in order that he might sleep more easily between divisions.

[16] Sufficiently so, at any rate, to produce on August 25 the almost unbelievable tedium of twenty-three divisions immediately following each other, and

many Liberals to take a short holiday. Progress on the Finance Bill was resumed on Wednesday, September 1. Thereafter, until the end of the committee stage more than a month later, only five parliamentary days were not devoted to it, and for the last three weeks, from September 20, it occupied the whole of the time. During this last lap (from September 1) the House did not sit quite so extravagantly late as it had been doing. There were no sittings that lasted until breakfast time; but there were four that lasted until after 3.0am and another five which lasted until 2.0am or later; and on only one occasion, except on Fridays (and there was a sitting until dinner time on one of these), was the business concluded before midnight.

The committee stage was finally concluded on Wednesday, October 6—the forty-second allotted day—and on the Friday the House adjourned for a week. After the reassembly, nine days, without late sittings, were devoted to report, and this stage of the bill was obtained on Friday, October 29. There remained only third reading, and this, after three days of debate, was carried by 379 votes to 149, at 11.30pm on Thursday, November 4. The bill was sent to the Lords, and the Commons went away for nearly three weeks.

In all, it had taken seventy parliamentary days to get the Budget through the House of Commons, and there had been 554 divisions—in the whole session there were no less than 895, as against a mere 383 in a very busy modern year like 1946-47. The strain on the Chancellor of the Exchequer had been immense, although he had received more help from his colleagues than would be normal today. Apart from his assistant at the

occupying the whole time from 9 pm until after midnight. The Finance Bill never subjected members to quite this form of torture.

Treasury[17] and the Solicitor-General, the Prime Minister, the Secretary of State for War, the President of the Board of Trade, the Chancellor of the Duchy of Lancaster, the Attorney-General and a number of junior Ministers all assisted him at the despatch-box. Haldane led for the Government throughout almost the whole of one all-night sitting, and Asquith on a number of occasions came down to the House after a short night and an early breakfast at Downing Street, and took over for the last hour or two of a long sitting. At more attractive times of day relief was still easier to obtain. Nevertheless, the brunt of the burden inevitably remained on the Chancellor's own shoulders. Some rough guide to the regularity of his attendance is given by the fact that he voted in 462 of the 554 divisions.[18] But his demeanour was more important than his presence, and there seems to be general agreement that at all stages of this arduous process his behaviour in the House was courteous, skilled and, where no point of principle was involved, conciliatory. It was a most distinguished parliamentary performance.

The strain of the summer on the Liberal back-benchers, while

----

[17] Charles Hobhouse. 1862–1941. Member for East Wiltshire, 1892–95. and Bristol, East, 1900–18. Financial Secretary to the Treasury, 1908–11. Chancellor of the Duchy of Lancaster, 1911–14. Postmaster-General, 1914–15. Succeeded his father as 4th Baronet, 1916.

[18] On the day after the bill received its third reading, Lloyd George gave a dinner to those of his colleagues who had assisted him in the House. The division records of those who attended were printed, a little invidiously perhaps, on the menu cards. (*See* Margot Asquith, *Autobiography*, vol. II, p. 123.) Of those present, only the Chief Whip and the Solicitor-General bettered the record of the Chancellor. Mr. Churchill, despite the pyjama incident, was bottom; but the Prime Minister, who voted in 202 divisions, was only a little above him.

obviously not so great as on the leaders, was also considerable; and they did not have the glory to compensate. Voting without speaking is always a dismal business. Fortunately the majority was such that a very rigorous system of whipping was not necessary. In none of the 554 divisions was there even the threat of a Government defeat. As a result, the Patronage Secretary was able to spread the burden fairly thin. There was not much indication, even during August, that many Liberal members were abroad or in the country, for the numbers voting early in the day were often surprisingly high—250–300 was quite common. But late at night only the minimum number was kept on duty. After about 2.0am the Opposition vote normally fell to between forty and sixty, and the Government obviously made little attempt to keep more than its 'closure vote'[19] and a margin of perhaps 15 to 20. In this way the strain of the session was made tolerable.

Sustained and severe though the struggle was in the House of Commons, it was little less so in the country; and here the issue was more open to doubt. At first the Budget did not appear to be popular. This impression came partly from a chance Liberal defeat at the Stratford-on-Avon bye-election which followed a few days after its introduction; partly from the greater speed with which the Unionist leaders took to the platforms; and partly from the fact that the City shouted so loudly that it seemed at first that there must be many others helping the financiers to make the noise. This campaign in the City reached its crescendo on June 23, when a crowded meeting of influential businessmen, under the chairmanship of Lord Rothschild, met in the Cannon

---

[19] Under the Standing Orders of the House a motion for the closure is not effectively carried unless there are at least 100 members voting in the 'Aye' lobby.

Street Hotel. Many of those present were normally supporters of the Liberal Party, and this, together with the fact that Lord Rosebery had used the previous day's issue of *The Times* to publish his first denunciation of the Budget, made some Liberals a little nervous of developments in their own party.

At this stage, however, the supporters of the Government re-took the initiative. On the same day as the City meeting, a meeting in the House of Commons set up the Budget League, with Mr. Churchill as president, to conduct a vigorous campaign in the constituencies; and on the following day Lloyd George delivered a sharp *riposte* to the businessmen. 'We are having too much Lord Rothschild,' he said. 'Some countries would not have their politics dictated by great financiers, and this country would join them.'[20]

Thereafter there was a spate of Liberal oratory. Mr. Churchill was perhaps the most indefatigable (and certainly one of the most violent) speakers in support of the Budget, but the Prime Minister did at least his fair share of campaigning, even braving a Cannon Street Hotel audience in July. The Chancellor himself, either by design or because he was fully occupied in the House, was very quiet. Apart from the speech in which he replied to Rothschild and one delivered at the Bankers' Dinner on July 16, in which, perhaps wisely but certainly unusually, he confined himself to a few technical revenue points, he made no public appearance until the end of July. Then, on the thirtieth of the month, he went to Limehouse and addressed an audience of 4,000 people at the 'Edinburgh Castle'. It was his first full-scale defence of his Budget before a popular audience, and he did not

---

[20] Speech at a luncheon given by the Land and Housing Reform Joint Committee. (*See Annual Register for 1909*, p. 146.).

neglect the opportunity. He justified the land taxes by quoting instances of extortionate profiteering by landlords—and he carefully chose his examples from amongst the dukes. He resisted the charge that these taxes would be a burden upon industry.

'We are placing the burdens on the broadest shoulders,' he said. 'Why should I put burdens on the people? I am one of the children of the people. I was brought up amongst them, I know their trials, and God forbid that I should add one grain of trouble to the anxieties which they bear with such patience and fortitude. When the Prime Minister did me the honour of inviting me to take charge of the National Exchequer at a time of great difficulty, I made up my mind that, in framing my Budget, no cupboard should be barer, no lot should be harder to bear. By that test, I challenge them to judge the Budget.'[m]

The speech produced sharp reactions. It provoked tumultuous applause from the audience, the most widespread and detailed attention in the newspapers, a letter of rebuke from the King, a howl of execration from some landowners, and an even more unfortunate attempt at reasoned reply from some others. Lord Lansdowne described the Chancellor as 'a robber gull', the Duke of Beaufort said that he would 'like to see Winston Churchill and Lloyd George in the middle of twenty couple of dog hounds', and the Duke of Rutland described the whole Liberal Party as a crew of 'piratical tatterdemalions'. The Duke of Portland, on the other hand, took up the point about 'bared cupboards', and attempted to show that a great many people's cupboards would in fact be bared as a result of the reduction in staff which great landowners would be obliged to undertake. The Duke of

Buccleuch gave practical shape to this principle by refusing a guinea to a Dumfriesshire football club because of the Budget proposals.[21] But neither this nor the Duke of Somerset's statement that he would have to discharge his own estate hands and reduce his gifts to charity were very well received by the public. People were getting a little tired of the troubles of the dukes and their excessively personal view of politics.[22] They were doing the Chancellor's propaganda for him even better than he could do it himself. This was widely felt, and a Conservative member of Parliament[23] went so far as to attack them very bitterly in a public speech:

'He only wished the Dukes had held their tongues, every one of them.... It would have been a good deal better for the Conservative Party if, before the Budget was introduced, every Duke had been locked up and kept locked up until the Budget was over.... These men who are going about squealing and say they are going to reduce their subscriptions to charities and football clubs because they were being unduly taxed ought to be ashamed of themselves, Dukes or no Dukes.'[n]

---

[21] This was replaced by shilling subscriptions from a number of Liberal members of Parliament.

[22] They perhaps contrasted the behaviour of these magnates with the 'silence and dignity' with which, Mr. Churchill had declared (Edinburgh: July 17), the working classes were paying their share of the new taxation.

[23] William Joynson-Hicks. 1865–1932. Later 1st Viscount Brentford, Unionist member for N.W. Manchester, 1908–10, Brentford, 1911–18, and Twickenham, 1918–29. Home Secretary, 1924–28.

Whether because of Lloyd George's Limehouse speech and the replies which it provoked or for more general causes, there was a very widespread impression at the beginning of August that the tide had turned in favour of the Government. *The Times* of August 4 said that the fate of the Budget had ceased to be precarious, and on the following day the *Daily Mail* (which was also owned by Lord Northcliffe) announced that outside the City the campaign of the Budget Protest League had fallen flat. Apparently its promoters had sometimes met the humiliating fate of having their resolutions defeated at their own meetings.*

Whether or not the issue was decided, however, the campaigns continued unabated throughout August and September and into October. On September 4, Mr. Churchill was telling a Leicester audience that 'the tax-gatherer would now ask, not what have you got, but how did you get it?' On the tenth, Lord Rosebery, who had just resigned the presidency of the Liberal League, was making his second public attack on the Budget, and defending the dukes as 'a poor but honest class'. A week later there began the Birmingham battle between the leaders of the two parties, when Asquith spoke to an audience of 10,000 people in Bingley Hall and an overflow meeting of 3,000 on September 17, and Arthur Balfour answered him at the same place on the twenty-second. Early in October there came Lloyd George's great series of meetings at Newcastle-on-Tyne. But more and more the issue was coming to be, not so much whether the Budget was desirable in itself, but whether or not the House of Lords was entitled to reject it, and what would be the constitutional consequences if it did. And this was another story.

V

To Reject or not to Reject

The peers had not rejected a Finance Bill for more than 250 years; and their attitude towards the Old Age Pensions Bill of the previous session had given a very recent indication that even in their most recalcitrant mood they went in some awe of the doctrine of Commons' supremacy on money matters. It was not therefore surprising that during the early stages of the battle of the Budget there was no open discussion on either side of the possibility of a Lords' rejection. The *Annual Register* recorded no reference to the matter before July 16, when Lord Lansdowne somewhat ambiguously announced that 'the House of Lords would do its duty, but would not swallow the Finance Bill whole without wincing'.[1] By August 9, with the Limehouse speech to encourage him, he was leaning much more openly towards

---

[1] In some newspapers this was apparently misprinted as 'without mincing', and provoked Mr. Churchill to engage in an involved controversy as to whether or not Lord Lansdowne would have to 'eat his mince'.

rejection, and Sir Edward Grey, in a reply on the following day, summed up the position by saying that 'Mr. Balfour and Lord Lansdowne are keeping two doors open. They are debating whether they should pass the Budget or not. We know their wishes, not the extent of their nerve.'[a] By the time of the Prime Minister's Birmingham speech on September 17 the indication that the Lords proposed to reject had grown stronger, and, in his own words, he 'thought it right to use the plainest language'.[b] 'Amendment by the House of Lords,' he said, 'is out of the question. Rejection by the House of Lords is equally out of the question. … Is this issue going to be raised? If it is, it carries with it in its train consequences which he would be a bold man to forecast or foresee. That way revolution lies.'

The Unionists paid little attention to his warning, and at their own meeting at the same place a week later Austen Chamberlain read out a letter from his father which expressed the hope that the Lords would force an election, while one of the supporting speakers[2] said that 'the peers are not worthy of their seats if they do not reject the Budget'. Arthur Balfour was far more guarded, but there can be little doubt that by this time his mind was quite firmly made up in favour of rejection.

Lansdowne's biographer, after quoting a letter to show that by October 2 Lansdowne had reached his own decision to reject, notes that 'Mr. Balfour had, from an even earlier period, believed that a compromise was impossible.'[c] When, therefore, the Unionist leaders were summoned to see the King on October 12 they had already come down quite decisively on the side of rejection.

---

[2] Sir George Doughty. 1854–1914. Liberal Unionist member for Grimsby, 1895-January, 1910 and December, 1910–14.

This audience took place on the initiative of the Sovereign himself, but with the full approval of the Prime Minister. At the end of September King Edward had the rumours of the summer confirmed by a memorandum, pronouncing strongly in favour of rejection, which Lord Cawdor, who was staying at Balmoral, drew up and presented to him. On receiving this the King summoned Asquith to Scotland, expressed his own desire to avoid a collision between the two Houses by the discovery of some *via media*,[3] and secured the agreement of the Prime Minister to his talks with Balfour and Lansdowne.

These talks served little purpose. The Unionist leaders informed the King that no definite decision had been reached, which was formally correct, as no meeting of the Unionist peers had taken place;[4] but they knew, and he knew, how utterly remote had become the chance of a moderate course being chosen.

The Liberals also knew how nearly the die was cast, and however fanciful may be the theory that Lloyd George had originally framed his Budget with the principal object of exciting the peers, there can be no doubt that he and Mr. Churchill and some others were now extremely anxious that rejection should take

---

[3] What was in his mind was that, if the Lords would accept the Budget, the Government should agree to a January dissolution. Asquith stressed the practical disadvantages of such a course—it would not be attractive to either party and would be likely to produce a parliamentary stalemate—and succeeded by this method in turning the King's mind away from it. He might well have added that to have conceded a dissolution at the point of their lordships' pistol would have been to give away the whole principle which was at issue.

[4] In the outcome the feeling in favour of rejection was so strong that a meeting was held to be unnecessary.

place. 'It would give the Government a great tactical advantage,' Mr. Churchill informed the National Liberal Club on October 8.[d]

The famous speeches which the Chancellor of the Exchequer delivered at Newcastle-on-Tyne during the week-end of October 9-11 were therefore designed to inject the maximum amount of heat into the already torrid controversy, and to make it as difficult as possible for the Unionists to retreat from the dangerously exposed positions they had already taken up.

'They are forcing revolution,' he said. 'But the Lords may decree a revolution which the people will direct. If they begin, issues will be raised that they little dream of, questions will be asked which are now whispered in humble voices, and answers will be demanded then with authority. The question will be asked "Should 500 men, ordinary men chosen accidentally from among the unemployed, override the judgment—the deliberate judgment—of millions of people who are engaged in the industry which makes the wealth of the country?" That is one question. Another will be, who ordained that a few should have the land of Britain as a perquisite; who made 10,000 people owners of the soil, and the rest of us trespassers in the land of our birth; who is it—who is responsible for the scheme of things whereby one man is engaged through life in grinding labour, to win a bare and precarious subsistence for himself, and when at the end of his days he claims at the hands of the community he served a poor pension of eightpence a day, he can only get it through a revolution; and another man who does not toil receives every hour of the day, every hour of the night, whilst he slumbers, more than his neighbour receives in a whole year of toil? Where did the table of that law come from? Whose finger inscribed it? These are the questions that will be asked. The answers are charged with peril for the order of things the Peers represent; but they are fraught with rare and refreshing fruit for the parched lips of the multitude who have been treading the dusty road along which the people have marched through the dark ages which are now emerging into the light.'ᵉ

It was a wonderful popular oratory, with enough weight of content—an explosively radical content too—for there to be no question of dismissing it as mere froth. Some of the imagery might be a little lurid for fastidious tastes—Lord Knollys begged the Prime Minister 'not to pretend to the King that he liked Mr. Lloyd George's speeches, for the King would not believe it, and it only irritated him'—but it was not intended for fastidious people. It was intended to rouse the mass support of the Liberal Party and to goad the peers into a rash truculence. Towards both these ends it was extremely conducive, although by October the former was more necessary than the latter.

The final decision was taken by the Unionist Party by November 10, a week after the Finance Bill had left the Commons, when Lansdowne gave notice that on second reading he would move 'that this House is not justified in giving its assent to the Bill until it has been submitted to the judgment of the country'. The motion was most carefully drafted, by Balfour and others, so as to present the intervention of the House of Lords in the most popular light possible. To this end it was as well-conceived as any motion could be, but the awareness of danger which this reveals makes it only more surprising that such an experienced party as the Unionist Party, under such experienced leaders as Balfour and Lansdowne, should ever have decided upon a course so reckless as a peers' rejection of a Budget. Their action did not kill the Budget, it greatly improved the electoral prospects of the Liberal Government, and it made the destruction of the Lords' veto inevitable; and all these consequences could have been predicted by any intelligent observer, and were predicted by many people. Why did the Unionist leadership ever agree to such a course?

It was not through lack of good advice. On the purely constitutional and legal plane they were not perhaps very well served, for, of the leading authorities, the Unionists, Anson and Dicey, by declaring that rejection would be perfectly proper (in sharp conflict with the Liberal, Pollock, who declared that it would be most improper), showed themselves to be no more objective than most men. But there were plenty of sage Unionist politicians to point out the foolishness of the course which was being taken. The old Duke of Devonshire, who would undoubtedly have exercised a strong influence on the side of caution, had died in 1908, and Lord Goschen,[5] who would have been on the same side, had predeceased him by a year.[6] Nevertheless there was still Lord James of Hereford, Lord St. Aldwyn, and Lord Balfour of Burleigh, all of them former members of Unionist Cabinets and all of them most unhappy at the thought of a peers' rejection.

'If we are to do anything,' St. Aldwyn wrote to Lansdowne on September 8, discussing a possible compromise policy of amendment, 'this seems to me a reasonable course; but I own that my House of Commons feeling on finance is against it, and that I think both the right and the wise course is to pass the Budget as it comes to us.' Lord James and Lord Balfour were, if anything, even more strongly opposed to action by the Lords, and they

---

[5] 1831–1907. George Joachim Goschen. Created 1st Viscount Goschen, 1900. First Lord of the Admiralty, 1871–74 and 1895–1902. Chancellor of the Exchequer, 1887–92.

[6] The attitude which both of them would have taken is well summed up by Goschen's remark: 'The Duke of Devonshire is like myself, a moderate man—a violently moderate man!'

were supported in this view by Lord Cromer and Lord Lytton. The last, in particular, argued very powerfully that rejection would be not so much wrong as catastrophically foolish.

'... a general election immediately following the rejection of the Budget,' he wrote, 'would, beyond all doubt, be disastrous to the fortunes of the Unionist Party. The Government would be returned with a sufficient majority to re-enact the Budget and to remain in office another five years. This would be bad enough, but it would be still worse if they obtained—as they must inevitably try to obtain— power to curtail the veto of the House of Lords. ... If, on the other hand, the Budget were allowed to pass, its burdens would soon prove odious in practice, and the comforting theory on which it is now founded would be exploded. By the end of another year the Government would have to go to the country and would, I believe, suffer defeat. A Unionist Government would then be in a position to amend the Budget, strengthen the House of Lords against further attack, and save the country from the Socialism and class warfare which are being fostered today.'[g]

This was a most prescient forecast of what was to happen when the Budget was rejected, and an attractive, and not altogether implausible, forecast of what might have happened had the opposite course been chosen. This was very much the point of view which F. E. Smith was urging upon Balfour at this time. In the words of his biographer, 'he (Smith) was convinced that the Lords should pass the Budget, so that when its brutalities were exposed and the Unionists returned to power, its terms could be altered and softened, its more violent clauses repealed'.[h]

He was a useful if surprising ally for the cause of moderation (his attitude at this time was very different from that which he was to take up when it came to the Parliament Bill, eighteen months later), for he was untouched by the heresy of free trade, and was in this respect unlike all the 'moderate' peers mentioned above.

This was the key to the whole difficulty. Tariff reform was the issue which rallied the Unionist enthusiasts in the country. From a party point of view it was the popular thing with which to be associated. Those who stood aloof found that the applause they received from their followers in the constituencies was less hearty than it might have been, and that they were always in danger of being regarded as bad party men. The free trade element in the party was therefore suspect, and the advice which came from it was given far less attention than it deserved.

Nor was it quite enough not to be a free trader. The Balfourians, as opposed to the 'whole-hoggers', were also in a difficult position. Arthur Balfour himself was leading a parliamentary party the great majority of which was far to the right of him on the protection issue. To equivocate on this, while retaining the lead, had been difficult enough, and it meant that he could not afford to restrain the fighting spirit of his party on yet a second major question. Lansdowne suffered a double disadvantage. He was not only a Balfourian, he was also an ex-Whig, and not even a member of the Carlton Club. At a time when it greatly needed firm and far-seeing leadership the Tory Party had thus succeeded, by internal schism and distrust, in destroying the self-confidence of its leaders and making them incapable of anything more adventurous or valuable than a little gentle swimming with the tide.

It was not an accident that those who were most vehemently in favour of rejection by the Lords were also, broadly speaking, ardent tariff reformers. Partly it was a question of temperament. No one could deny that to hitch the Tory wagon to the star of protection was a bold act; those who had done this preferred the boldness, or foolhardiness, of a peers' rejection to the nicely calculated tactics of calling off the battle at this stage. But there was more to it than this. There was also the fact that the protectionists feared the Budget *per se* more than did the free-fooders and the Balfourians. They had come to believe the propaganda of their opponents to the extent of accepting the view that Lloyd George's proposals constituted the only effective revenue-raising alternative to a general tariff. They agreed with the substance if not with the form of the argument which the Prime Minister had used in the third reading debate:

> 'What, then, are the two ways, and the only two ways, before the country of meeting the necessities of the nation? On the one hand you may do as we are doing. You may impose, simultaneously and in fair proportion, taxes on accumulated wealth, on the profits of industry, on the simpler luxuries, though not the necessities, of the poor.... That is one way—that is the way proposed by this Budget. What is the other, the only other, that has yet been disclosed or even foreshadowed to Parliament and the country? It is to take a toll of the prime necessaries of life; it is to raise the level of prices to the average consumer of the commodity; it is to surround your markets with a tariff wall.... That, Sir, is the choice which has to be made....'[i]

And because they agreed they were doubly anxious to destroy a Budget which would destroy part of the case for their beloved protection.

The forces of wealth, and particularly of landed wealth which counted for so much in the Unionist Party, were also against any retreat. The platform activities of some of the dukes might not have been well-regarded by many Conservative politicians, but when it came to a behind-the-scenes discussion of policy, the influence of these magnates was much too great for their point of view to be ignored. The liquor trade, which had clearly demonstrated its power over the Unionist Party in the previous session, was also all for a fight. And the Unionist organisation in the country, which had responded with zeal, as constituency organisations do, when their parliamentary army had marched up to such advanced positions during the battle in the House of Commons, was now by no means anxious that these positions should be evacuated. As Lord James of Hereford succinctly summed up the pressure for rejection: 'The agents, the organisations, and the Licensed Victuallers' Trade all demand it. They know nothing of, and care nothing for, Constitutional Law.'[j]

This was the clamour which carried Balfour and Lansdowne along. It is sometimes suggested that they were the victims of intense pressure from a small number of tariff reform peers who had secured an alliance with important sections of the Tory press. This was not the case. Lord Milner's famous 'Damn the consequences' Glasgow speech, which is often thought of as an example of this sort of pressure, was not in fact delivered until November 26, during the course of the rejection debate in the House of Lords, and long after all the decisions had been made. If pressure there was, it came not from a few peers, but from the whole of the unthinking section of the Unionist Party—always a formidable force—and from much of the thinking section as well; and if the pressure was not resisted, that was because Balfour and Lansdowne themselves half-believed rejection to be the right course, and because the weakness of their position dictated that they should follow those halves of their minds rather than the other.

The debate in the Lords began on November 23. It continued for five parliamentary days. Most of the peers of note on both sides and on the cross-benches took part,[7] and, as is so often the case when the House of Lords is engaged in reaching a peculiarly silly decision, there were many comments on the high level of the debate and on the enhancement it gave to the deliberative quality of the chamber.

After Crewe had formally moved the second reading, Lansdowne opened the debate by proposing his amendment. In the view at least of Morley, this was the best statement of the case heard from the Opposition benches. Lansdowne argued that 'tacked' on to the Finance Bill were a number of extraneous matters. 'Tacking' was a practice of which the House of Commons had become increasingly guilty, and it fully justified the Upper House in reviving the right to reject a money bill which had been expressly conceded in the Commons' arguments of 1689. On the tactical issue, he put forward the point that the House of Lords would do itself less harm by standing and fighting than by running away and abandoning for all time the right to interfere with the financial policy of a radical Government, however outrageous that policy might be.

Of the other speeches for the amendment, those of Halsbury and Curzon[8] were among the most extreme, and that of Ritchie

---

[7] Except for one or two, like St. Aldwyn, who deliberately absented themselves.

[8] George Nathaniel Curzon, 1859–1929, later 1st Marquess Curzon of Kedleston. Eldest son of Lord Scarsdale. Conservative member for

of Dundee, who had opposed his party and voted with the Government when the Lords were engaged in mutilating the Education Bill of 1906, was among the most surprising.

Balfour of Burleigh argued with great force on the other side. He pointed out the full enormity of the claim which the Upper House was making for itself.

'Finance differs from all other legislation in this respect. If a Bill is rejected either by a vote of this House or by disagreement between the two Houses the *status quo* which existed before the Bill was proposed survives and remains. It is not so in finance. If you are to establish a system whereby this House or any other authority has the right to establish a referendum as it is called—a reference to the people in matters of finance—you would spoil and destroy the control of the other House of Parliament over the Government, and would make, I venture to say, perhaps the most momentous change in the Constitution, as it has grown up, which has been made in the whole history of that Constitution.... My Lords, if you win, the victory can at most be a temporary one. If you lose you have altered and prejudiced the position, the power, the prestige, the usefulness of this House....'[k]

South-port, 1886–98. Viceroy of India, 1898–1905. Lord Privy Seal, 1915. Lord President of the Council and member of War Cabinet, 1916–19. Secretary of State for Foreign Affairs, 1919–24. Given an Irish peerage, 1898, and became an Irish representative peer, 1908. Created an Earl, 1911, and a Marquess, 1921.

He ended by warning the peers against walking into a trap set by their enemies, by doing which they would 'offend the deeper conservative instincts of the country'.

Lord James added similar counsel; Lord Reay remarked ominously that 'oligarchies are seldom destroyed and more frequently commit suicide'; Lord Rosebery denounced the Bill, but announced, to the great disappointment of the Unionists, that 'he was not willing to link the fortunes of the Second Chamber with opposition to the Budget', and said that he would not vote; and Lord Morley combined an accusation that the Lords were in effect repealing the Septennial Act with a curious homily about socialism and the 'fertilising residue of good' which he believed that 'socialistic movements and experiments would leave'.

Loreburn, the Lord Chancellor, read out a Government declaration saying, 'It is impossible that any Liberal Government should ever again bear the heavy burden of office, unless it is secured against a repetition of treatment such as our measures have had to undergo for the last four years.' And Crewe, who wound up the debate, announced that '… we must… set ourselves to obtain guarantees, … fenced about and guarded by the force of statute, guarantees which will prevent that indiscriminate destruction of our legislation of which your work tonight is the climax and crown'. He also assured their lordships that 'they were not the victims of a Ministerial plot; the great majority of the Ministers, including the Chancellor of the Exchequer, had hoped to the last that the Bill would pass'.

These late warnings, not surprisingly perhaps, were unheeded. When the question 'that the Bill be now read a Second Time' was put, the contents were seventy-five and the not-contents were 350; so the not-contents had it. There were few surprises in the division lists. A fine collection of Lloyd George's 'backwoods-men' turned up. Balfour of Burleigh was almost the only dissenting Unionist who voted for the bill. The great majority of bishops, including the Primate, abstained, although the Archbishop of York[9] and three others voted for the Government. The Bishop of Lincoln voted with the Opposition.

What reactions did this decisive rejection produce? The Liberal leaders were certainly not greatly distressed. A *Punch* cartoon—and *Punch* was then rather pro-Government— which showed the news being discussed at a hilariously happy Cabinet, was probably somewhat wide of the mark, although more in form than in substance perhaps. What was the Chancellor of the Exchequer's personal position? There are two pieces of directly contradictory evidence to be reconciled. There is Lord Crewe's statement, which is of importance both because he was a man most unlikely to say something which he knew to be untrue for the sake of oratorical effect, and because of its precision. He did not say that all Ministers wished to see the bill pass; he said 'the great majority[10]... including the Chancellor of the Exchequer'. It is difficult to see why, if he was not bound by the truth, he should have chosen this intriguingly qualified degree of misrepresentation.

---

[9] 1864–1945. Cosmo Gordon Lang. Archbishop of York, 1908–28, Archbishop of Canterbury, 1928–42. Created 1st Lord Lang of Lambeth. 1942.

[10] Who was in the minority? Was it only Mr. Churchill, who is recorded as saying that 'his hope and prayer was that they (the peers) would throw out the bill, as it would save the Government from certain defeat if the elections were put off'? (Wilfred Scawen Blunt: *My Diaries*, p. 689.) Or were there others too?

On the other hand, we have a biographer of Lloyd George, Mr. J. Hugh Edwards, who was clearly very much *persona grata* with his subject, and whose book, published in 1930, tells how, at the dinner which the Chancellor gave to celebrate the passing of the Finance Bill through the House of Commons, only one toast was drunk, that of 'May the Lords reject the Budget!'[m] This story, for which no corroboration can be found, is a little implausible when it is remembered that the Prime Minister and Haldane, as well as Lloyd George and his henchmen, were present at the dinner. Nevertheless, its spirit is more in keeping with Lloyd George's behaviour at this time than is Crewe's statement. It is not necessary to accept the theory that the Budget was designed from the first as a trap for the peers in order to believe that when rejection occurred the Chancellor of the Exchequer was very well satisfied.

> 'If the Budget has been buried,' Lloyd George declared, 'it is in the sure and certain hope of a glorious resurrection.' 'Liberty,' he went on, 'owes as much to the fool-hardiness of its foes as it does to the sapience and wisdom of its friends. ... At last the cause between the peers and the people has been set down for trial in the grand assize of the people, and the verdict will come soon.'[11]

The Liberal leaders were pleased, but the public showed no signs of excitement. A demonstration in Parliament Square, called by the Political Committee of the National Liberal Club for the evening on which it was thought that the vote would take

---

[11] Speech at a National Liberal Club Luncheon on December 3.

place in the House of Lords, was a complete failure,[12] and throughout the country the spontaneous protests of 1831 and 1884 were entirely absent.

Conservative spokesmen, naturally enough, gave loyal support to the action of Lansdowne and his followers. 'Is he wrong?' Arthur Balfour asked a Manchester audience. 'He is abundantly right, and there never was an occasion when this power, rested by the Constitution in the Second Chamber, was more abundantly justified.'" But there were many people, far from the ranks of the Liberal Party, who disagreed sharply with Mr. Balfour. Lord Knollys,[13] the King's private secretary, told the Clerk to the Privy Council 'very gravely and emphatically that he thought the Lords mad'.° Balfour of Burleigh and not Lansdowne had been right: 'the Lords had not merely treated the Liberal Government outrageously, they had also succeeded in offending the deeper conservative instincts of the country'; and Lord Reay had been right too: an oligarchy was performing the act of suicide.

---

[12] This may have been partly due to the organisers' selection of the wrong night.

[13] 1837–1924. Francis Knollys. Created 1st Lord Knollys of Caversham, 1902. Private secretary to King Edward VII as Prince of Wales, 1870–1901, and as King, 1901–10. Joint private secretary to King George V, 1910–13.

VI

The Verdict of the Nation

Any course other than immediate dissolution was out of the question. The legislature had refused Supply, and in these circumstances no government could carry on. It was this, most of all, which gave the full measure of what the Lords had done. They had not merely confronted the Government with the choice of an immediate election or of acceptance of the loss of a particular measure, as they had frequently done before. They had left the Government with no choice, and had taken upon themselves the right of deciding when a Government could carry on and when it could not, when a Parliament should end and when it should not. It was a claim which, if allowed, would have made the Government as much the creature of the hereditary assembly as of the elective assembly.

Asquith responded to the challenge on December 2, when he moved in the House of Commons 'that the action of the House of Lords in refusing to pass into law the financial provision made by this House for the service of the year is a breach of the

Constitution and a usurpation of the rights of the Commons'. He commended his motion to the House in what his biographers describe as 'a serious argument enlivened by brilliant raillery',[a] which was very well received by his followers. In the course of his speech he announced an immediate dissolution— 'at the earliest possible moment we shall ask the constituencies of the country to declare that the organ and voice of the free people of this country is to be found in the elected representatives of the nation'. The resolution, supported by both the Irish and the Labour Party, and opposed by a sick Arthur Balfour,[1] was carried by 349 votes to 134.

Prorogation took place on the next day, and the King's Speech, after thanking the Commons for the 'liberality and care with which (they) provided for the heavy additions to the national expenditure due to the requirements of imperial defence and social reform', noted with regret 'that their provision had proved unavailing'. The dates of the election were not known at once, but on December 23 it was announced that the writs would be issued on January 10, and that polling would be spread over the fortnight beginning January 15. Nevertheless the campaigns, which had begun sporadically as soon as the dissolution was announced, were formally opened on December 10, when Balfour issued his address to the electors of the City and Asquith spoke at the Albert Hall.

The Prime Minister's audience, which numbered 10,000 and was described by *The Times* as 'boiling over with enthusiasm, was by careful design exclusively male, for the suffragettes were very

---

[1] He developed pulmonary catarrh, which prevented his participation in the election campaign until the beginning of January.

active at the time,[2] and strict precautions were thought necessary. Its members were told that the three major issues on which the country had to pronounce were 'the absolute control of the Commons over finance, the maintenance of Free Trade, and the effective limitation and curtailment of the legislative powers of the House of Lords'. In amplification of the last point he had said:

'The people in future, when they elect a new House of Commons, must be able to feel, what they cannot feel now, that they are sending to Westminster men who will have the power not merely of proposing and debating, but of making laws. The will of the people, as deliberately expressed by their elected representatives, must, within the limits of the lifetime of a single Parliament, be made effective.'[b]

And on Home Rule he expressly freed the Liberal Party from the 'self-denying ordinance' which had made it eschew this subject in the 1906 Parliament.

Arthur Balfour's election address deployed arguments which have since become familiar. The attack on the House of Lords, he said, was only the culmination of a long-drawn conspiracy to

---

[2] A few weeks before, Mr. Churchill had been dog-whipped at Bristol, and a few days afterwards the Chancellor of the Exchequer was to be locked into his car, outside the Queen's Hall, by and with a militant young female, who lectured him for some time before he was able to escape. Even at the Albert Hall meeting immunity was only secured by extricating one woman from the organ shortly before the commencement, and by preventing another, who was disguised as a telegraph boy, from entering during the Prime Minister's speech.

secure a single-chamber legislature. These 'conspirators' wished the Commons to be independent not only of the peers, but of the people. This plot was ingeniously contrived, but was proving unsuccessful. The people were not insulted by having their opinion asked on the Budget, and they did not think that the House of Lords had exceeded its duty in asking for a dissolution on this point.

The day before this address was issued the Chancellor of the Exchequer had begun his own campaign at Caernarvon. After arousing great enthusiasm by his announcement that he proposed to decline the offer made to him to contest Cardiff and to remain in his old constituency,[3] he went on to employ, most effectively, a metaphor in his familiar pastoral style:

'Yesterday I visited the old village where I was brought up,' he said. 'I wandered through the woods familiar to my boyhood. There I saw a child getting sticks for firewood, and I thought of the hours which I spent in the same pleasant and profitable occupation, for I also have been something of a backwoodsman; and here is one experience taught me then which is of use to me today. I learnt as a child it was little use going into the woods after a period of calm and fine weather, for I generally returned empty-handed.... But after a great storm I always came back with an armful.... We are in for rough weather, we may even be in for a winter

---

[3] Why the offer was regarded as attractive is not clear, for the Cardiff District seat, for which D. A. Thomas (later Lord Rhondda) then became the candidate, was, on paper at any rate, a much less safe Liberal division than Lloyd George's own Caernarvon District. At the second 1910 election it was lost to the Unionists by a majority of 300.

of storms which will rock the forest, break many a withered branch, and leave many a rotten tree torn up by the roots. But when the weather clears you may depend upon it that there will be something brought within reach of the people that will give warmth and glow to their grey lives, something that will help to dispel the hunger, the despair, the oppression and the wrong which now chill so many of their hearths.'[c]

Throughout the campaign Lloyd George remained in strong oratorical form. He joined eagerly in a 'war scare' with Germany[4] argument which Balfour introduced, and told a Peckham audience on January 7 that 'the believers in inevitable war are the men who make them. The Unionists, after having destroyed the Constitution, are prepared to destroy the fiscal system and to risk war with a European power, and all just to avoid valuation of their land.'[d] And he kept up his rhetorical pressure to the last moment, even to the extent of addressing a large meeting at Grimsby on the day of the poll, an intervention which was commonly thought to have had much to do with the Liberal gain which was achieved there. His visit incensed the local Unionists to the extent of making him repeat, in a less dramatic and ingenious form, his Birmingham escape of ten years earlier.[5]

---

[4] In one way and another the Germans figured very prominently in Unionist propaganda at this election. They were portrayed as dangerously aggressive in order to justify an attack on the Government's naval policy, and as contented and well-fed in order to justify a policy of tariff reform.

[5] The political attention paid to Grimsby at this time was remarkable. At the second 1910 election, after Balfour had addressed an audience of 10,000

The election campaign generally was in no way outstandingly exciting—even the suffragettes called off their attempts to break up meetings after Christmas—although public interest remained high throughout. Inevitably, the attention of the voters strayed from the rather involved constitutional point at issue, and the Budget versus tariff reform was probably the main question upon which electors in Great Britain made up their minds. In other words, the Unionists got what they wanted: an election on the merits of the Budget rather than on the propriety of the peers' behaviour. In Ireland, of course, the position was entirely different. The Budget itself would have won very few votes, but it had come to possess the contingent merit of opening up a way by which the veto might be destroyed; and to this end, which they knew to be a necessary step towards Home Rule, the bulk of the Nationalists were prepared to swallow the Budget and give close support to the Liberal Party. A minority of the Nationalists, however, rejected such a policy of compromise, and nine members, who had accepted Redmond's leadership in the last Parliament, fought and were elected under the label of 'Independent Nationalists'.

The earlier part of the campaign was notable for the platform activity of the peers. Hitherto the regular sessional order of the House of Commons declaring that no member of the other House should concern himself in parliamentary elections had been fairly strictly observed, even when, as in 1880, it put the Unionists at a grave disadvantage by precluding their three

---

there during the day, Mr. Churchill, who had spoken in Cheshire that evening, travelled across by special train, stopping to have Balfour's speech supplied to him in instalments *en route*, and delivered a rumbustious reply, to a well-filled meeting, at midnight.

leading figures[6] from participation in the campaign. In the 1906 Parliament an apparent breach had occurred when the Duke of Norfolk wrote a public letter of support to the Unionist candidate in the High Peak bye-election,[7] and the fact that the Committee of Privileges, to which the matter was referred, recommended no action may have encouraged peers to apply the rule more loosely at the general election than had before been the practice. Many of them decided that to participate fully up to the day on which the writs were issued, and then to abstain, would be a fair compromise.[8]

Until January 10, therefore, there was a spate of senatorial oratory from Unionist platforms. Whether it helped the cause it was designed to promote is doubtful. Mr. R. C. K. Ensor has commented that 'it had in some cases the disadvantage which the act permitting a prisoner to give evidence is generally allowed to have entailed for the prisoner'.[e] Lord Cawdor and Lord Curzon were perhaps the most vehemently immoderate of spokesmen in their own defence. Cawdor combined his vehemence with an engagingly demagogic approach, as when, at Leeds on December 18, he accused the Government of 'wanting us to copy Bulgaria and Greece in getting rid of a Second Chamber, and Nigeria in its land law'.[f] Curzon was very different, and it is difficult now to imagine the reaction of his audience at Oldham on December 16 to his denunciation of the House of

---

[6] Beaconsfield, Cranbrook, and Salisbury.

[7] With the object of swinging the Roman Catholic vote.

[8] When the usual sessional order was moved on the first day of the new Parliament, a Unionist amendment to restrict it to peers who were also Lords-Lieutenant of counties was proposed, and this was accepted by Asquith and carried without a division.

Commons for containing 'no great generals or ex-Colonial Governors', and his revelation that 'Renan had said that all civilization had been the work of aristocracies,[9] and Maine that a democracy in England would have prevented the Reformation and a series of other great political and economic reforms'.[g]

In Birmingham they were less concerned with proclaiming the merits of aristocracy, a theme which would still have been uncongenial to both the leaders and the supporters of the Chamberlain faction, than with turning everything to the advantage of the cause of tariff reform. Joseph Chamberlain, who was again candidate for West Birmingham, was unable to leave the Kensington house where he had remained, incapacitated by a stroke, since 1906, but he poured out letters of encouragement to chosen candidates; and Austen, operating from Highbury and fighting East Worcestershire, was a willing if not altogether effective substitute. The tariff reform cause undoubtedly made some progress during this campaign,[10] within the ranks of Unionist workers and outside, and Balfour, on the eve of the first day's polling, both made it the principal subject of his last-minute message to the electors and joined with Joseph Chamberlain in

---

[9] Lloyd George replied to this, characteristically but effectively, by saying that he 'thought the Carpenter of Galilee had more to do with the best and highest element of civilization'. *(Annual Register for* 1909, p. 269.)

[10] Although not quite to the extent that Austen Chamberlain suggested when he wrote to Balfour after the election and said: 'Tariff Reform was our trump card. Where we won, we won on and by Tariff Reform. Even where we lost, it was the only subject in our repertoire about which people really cared.' (Petrie, *op. cit.,* vol. 1, p. 242.) Austen's loyalty to his family cause, combined perhaps with his Liberal Unionism, made him under-estimate the effect of true Tory scepticism, of blank, negative opposition, as a vote-winning force for the Unionist Party.

signing a categorical denial that protection would affect the working-class cost of living.

Asquith was always at home with this subject, and he responded eagerly to any gauntlets which were flung down before him by the Opposition leaders. 'After seven years' controversy,' he said at Crieff on January 15, 'the world is strewn with the wreckage of Mr. Chamberlain's prophecies on Tariff Reform. Our oversea trade has expanded beyond expectation; the census of production has shown that we are more than holding our own, and that the injury of "dumped" goods is imaginary.'[h]

He was glad to have something into which he could get his teeth, for many of the Unionist pronouncements on other topics (and some on this) presented the controversialist with nothing but a smooth, round surface. 'We seek to build up; our opponents to destroy,' wrote Austen Chamberlain, in a mystical mood. 'We seek to promote union; our opponents to promote separation.'[i] 'Liberal policy runs counter to the best thought of the time,'[j] said Arthur Balfour, in one of the most unprecise and arrogant remarks which can ever have come from such normally precise, if not, in big things, over-modest lips.

Polling began on January 15. Both parties were optimistic, as parties must always be, although the calmer spirits in both would probably have admitted that a near balance with the Irish holding control was the most likely result. London and Lancashire were regarded as the key areas, in which sweeping Conservative gains would be registered if the left-wing majority was to be destroyed.

The first results were not discouraging for the Unionists. There were three gains for them in London, three in Lancashire and two in the three-member industrial borough of Wolverhampton; and in Birmingham the safe seats became still safer. But this early promise was not quite fulfilled. By the end of a week, with about three quarters of the results in, a net Unionist gain of seventy-five was shown, and it was certain that neither of the two main parties could secure a clear majority, but that the Government, with its allies, would be fairly comfortably placed.

By the end of the month all the returns, with the usual exceptions of the Scottish Universities and Orkney and Shetland, were complete, and it was possible to see the picture in detail. The Unionists had achieved a net gain (over their 1906 position) of 116 seats, and had brought themselves to within two of the strength of the Liberal Party itself; they were 273 and the Liberals were 275. The Nationalists, in addition to the defection of the 'independents', dropped one county division, and the Labour members, despite a gain from the Unionists at Wigan and the spur of the Osborne judgment (which had been given on December 22), sustained a net reduction of eleven, and fell back to forty.

The Government coalition therefore had a nominal majority of 124, which, although very far short of the preponderance of 1906, was nevertheless the next largest majority which a Liberal Government had enjoyed since 1832.[11] But it was not a very cohesive majority. To call the Independent Nationalists allies of the Government in any sense was to strain the meaning of language. They certainly could not be counted upon for support. And even the support of Redmond and his followers was highly conditional. But it was quite essential, for, even with the Labour Party solidly in the Government lobby, a temporary alliance of Unionists and Nationalists could defeat Asquith by forty. It was not an easy prospect which faced the Prime Minister.

[11] Even in 1868 Gladstone had a majority of only 116.

Where had the losses occurred which made the Liberal strength so much less than in 1906? Not, to any extent, in Wales, Scotland, or Ireland. The Celtic fringe, which in 1906 had given the Government parties 175 seats (out of a possible 235), gave them only four less in 1910. In Scotland there was even a net gain of one, for losses further north were more than balanced by an increase in Liberal strength on the Clyde. In Wales the 'clean sweep' of 1906 was not repeated, but there were only two Unionist gains, one in Radnorshire and one in the Denbigh District. In Ireland, as has already been mentioned, the Nationalists lost one seat (at Mid-Tyrone) and sitting Liberals were defeated by Unionists at North Antrim and South Tyrone.

In England the position was markedly different. In 1906 the Government had held 338 of a total of 465 seats, but in 1910 they sustained a net loss of 112 and fell back to a minority —226, as against the Opposition's 239.[12] These losses, of course, were not evenly spread over the whole country.[13] They were much heavier in the south than in the north, and they occurred more in county divisions and in small boroughs than, with the exception of London, in big towns. Asquith expressed at least some of

---

[12] This enabled the Unionists, when the issue of Home Rule came more to the fore (and when the second 1910 election had confirmed the verdict of the first), to develop the constitutional sophistry of saying that no Government should attempt to carry through a structural change in the relations of the four countries—such as the setting up of a separate Parliament for Ireland—without the support of a majority of the electors of the 'predominant partner.' It was an ingenious, if not very creditable, attempt to erect a sort of Anglo-Saxon veto to replace the veto of the peers which had then been destroyed.

[13] A list of the seats which in January, 1910, produced a result different from that of 1906 is given in appendix B.

the truth when he told his constituents at East Fife, after a few days' polling, that 'the Unionist gains have been chiefly in the smaller boroughs and cathedral cities; the great industrial centres have mainly declared for Free Trade....'[k]

Examples of 'the smaller boroughs and cathedral cities' which changed hands were to be found in Bath, Bedford, Cambridge, Chester, Colchester, Exeter, Gloucester, Kidderminster, Rochester, Salisbury and Warwick; and there were a number of others. The solidarity of 'the great industrial centres', on the other hand, was best illustrated in Lancashire and Yorkshire, where in the whole of the two counties, including the borough constituencies, the Government sustained a net loss of no more than six seats, one in a seaside resort and two in rural Yorkshire. But there were other features in the picture. There were the sharp Liberal reverses in the dockyard towns, with both the seats changing hands in Devonport and Portsmouth and the single seat at Chatham going the same way.[14] There was London, where of a total of sixty-two seats the Unionists gained twelve, including not only the present-day 'marginals' like North Kensington and North Paddington, but also divisions which should have been much more solidly left-wing—Southwark West, Mile End, Bow and Bromley, Lambeth North and a number of others. These gains gave the Unionists a majority of six in London.

There were the West Midland industrial boroughs (apart from Birmingham), where the Liberal tide ebbed sharply, with losses in Walsall, Wednesbury, West Bromwich and two of the three

---

[14] The Unionists appeared to have been successful in convincing the dockyard workers that they would build more warships, even if not in convincing the rest of the country that more warships were necessary.

111

Wolverhampton seats. Last, and most striking of all, were the Liberal reverses in the southern agricultural counties (east of the Devon border) and in the suburban fringes of the Home Counties. Two seats were lost in Berkshire, two in Dorset, four in Essex, two in Hampshire, two in Hertfordshire, three in Kent, three in Middlesex, three in Oxfordshire, three in Somerset, four in Suffolk, three in Surrey, two in Sussex, and four in Wiltshire. The turn-over in this belt amounted to a half of the total number of seats, and gave the Unionists a third of their total gains.

A feature of this election was the extent to which the gains were not all one way. The balance, of course, was enormously in favour of the Unionists, but their gross gains were offset by the Liberals winning twelve seats which the Unionists had won in 1906, and by the Labour Party winning one. This was quite different from the position in 1945, for example, when the sweeping Labour gains were not offset by a single Conservative gain from Labour; the contrast may be explained by the greater influence which was exerted by the local campaign and the personalities of the candidates in 1910. Without doubt it was widely held at the time that electors were more open to the influence of a powerful speech delivered in the constituency or of some other local factor than is now usually thought to be the case. The results attributed to Lloyd George's polling-day intervention at Grimsby have already been noted; and Austen Chamberlain, writing to Balfour a few days after the contests and discussing the failure of the Unionists to make gains in Devonshire, said '... we were overwhelmed at the last moment by the weight of oratory on the Government side—three Cabinet Ministers and other lesser lights, against whom we could set none but local men. But for this we ought to have won three or four more seats down there'.[1] This may have been an exaggerated view even then, however.[15]

Another feature of the results was the almost complete unanimity with which the seats where the Unionists had made bye-election gains during the previous Parliament swung back to the Liberals. North-West Manchester, where Mr. Churchill had been defeated in 1908, Ashburton, Newcastle-on-Tyne (where the Unionist had broken through a huge Liberal majority) Pudsey, Bermondsey, and a number of others all returned to their 1906 allegiance by substantial majorities.

Bye-elections are always an uncertain guide; and those who have assumed that the behaviour of the Lords was almost wholly responsible for the contrast between the general election result which a projection of bye-election returns before the introduction of the Budget would have given and the result which was in fact obtained nine months later may well have applied too mechanistic an interpretation to events. The approach of a general election in itself rallies support to the Government, and this, combined with the fact that the Budget, both for its own merits real or supposed and as an alternative to tariff reform, was a vote winner, is enough to explain the recovery in the strength of the Government. It is therefore by no means certain that Lord Lansdowne and his followers lost the first general election of 1910 for their party. Their action in November did not make the Budget popular. It was already so—although the opposition of the dukes had had something to do with this. What the peers' rejection did was to make the Budget an effective stepping-stone

---

[15] Although it is perhaps worth noting that in the second 1910 election, when Lloyd George was not at Grimsby and when the South West may have been better served by Opposition orators, there were Unionist gains in Grimsby and in three of the Devon divisions.

towards the destruction of the veto and the implementation of much legislation which had hitherto been blocked; and it therefore made the Liberal electoral victory not necessarily greater, but far more fertile, than it would otherwise have been. It was a more modest victory than that of 1906, but it was to be a less sterile one.

VII

The Beginnings of the
Parliament Bill

The new parliament, which had looked as though it might be
difficult to lead, did nothing to belie this reputation in its
first few weeks of life. But this may have been due more to
Asquith's temporary loss of nerve and touch than to the inherent
complexity of the situation. The left-wing parties had between
them a very substantial majority, and they were firmly united on
the two main issues of the day: they were all anxious to curb the
veto and to give Home Rule to Ireland. The Irish (and *a fortiori*
the Labour Party) could have found no basis of alliance with the
Unionists, and while they had their differences with the Liberals,
it was never likely that they would carry a dispute to the extent
of putting the Government out. The dispute on the Budget,
which even in the freedom of the previous Parliament had not
led the Nationalists to vote against the third reading of the
Finance Bill, was about the Irish share of a £1,200,000 increase

in the spirit duty. It was a trivial item to set against the other issues at stake.

The essentials of the situation were therefore that the Government was committed not by the exigencies of the parliamentary position but by its own desires to giving the Irish the main things they wanted, and that, this being so, the Irish could easily be brought to heel on points of detail or precedence.

The Prime Minister did not appear to see this as clearly as he should have done. He may have been frightened by the rather threatening tone of Redmond's speech at Dublin on February 10, or by the independent attitude which was taken up by the Labour Party at its Conference at Newport on February 8, but it was unlike Asquith not to be able to ride out heavier storms than these without concern. The probability is that the end of the election found him mentally exhausted and with a temporarily relaxed grip on affairs, that he found it difficult to adjust himself to governing with a greatly reduced and less cohesive majority, and that his equanimity was troubled by his failure to extract, before the election, a definite promise from the King to sustain the Government by a wholesale creation of peers if this should prove necessary.

This question of the 'guarantees', as they were called, gave the Government a very bad start in the new Parliament. Asquith, it will be remembered, had stated in his Albert Hall speech at the beginning of the campaign that 'We shall not assume office and we shall not hold office unless we can secure the safeguards which experience shows us to be necessary for the legislative utility and honour of the party of progress....'[a] It was widely assumed that this meant that he had obtained from the King a promise, if the Liberals won the election and if the peers proved recalcitrant, to exercise the prerogative to the extent of creating

116

a Government majority for the passage of a 'veto' bill through the House of Lords. In fact, however, he had not even a hint of such a guarantee when he spoke. And five days later Asquith's private secretary had an interview with the King's private secretary which was recorded in the following terms for the Prime Minister:

'Lord Knollys asked me to see him this afternoon and he began by saying that the King had come to the conclusion that he would not be justified in creating new peers (say 300) until after a second general election and that he, Lord K., thought you should know of this now, though for the present he would suggest that what he was telling me should be for your ear only. The King regards the policy of the Government as tantamount to the destruction of the House of Lords and he thinks that before a large creation of peers is embarked upon or threatened the country should be acquainted with the particular project for accomplishing such destruction as well as with the general line of action as to which the country will be consulted at the forthcoming elections.'[b]

How long the Prime Minister was intended to keep this rather heavy confidence to himself is not clear. It must, in any event, have been confided to all his Cabinet colleagues soon after the result of the polling was known, when they were called upon to determine whether they should continue to hold office, and then, having decided to do so, what their line of action should be. Early in February the King was asking to be informed of the intentions of the Government, and a Cabinet minute dated February 11 told him that they involved no request for the exercise of the Royal prerogative until plans had been submitted to Parliament and the actual necessity arose. Asquith then had to perform the more difficult task of informing the House of Commons and the nation of the position and of the limited extent to which anything had been settled by the general election. This he did in no spirit of apology.

'I tell the House quite frankly,' he said on February 21, in the debate on the Address, 'that I have received no such guarantee, and that I have asked for no such guarantee ... to ask in advance for a blank authority for an indefinite exercise of the Royal prerogative in regard to a measure which has never been submitted to or approved by the House of Commons is a request which in my judgment no constitutional statesman can properly make, and it is a concession which the Sovereign cannot be expected to grant.'[c]

That was that, and it had to be accepted, although, as Asquith's biographers have commented, 'it provoked cries of disappointment from even loyal members of the Party'.[d] Part of the concern, however, arose not from disappointment about 'guarantees' but from uneasiness that the Government was going to get itself lost in the morass of House of Lords reform instead of keeping to the firm if difficult road of dealing with its powers. Sir Charles Dilke,[1] after presiding over a meeting of about thirty advanced radicals, led a delegation to the Prime Minister which

---

[1] 1843–1911. Liberal member for Chelsea, 1868–86, and for the Forest of Dean, 1892–1911. President of the Local Government Board from 1882 until cited as co-respondent in a divorce case in 1885.

demanded concentration upon the veto and threatened, if this were not done, to put down a motion declaring that the Government had no mandate for the reconstruction of the Upper House. Sir Henry Dalziel,[2] the President of the National Liberal Federation, took similar action, and Hilaire Belloc abstained from voting on the motion for the Address because he thought that the Speech from the Throne, which mentioned no assurances that the curtailment of the veto would become law, was nothing but 'a party sham'. As, however, he considered the House of Lords 'by its constitution a committee for the protection of the Anglo-Judaic plutocracy',' it may be thought that a demand for reconstitution would have been a more logical outcome of his thought and that his views were substantially less representative than those of Dilke and Dalziel.

The non-Liberal part of the Government's majority was equally or more worried. Keir Hardie declared that 'Ministers were returned not to reconstitute but to destroy the House of Lords', and there were continual warnings from Redmond and the other Irish that it was the immediate restriction of the veto and not more sophistical solutions in which they were interested.

This concern was not entirely misplaced. Some leading members of the Cabinet were most unattracted by the suspensory veto and by the conflict with the Sovereign in which it seemed likely to involve the Government. Reform of the Upper House looked to them a far more promising prospect. Sir Edward Grey was the protagonist of this school of thought. As late as March 14 he told a Liberal banquet at the Hotel Cecil that the

---

[2] 1868–1935. Later 1st Lord Dalziel. Member for Kirkcaldy Burghs, 1892–1921.

country would not tolerate single-chamber Government, and that to leave reform to the Unionists would mean 'disaster, death, and damnation' to the Liberals.[f] Haldane, as was usually the case, was with Grey. He was in favour of proceeding simultaneously and at once with the Budget and with reform of the Lords. Despite his subsequent swing to the left there seems little doubt that at this time Haldane was too preoccupied with dislike and distrust of Lloyd George to be a very loyal member of a radical Cabinet. He recorded with unattractive satisfaction an audience which he had with the King soon after the election.

'He (the King) said the result of the election was inconclusive,' Haldane wrote, 'and (that) he could not possibly consider the creation of peers without a much more definite expression of opinion from the country. I told him that I had every hope that it would not be necessary to proceed to that extreme.... As I was taking leave he said "This Government may not last. I say nothing of some of my Ministers, but I wish you may very long be my Minister." '[g]

To add to the suspicions of the radicals, two members of the Government who were seeking new homes after defeats at the general election—J. A. Pease,[3] the former Chief Whip who had become Chancellor of the Duchy of Lancaster, and Colonel Seely,[4] the Under-Secretary at the Colonial Office—both made

---

[3] 1860–1943. Liberal member for Tyneside, 1892–1900, Saffron Walden, 1901–10, and Rotherham, 1910–16. Created 1st Lord Gainford, 1917. President of the Board of Education, 1911–15. Postmaster-General, 1916.
[4] 1868–1947. Secretary of State for War, 1912–14. Created 1st Lord Mottistone, 1933.

byc-clection speeches which were concerned with reform rather than with reduction of powers.

Where did Asquith stand on this issue? Grey and Haldane were his closest political associates, and by the views of the former at least he still set the greatest store, depending on his advice more than on that of any member of the Cabinet except one. We know, too, that in 1907 he had been most reluctant to accept the suspensory veto, and we can guess that he did not relish the prospect of the difficult Court and social relations which a bitter constitutional struggle was likely to bring in its train. On February 18, Lord Hugh Cecil[5] wrote Margot Asquith a brief letter, which read as follows: 'Lloyd George has got you into a nice mess: nothing left for you but to try and create 500 peers and perish miserably attacking the King. That's what comes of making an irresponsible demagogue Chancellor of the Exchequer.'[h] Mrs. Asquith quotes this as being 'among the best' of the 'many and amusing letters' which she and her husband received after the election, and it would be easy to believe that it struck an answering chord in the Prime Minister.

On the other hand we have Asquith's steady loyalty to causes he had espoused and to colleagues he had chosen—the essential quality which enabled a conservative-minded man to be a great radical Prime Minister; we have his sureness of touch in all constitutional matters; and we have the knowledge that, apart from Grey, his closest adviser was Crewe, who had shown when dealing with Lord Newton's bill in 1907 that on matters relating to the Second Chamber he was a clear-sighted radical. Furthermore, there is the assurance of Asquith's biographers

[5] 1869–1956. Created 1st Lord Quickswood, 1941. Unionist member for Greenwich, 1895–1909, and for Oxford University, 1910–1937.

that: 'In his own mind Veto and Reform were always in separate compartments. With or without Reform the curtailment of the Veto was essential, and no Reform which he ever contemplated was to involve the restoration of the Veto.'[i]

It may therefore be assumed that Asquith, who had also to live with the facts of party politics in a way which Grey or the other side of Downing Street did not, was an influence, and no doubt the decisive influence, in favour of the more radical course. Nevertheless there could be no question of his giving Redmond the assurance which the latter was constantly demanding—that if the Irish voted for the Budget a veto bill would be passed into law within a year. On February 25 the Prime Minister reported to the King that 'certain Ministers were of opinion that the wisest and most dignified course for Ministers was at once to tender their resignation to your Majesty', and on the same day he instructed the new Chief Whip, the Master of Elibank,[6] to tell Redmond that there could be no assurance and that he must act on his responsibility as the Government would act on theirs.[7]

---

[6] 1870–1920. Alexander Murray. Heir to Viscountcy of Elibank, but created 1st Baron Murray of Elibank, 1912. Member for Midlothian, 1900–5, Peebles and Selkirk, 1906–10, and Midlothian, 1910–12. Chief Liberal Whip, 1909–12.

[7] Irish threats were taken sufficiently seriously at this time for the King to make an informal approach to Balfour, no doubt with the approval of Ministers, to see whether, in event of the Irish deciding to vote against the Budget, Unionist support for it could be obtained. Balfour replied in a memorandum dated February 15, that 'great as would be the embarrassment to all parties which would follow upon an immediate defeat of the Government ... it would be vain to ask the Unionist Party on tactical grounds to vote black where they had before voted white'. (*See* Newton, *op. cit.*, p. 389.)

Three days later the morale of Ministers seemed to have rallied somewhat, and Asquith, in moving to take the whole time of the House until Easter for Government business, was able to announce some of the intentions of his Cabinet. Until March 24 the time would be taken up with routine but essential business, mainly relating to Supply. Then, after the Easter week-end, the Government would press on with their detailed proposals on relations between the two Houses, which would be embodied in the first instance in a set of resolutions. These changes in the powers of the House of Lords would be based on the assumption that in a subsequent session a reform bill would be brought forward. No date for proceeding with the Budget was given.

Balfour, rather to the disgust of some of his followers, gave Asquith his motion without a division, and so the decision of the Irish to abstain was of no importance. Trouble then arose over the Government's need to borrow money to replace the revenue temporarily lost by the failure of the 1909 Finance Bill to reach the statute book. No great sum was involved, for, whether legally or not, the collection of everything except income tax, super-tax and certain other new taxes to the total extent of £30 million was proceeding normally. The Chancellor of the Exchequer sought to fill this gap by the Treasury (Temporary Borrowing) Bill, and the second and third readings of this measure, as well as its passage through the House of Lords, provided the Opposition with opportunities somewhat brazenly to accuse the Government of creating 'financial chaos'. The Unionist leaders claimed that the correct course for Ministers was to split the Budget into parts and to proceed immediately with those sections, including an income-tax resolution, to which the Lords had no objection. To create further embarrassment they caused, in the Prime Minister's words, 'the stream of criticism (on Supply) mysteriously to run dry', and thus gave the Government an unwanted abundance of parliamentary time. 'Why was it not used to get on with the financial business?' was continually asked.

Asquith and Lloyd George very wisely refused these enticements. To have split up the Finance Bill and allowed the peers to pick and choose would have been to go back on the position which Gladstone had established in 1861 after the rejection of his Paper Duty Bill. At the same time Ministers' inability to announce a definite date for the reintroduction of the Budget gave an impression of weakness and confusion, and undoubtedly impaired the prestige of the Government. Disputes outside the Cabinet as to the terms on which the Irish could be persuaded to vote for the Budget, and within the Cabinet as to the relationship between reform and the veto, were still proceeding.

Asquith's next important pronouncement was made before a public meeting in the Oxford Town Hall on March 18. He first declared, with almost unnecessary frankness, that 'the Ministry had hesitated whether they ought to go on'. But, he continued, they had resolved not to run away from their tasks—the passing of the Budget and the abolition of the financial, and limitation of the legislative, veto of the Lords. The Liberal Party further held that the Lords 'must be rebuilt on a democratic basis'. The resolutions were then put on the paper of the House of Commons on March 21. They were three in number and corresponded very closely with Camp-bell-Bannerman's 1907 scheme. The Lords could neither amend nor reject a money bill, and the definition of a money bill was to rest with the Speaker, acting in accordance with certain specified rules. For other legislation the Lords were to retain a power of delay of two years and one month. A bill sent up from the Commons in three successive sessions was to become law without the assent of the peers if, on the third occasion, it had not been passed by the House of Lords without amendments, other than those agreed to by both Houses, within twenty-eight days of being received by the Upper House. The maximum duration of a Parliament was to be reduced from seven years to five. The only differences between these proposals and those of Campbell-Bannerman were that the provision for a conference between the two Houses had been abandoned, the restriction of the life of Parliaments was new, and so was the drafting of the second resolution in such a way that the three sessions could be spread over more than one Parliament; the last two years of a Liberal Parliament need not therefore be barren, provided the Government was successful at the subsequent general election.

At this stage the plan was to take the resolutions, then obtain a first reading for a Parliament Bill based on them, and immediately afterwards to begin again with the Budget. The Budget remained an adventure for the Government, because the Irish, although now offered precedence for the veto over reform, were still unwilling to commit themselves to sinking financial differences without an assurance that a Lords' rejection of the resolutions would be followed by a demand for the exercise of the prerogative, backed if necessary by a determination to dissolve again. This Asquith was still unable or unwilling to give. On March 3, when asked by a Unionist member what he would do if these circumstances arose, he had first used a famous phrase, which he was later to repeat on a number of occasions. 'We had better wait and see,' Hansard recorded the Prime Minister as saying.

The resolutions were exhaustively debated at their various stages in the House of Commons, and were eventually got through, by a free use of the closure, after eleven parliamentary days. Government majorities varied somewhat, but the general pattern was given by the vote rejecting a Unionist amendment to Asquith's motion to go into committee on the resolutions. A 'No' lobby of 351 was made up of 256 Liberals, thirty-four Labour members, sixty-five of Redmond's Nationalists and two Independent Nationalists. On the other side were 250—all Unionists. It was generally agreed that this and other highly satisfactory Government majorities meant that the Cabinet had at last made up its mind to satisfy the Nationalists that it was prepared to coerce the Lords by advising the use of the prerogative. This appeared the more likely as William O'Brien, the strongly anti-Government Independent Nationalist member for Cork City, had used the week-end before the vote to increase Redmond's difficulties by making public a private interview with Lloyd George in which, O'Brien claimed, it had become clear that substantial concessions could have been secured on the Finance Bill had the Nationalists been prepared collectively to demand them.

This widespread public impression proved to be correct.[8] On April 15, shortly before the guillotine was due to fall on the consideration of the second resolution, the Prime Minister rose to explain the intentions of the Government if the Lords proved recalcitrant, but, the Chairman of Ways and Means having ruled that he could not do so without a general consent, which Balfour refused to give, he was forced to sit down again amidst loud

---

[8] Although, as late as April 13, the Prime Minister had telegraphed to the King at Biarritz that recent Government decisions to make no changes in the Budget might well involve their defeat. (Spender and Asquith, *op. cit.*, vol. I, p. 278.)

conflicting demonstrations on both sides of the House. Later, when the third resolution had also been cleared and he had presented the Parliament Bill for its first reading, he made his statement on the adjournment:

'If the Lords fail to accept our policy, or decline to consider it as it is formally presented to the House, we shall feel it our duty immediately to tender advice to the Crown as to the steps which will have to be taken if that policy is to receive statutory effect in this Parliament. What the precise terms of that advice will be—(an Hon. Member: "Ask Redmond")—I think one might expect courtesy when I am anxious, as the head of the Government, to make a serious statement of public policy—what the precise terms of that advice will be it will, of course, not be right for me to say now; but if we do not find ourselves in a position to ensure that statutory effect shall be given to that policy in this Parliament, we shall then either resign our offices or recommend the dissolution of Parliament. Let me add this, that in no case will we recommend a dissolution except under such conditions as will secure that in the new Parliament the judgment of the people as expressed at the elections will be carried into law.'[j]

Asquith was followed by Balfour, who denounced the anticipation by months of prospective advice to the Crown and charged the Prime Minister with having concluded an unworthy bargain with Redmond. 'He has bought the Irish vote for his Budget, but the price is paid in the dignity of his office.' The brief debate terminated in great excitement, with a Nationalist and a Unionist member almost coming to blows.

Asquith replied to Balfour's charges in a letter to *The Times* published four days later. There had been no meeting between himself and Redmond after the Government's decision and before his statement, he said. In any event, it would be difficult to see in what the unworthiness of the Government action lay. Their decision was just as welcome to the majority of their followers as it was to the Nationalists, and if a decision so taken brings in its train a substantial block of support in the division lobby there is nothing inimical to the best traditions of parliamentary practice in that. Minority governments usually have to compromise with their principles to a far greater extent than did Asquith in these early months of 1910. The real truth is that the Unionists had worked themselves into a position of unusual prejudice and illogicality. They were determined, at almost all costs, to keep the Irish members against their will in the Parliament of the United Kingdom. At the same time they regarded them almost as 'second-class citizens', and therefore viewed any majority of which these involuntary intruders formed a decisive part as something of a fraud. It was Anglo-Saxon hypocrisy carried to its ultimate degree.

This is not to deny, of course, that Asquith's statement enabled him suddenly to become decisive about the Budget. The period of 'wait and see' was over. He moved a 'timetable' resolution on April 18 for the reintroduced Finance Bill and firmly declared that the fortunes of the Government and of the Liberal Party were bound up with the measure. A day and a half was to be devoted to the preliminary resolutions, two to second reading and one to third reading, while at the committee stage the only amendments permitted were to be those relating to changes which had been made in the bill since its previous passage through the Commons. The debates to which these various stages gave rise, and which began almost immediately after the 'time-table' resolution and followed each other in quick succession, necessarily involved the flogging of very old horses. The main point of interest was the attitude of the Irish members. The Independent Nationalists remained implacable in their opposition, and O'Brien, who on a different occasion in the same week had spoken in almost Tory terms of the Chancellor of the Exchequer having decided 'that the Irish votes should be bargained for at the expense of the King rather than the Treasury', moved the rejection of the second reading. Redmond, however, was firm in his support (one of his followers, Joseph Devlin, who spoke on third reading, reminding O'Brien that there were other people in Ireland besides landlords and distillers), and the motion to reject was defeated by 328 to 242, a majority only a little smaller than that which had been secured in the first division on the veto resolutions. Third reading was obtained on April 27 by 324 to 231.

On the next day the bill was taken into consideration in the Lords. Here the second reading debate lasted only three hours. Lord Lansdowne made a few old points about the national credit and negotiations with the Irish, and Lord Russell[9] some new ones about motor cars; the Lord Chancellor replied for the Government; and that was about all. There was no division, and the remaining stages passed without debate. On this issue at least the Lords were prepared to accept the fact that they had been defeated in the appeal to the country which they had forced. It needed only another twenty-four hours to secure the Royal

_____

[9] 1865–1931. Francis Stanley. 2nd Earl Russell. Later joined Labour Party. Parliamentary Secretary to Ministry of Transport, 1929. Brother of Bertrand Russell (3rd Earl Russell).

Assent, and the Finance Bill of 1909 therefore passed into law precisely a year after Lloyd George had opened the Budget upon which it was based.

During the difficult weeks at the end of March, Ministers had not only had the tasks of deciding upon the order in which they were going to proceed and of agreeing to the form of the veto resolutions. There had also to be produced an acceptable draft of the Parliament Bill. In substance it was the same as the resolutions. But this alone would not have satisfied Grey and the other advocates of reform, nor would it have left others like Asquith himself and Mr. Churchill, who were very willing to put the veto first but who none the less believed that reform was desirable and should not be lost sight of, entirely happy. The difficulty was solved by a preamble, which was an expression of the wishes of the Government, but which would, of course, if and when the bill passed into law, have no legal force.

'Whereas it is intended to substitute for the House of Lords as it at present exists,' it ran, 'a Second Chamber constituted on a popular instead of hereditary basis, but such a substitution cannot immediately be brought into operation: And whereas provision will require hereafter to be made by Parliament in a measure effecting such substitution for limiting and defining the powers of the new Second Chamber, but it is expedient to make such provision as in this Act appears for restricting the existing powers of the House of Lords.'

The suggestion that a reconstituted Upper House might be invested with greater powers than those which the bill would leave the House of Lords was a little sinister, but it was all so vague as not to cause great radical agitation.

In this form the bill was sent out to the King, who was at Biarritz. He acknowledged it in his own not over-literate hand. His letter, dated April 19, read as follows: 'The King has received from the Prime Minister the draft of a Bill to make provision with respect to the powers of the House of Lords in relation to those of the House of Commons and to limit the duration of Parliament. The King notices that the date of this Bill is the first of this month.'[k]

The Government had at last made their intentions clear and thrown a difficult ball to the House of Lords. But when Parliament rose for a short spring recess on April 28, great difficulties still lay ahead for Asquith and his colleagues. Their trump card was the exercise of the prerogative, but this involved the King as well as themselves, and there was no doubt that he was distrustful of the whole constitutional policy of the Government and would approach such action with great distaste.

VIII

The Reply of the Peers

In 1907, as was described in chapter 111, Lord Newton's House of Lords Reform Bill was given modified support by the Unionist leaders and rendered temporarily innocuous by reference to a Select Committee. This committee deliberated for a year. Despite its strength—it had Rosebery as chairman, the Archbishop of Canterbury and an ex-Speaker[1] among its independent members, and Lansdowne, Curzon, St. Aldwyn, and Midleton[2] from the Opposition benches—it was not an entirely satisfactory body. Newton has made it clear how difficult it was to work with Rosebery.

---

[1] Lord Selby. 1835–1909. Formerly Mr. Speaker Gully.

[2] 1856–1942. St. John Brodrick. Succeeded to Viscountcy, 1907. Created 1st Earl of Midleton, 1920. Conservative member for Surrey, West, 1880–85, and for Guildford, 1885–1906. Secretary of State for War, 1900–3, and for India, 1903–5.

'It must be admitted, however,' he wrote, 'that Lord Rosebery was less successful as a chairman than might have been anticipated, for he allowed the members to stray from the point under discussion, frequently made discursive if entertaining speeches himself, and conveyed the impression that he was physically unequal to the moderate strain of work involved. He was also liable to fits of discouragement....'[a]

Despite these handicaps, the committee eventually produced an agreed report. This adopted most of the proposals of the bill of 1907, notably those limiting and reducing the hereditary qualification. But it created little stir, and was not even debated in the House of Lords. Leisurely unconcern was the attitude of most of the Unionist peers. The result of the first 1910 election drastically changed this atmosphere. In the first place it made a Liberal attack upon either the powers or the composition of the House of Lords inevitable. In the second place it revealed the not very surprising fact that in the constituencies, and particularly in Scotland and the North of England, the hereditary principle, so far from being treated with reverence, was decidedly unpopular. Already by January 3, Lansdowne was writing to Balfour saying that he had 'received several letters pressing us for a strong declaration as to House of Lords reform', but adding that, in his view, 'we ought not to allow ourselves to be rushed by Sir Reginald MacLeod[3] or anyone else'.[b] Balfour was never inclined to rush anyone, and certainly not Lord Lansdowne on this occasion. Even when he had received word, in the interval between the end of the election and the beginning of the

---

[3] The chief Conservative Agent in Scotland.

session, that proposals for reform might strengthen the hand of the King and of the 'moderates in the Cabinet', he remained unenthusiastic.

'The only objections that I can see to this course,' he wrote to Lansdowne on January 29, 'are (1) that it a little savours of panic, and (2) that we may not find it easy to agree upon a scheme of reform which would be agreeable to the House of Lords, which would meet the views of the Unionist doctrinaires in the constituencies, and which would be workable. Still if the announcement that you mean to try your hand at the problem would strengthen the hands of the King and of the moderates within the Cabinet in resisting unconstitutional pressure by the extremists, I see no reason why it should not be made....'[c]

Lansdowne himself was, if anything, still less enthusiastic, both because of his own predilections, and because, as leader of all the Unionist peers, he could hardly fail to be cautious of a scheme which, whatever its details, would inevitably deprive a substantial number of his followers of their right to sit and vote. Nevertheless in his speech in the debate on the Address he not only indicated his willingness to consider proposals for reform but went further, saying that if the Government refused its co-operation, the peers would bring forward proposals of their own.

This was an invitation which Rosebery, who was indefatigable in taking a series of first steps towards reform, if in nothing else, was eager to accept. He quickly announced that he would move a resolution that the House of Lords should go into committee on the question of its own reform, and that if this were carried he

134

would follow it up with three substantive resolutions in the following form:

'(1) That a strong and efficient Second Chamber is not merely an integral part of the British Constitution, but is necessary to the well-being of the State, and to the balance of Parliament.

'(2) That such a chamber can best be obtained by the reform and reconstitution of the House of Lords.

'(3) That a necessary preliminary of such reform and reconstitution is the acceptance of the principle that the possession of a peerage should no longer of itself give the right to sit and vote in the House of Lords.'

The debate on these resolutions began on March 14. Rosebery himself led off with a speech of great oratorical distinction. He praised the House of Lords both because of its deliberative qualities and because it could claim to be the direct lineal descendant of the Witenagemot. But on the other hand there were the insuperable objections of Scotland and the North of England to the hereditary principle and a majority of 125 in the other place bent on the destruction of the existing chamber. The peers must act first, so that an Upper House able to see 'that the voice of the people should be deliberate' remained in being. He proposed that there should be an elected element in the new House, and that it should be chosen by corporations and county councils, existing members of the House being eligible for election. 'I believe that at this critical moment,' he concluded, 'you have an opportunity of rendering your country a greater service than has fallen to any body of men since the Barons wrested the liberties of England from King John at

Runnymede.… What is the alternative? The alternative is to cling with enfeebled grasp to privileges which have become unpopular, to powers which are verging on the obsolete, shrinking and shrinking until at last, under the unsparing hands of the advocates of single-Chamber Government, there may arise a demand for your own extinction, and the Second Chamber, the ancient House of Lords, may be found waiting in decrepitude for its doom.'[d]

Support for Rosebery, varying greatly both in its enthusiasm and in the assumptions on which the speakers were acting, came from Curzon, Salisbury, the Archbishop of Canterbury, Newton, Cawdor, Cromer, and Lansdowne. Curzon was probably the most enthusiastic, although he thought that Rosebery had overstated the case against the hereditary principle and claimed that 'in India the House of Lords was regarded with enormous veneration and respect, largely because its composition rested on a basis familiar throughout Indian society'. The Archbishop set the tone for a rather condescending speech by telling their lordships that his title to sit in the House was 600 years older than that of any hereditary peer. In the quarrel between the Lords and the Government there had been exaggeration on both sides. Rosebery's proposals, 'got into shape', should produce the adjustment necessary to relieve the strain. The bishops were ready to help. It all sounded very easy.

Cawdor devoted most of his speech in favour of a new House of Lords to defending the existing one. On Home Rule, the Education Bill, the Licensing Bill, and the Budget it had represented the mind of the people far better than had the Commons. His conclusion did not seem to follow very obviously from his premises. Salisbury was another rather static reformer. The character and reputation of the House of Commons had declined, and so had the independence of its members. But in the House of Lords there was perfect independence (a perfection which was somewhat blemished, however, by Crewe's reminder that the only Scottish representative peer[4] who had voted for the Budget had been deprived of his seat). The hereditary principle had the merit of 'trusting a man because of his sense of public duty; it meant that a man reverenced the example of his fathers and avoided prejudicing his son's prospects'. But some reform appeared to be necessary and the best plan was the selection of representative peers and the nomination of some members by the Crown. Cromer interpreted the 'silent voters'—*ex hypothesi* a safe body of men to whom to attribute views—as being frightened of single-chamber government, and insisted that a reformed House should have full powers over finance.

Lansdowne made the most important speech. He was in favour of going into committee, but reform must result in preserving the historic continuity of the House of Lords. He was not prepared to change its name, to renounce the hereditary principle, or greatly to reduce the number of hereditary peers. He was against election by the county councils or anyone else, but thought that a certain non-hereditary element might be secured by life peerages and by Government nominations for a substantial term. This speech greatly disappointed Rosebery.

'I honestly think,' he wrote to Lansdowne. 'that if you cannot go beyond the limits you laid down last night, the House of Lords plan will be stillborn. The great mass of

---

[4] Lord Torphichen. 1846–1915. 12th Baron, representative peer for Scotland, 1894 to January, 1910, and December, 1910–15.

the Lords are not solicitous about reform at all; if they must have it, they will go for the minimum, and it is the minimum which their leader offers and declares to be sufficient.'[c]

Two members of the Government—Morley and Crewe—took part in the debate. They were even less enthusiastic than Lansdowne. Morley thought that the changes proposed would not free the House of Lords from the imputation of class prejudice, nor did they contain any provision for removing or diminishing deadlocks. Crewe, with his usual good sense, said that 'the Liberals in the House of Commons and the country would believe that the object of the reforming peers was to consolidate the power of the Unionist party and to increase it by limiting the prerogative of the Crown. The real point at issue was the deadlock between the two Houses, and any considerable reform must destroy or weaken the unwritten understanding between them.' This was the essence of the problem: a reformed House of Lords would inevitably destroy the constitutional safety-valve of large-scale creation, and the Unionist reformers, who from almost every other point of view were perfectly satisfied with the existing chamber, were urged forward by the knowledge that this would be so.

Crewe's prescience, however, did not lead him to oppose Rosebery in the division lobby, either on the motion to go into committee or on the substantive resolutions. This task was left to Lord Halsbury, who could be depended upon, rather like a comedian achieving his laughs by the repetition of a well-known series of catch-phrases, to put up his standard performance of opposition to all change. 'It was impossible to make an institution more practically useful for its purpose than the present House,' he declared on this occasion. He was supported by one or two die-hard peers like Willoughby de Broke[5] and Oranmore and Browne. But he divided only against the last resolution, and mustered a lobby of no more than fifteen. The Government peers voted with the majority.

Before the debate a private Unionist colloquy on the subject had been held at Lansdowne House, and Rosebery had stretched his cross-bench conscience to the extent of attending what was virtually a meeting of the Conservative Shadow Cabinet. Austen Chamberlain has left an account of what took place, which is notable chiefly for a statement of Balfour's putting the opportunist Unionist case with such lucidity that the elegant cynicism of his words was not obscured by Austen's rendering of them:

'I agree with what I believe Austen thinks,' the account characteristically opens. 'I dislike the whole thing. I would like to leave things as they are if we could. I don't believe you can make a better House. But that is not the question. The question is: can you make a Second Chamber strong enough to stand and resist assault? Can you make such changes as will enable our men (surely Austen's phrase and not Balfour's) to fight with success in Yorkshire, Lancashire and Scotland against single-chamber government? I don't think you can in our democratic days unless you admit an elective element, and although at first I thought the elective and non-elective elements would at once clash, and the remaining hereditary element be thrust out, I have come to the conclusion on reflection that this danger is not as great

---

[5] 1869–1923. Richard Greville Verney. 19th Lord Willoughby de Broke. Conservative member for Rugby, 1895–1900.

as I at first thought, and that such a House as we are discussing might stand at any rate for fifty years.'[5]

This suggests that Balfour had moved a little ahead of Lansdowne. And Austen Chamberlain, Walter Long, Curzon, and Akers-Douglas[6] appear to have been with or in front of the leader of the party, with Salisbury, Midleton, and Lansdowne urging greater caution. In the event, however, these various currents of opinion became of little immediate importance. The spring recess, as we have seen, found the Commons with their veto resolutions complete and with the Parliament Bill given a first reading, but with no further progress made. Equally, it interrupted the Lords at a stage at which the Rosebery resolutions had been passed but when the moment had not arrived to give them more concrete shape. And before Parliament reassembled the whole political atmosphere had been transformed by the death of the King.

It was a comparatively sudden death, and for that reason it was all the more politically cataclysmic in its effects. On April 27, His Majesty had returned to London after spending most of the previous two months at Biarritz. After his return he had attended a performance of *Rigoletto* at Covent Garden, visited the Royal Academy Summer Exhibition, and spent a week-end at Sandringham. As late as May 5, he received the new Governor of New Zealand in audience. On that afternoon the first warning

---

[6] 1851–1926. Aretas Akers-Douglas. Created 1st Viscount Chilston, 1911. Conservative member for St. Augustine's division of Kent, 1880–1911. Chief Conservative Whip, 1883–95. First Commissioner of Works, 1895–1902. Home Secretary, 1902–5.

bulletin was issued. On the following morning he was up and transacting a little business. At 11.45 pm on that evening—May 6—he was dead.

Asquith received the news at sea. He had gone with McKenna, one of his closest friends in the Cabinet, on an Admiralty yacht cruise to Spain and Portugal. Near Gibraltar the first disturbing bulletin had been received. The yacht had been ordered to turn round and make full steam for Plymouth. Before reaching the Bay of Biscay the final news had been received. Asquith has recorded his thoughts that night:

'I went up on deck, and I remember well that the first sight that met my eyes in the twilight before dawn was Halley's comet blazing in the sky.... I felt bewildered and indeed stunned. At a most anxious moment in the fortunes of the State, we had lost, without warning or preparation, the Sovereign whose life experience, trained sagacity, equitable judgment, and unvarying consideration, counted for so much. For two years I had been his Chief Minister, and I am thankful to remember that from first to last I never concealed anything from him. He soon got to know this, and in return he treated me with a gracious frankness which made our relationship in very trying and exacting times, one, not always of complete agreement, but of unbroken confidence. It was this which lightened the load which I should otherwise have found almost intolerably oppressive: the prospect that, in the near future, I might find it my duty to give him advice which I knew would be in a high degree impalatable.

'Now he had gone. His successor, with all his fine and engaging qualities, was without political experience. We were nearing the verge of a crisis without example in our constitutional history. What was the right thing to do? This was the question which absorbed my thoughts as we made our way, with two fast escorting destroyers, through the Bay of Biscay, until we landed at Plymouth on the evening of Monday, May 9.'[g]

The shock affected different people in different ways,[7] but few in the world of politics were unmoved by it. And many much further away from the Throne were equally affected. The Victorian age had accustomed the British people to long reigns and to the occupation by their Sovereign of a dominant position in the family of European royalty. King Edward's death destroyed both these conventions. The Edwardian period, which in fact possessed little of that tranquil and assured dignity with which the personality of the monarch has since invested it, had shown itself to be but a brief epilogue to the reign of the old Queen. And King George was very different from his father. He had not been brought up to reign. He had lived, first as a naval officer and then as a country gentleman, a life far removed from high politics. He was bored by foreigners, he disliked smart society, he had no interest in clever conversation. He did not inspire the German Emperor, as his father had done, with feelings which were a mixture of

---

[7] Mrs. Asquith's grief, for example, was of a less Roman quality than her husband's. She has described how on the morning of May 7 she wept on a sofa in Downing Street with Sir Ernest Cassel, and in the evening attended a dinner party at which Mr. Churchill said 'Let us drink to the health of the new King', and Lord Crewe with a slight rebuke replied 'Rather to the memory of the old.' (*The Autobiography of Margot Asquith.* vol. 11, p. 138.)

respect and resentful envy. He had not been, and was never to become, a leader of European society.

From the Prime Minister's point of view the most important difference between the new King and his father was the former's lack of political experience. In fact, King George had seen far more of state papers during his period as Heir Apparent than had King Edward. Perhaps therefore he appeared as a tyro more because of his unsophisticated mind and tastes than because of newness to the job. But whatever the reason it is undoubtedly true that Asquith felt that King Edward had been able to look after himself and find his own way through constitutional difficulties in a way that King George was not. However unlikely the principals, most Prime Ministers at the beginning of a new reign have half a desire to play the Melbourne.

It was therefore natural that Asquith, who, we have seen, had been in no hurry to tender unpalatable advice to King Edward, should have found procrastination given a new lease of life by the accession of King George. At one of his first private audiences the Prime Minister, as recorded in the King's own words, 'said he would endeavour to come to some understanding with the Opposition to prevent a General Election and (that) he would not pay attention to what Redmond said.'[h]

This endeavour took the form of an approach to Arthur Balfour for a two-party constitutional conference. The suggestion was eagerly taken up by the Unionists—the *Morning Post* and the *Observer* had indeed advocated a move along these lines within a day or two of the death of King Edward, and Austen Chamberlain had told Lansdowne during the train journey back from the funeral at Windsor that any further move by the Lords on the reform resolutions would be most unfortunate. Opinion on the Government side, not unnaturally, was less enthusiastic.

The Nationalists (except, paradoxically, for O'Brien and his followers) were very restive, the Labour Party was suspicious, and Josiah Wedgwood[8] led a mild revolt of advanced Liberals. But Asquith had committed himself with the King and was, in any event, firm in his own mind; and so the plan went forward. For six months the constitutional struggle retired behind closed doors.

---

[8] 1872–1943. Later 1st Lord Wedgwood. First Liberal and then Labour member for Newcastle-under-Lyme, 1906–42.

IX

The Attempt at Compromise

On June 16 the arrangements for the conference were completed. It was to have eight members: the Prime Minister, Lloyd George, Crewe, and Birrell from the Government; and Balfour, Lansdowne, Austen Chamberlain, and Cawdor from the Opposition. A statement was issued that the negotiations were to be entirely untrammelled and the proceedings strictly confidential. The press was informed when meetings were held, but of nothing else. Asquith and Balfour agreed upon a general scheme of discussion, which, in the words of Asquith's biographers, was to cover the following points:

'1. The relations of the two Houses in regard to finance.
2. Provision of some machinery to deal with persistent disagreement between the two Houses, whether by limitation of veto, joint sitting, referendum or otherwise.
3. The possibility of coming to some agreement as to such changes in the composition and numbers of the Second

House as would ensure that it would act, and would be regarded as acting, fairly between the great parties in the State.'[a]

This outline was not published.

The first meeting took place in the Prime Minister's room in the House of Commons on June 17, and there were twelve meetings between then and the end of July. As a result of them the Prime Minister was able to report to the House of Commons before its adjournment for the summer recess 'that our discussions have made such progress, although we have not so far reached an agreement, as to render it, in the opinion of all of us, not only desirable but necessary that they should continue'. He added that there 'is no question of their indefinite continuance, and (that) if we find as a result of our further deliberations during the recess that there is no prospect of an agreement that can be announced to Parliament in the course of the present Session, we shall bring the Conference to a close'.[b]

The question of where the summer meetings should take place then arose. Crewe offered his country house as a *venue*, but Lansdowne was hostile to this suggestion. Any agreement which might be reached would be subjected to criticism by extremists on both sides. 'Would not that criticism be more severe,' he wrote, 'if it can be said that we had been "softened" by the excellence of Crewe's champagne and the other attractions of a hospitable and luxurious country house.'[c] The suggestion was dropped, and Lord Lansdowne's followers could feel that their leader was maintaining his principles intact amidst the austerities of Bowood, Lansdowne House, Derreen, Meikleour or Tulliallan. But this involved no further meetings until Ministers and Opposition leaders returned to London in October. There was a brief but intensive series of meetings until the middle of the month, a fortnight's adjournment, and then another series of meetings until the end came on November 10.

Even then no public statement was issued. There were, not unnaturally, a number of reports in the press even while the conference was in progress purporting to describe what was going on, and subsequently more detailed but still unverifiable accounts were published by journalists. Now the memoirs or biographies of all the participants and of some others who were closely concerned are available. Even so the task of unravelling the course of the negotiations does not become a straightforward one, for there are many statements which lack corroboration, and a few cases of direct contradiction between the interpreters of one participant and those of another. But the main lines stand out fairly clearly.

A Unionist memorandum, presented at the beginning of the conference, proposed that legislation should be divided into three categories: financial, ordinary, and constitutional. So far as the first category was concerned it was suggested that the Lords should abandon their claim to reject money bills, provided that tacking could be prevented. Tacking was defined in the memorandum as occurring in the case of bills which, 'although technically dealing with little or nothing but finance, have social or political consequences which go far beyond the mere raising of revenue'.[d] On this point substantial agreement was reached. The Chancellor of the Exchequer was responsible for a proposal that a joint committee of both Houses—seven representatives from each with the Speaker presiding and exercising a casting vote—should determine whether or not a measure was a money bill. Austen Chamberlain's biographer, apparently quoting from an unspecified document, adds the gloss that this committee was to work within the very restrictive rule that 'if it appears that any provision of a bill, although dealing with taxation, would effect important social or political changes through expropriation or differentiation against any class of owners of property these provisions shall not be treated for the purposes of this act as provisions dealing with taxation'.*

Whether this was accepted by the Government representatives is not certain. On the one hand, Asquith, in a letter to Balfour, most uncharacteristically undated but presumably written towards the end of the conference, referred to the concessions he and his colleagues had made in regard to finance as 'of the most substantial character, and extremely difficult for us to defend against the criticism of our own supporters'.* On the other, Lansdowne, in a memorandum dated September 10 (such agreement as was reached on finance is commonly thought to have been arrived at in the summer sittings) and also addressed to Balfour, notes that: 'No one has yet been able to suggest a formula which, to my mind, would be really satisfactory for the purpose of dividing pure finance from legislation partly financial but important quite as much from its political as from its financial effects'.* If Ministers did go as far as Sir Charles Petrie suggests and the conference had succeeded, hardly a single Budget since presented would have been statutorily protected from the interference of the peers.

So far as 'ordinary' legislation was concerned, progress was made by accepting a suggestion that when a bill which fell within this category had been twice rejected by the House of Lords, its fate should be determined by a joint sitting of the two Houses. What was to be the composition of such a joint session? Mr. R. C. K. Elisor states that it was agreed 'that the representation of the Lords ... should be so scaled down that a Liberal Government

148

with a Commons majority of fifty would be able to pass its bills'.[h] But all the other evidence is that this was never accepted by the Unionist representatives. The form in which it was put forward by the Government was that the whole of the House of Commons (670 members) should take part in the joint sitting, together with a hundred representatives—chosen on a basis of proportional representation—of the House of Lords.[1] Lansdowne wrote at some length on the point, but never got nearer to a solution than to suggest that a reformed House of Lords (the plenum of which could be admitted) was the key to the problem of joint sittings. And agreement on a scheme for reform was never near. Asquith, in a memorandum dated May 28, had committed himself to reform, and according to Lansdowne, had subsequently 'admitted casually that the hereditary element must not disappear, and that any House of Lords must of necessity be conservative in its general complexion'.[i] But the Government representatives, again in Lansdowne's view, had thereafter 'shown an ill-concealed desire to "shunt" this part of the case'. This, Lansdowne thought, was because they were hopelessly divided as to how reform should be effected. Largely for this reason he decided to concentrate upon the point. It was where his opponents were weakest.

---

[1] Sir Robert Finlay, former Attorney-General, in a note which he took of Balfour's statement at a Shadow Cabinet held after the breakdown of the conference (see Newton: *op. cit.*, pp. 402–3), says that twenty of the representative peers were to be 'members of the Government', leaving only eighty to be chosen by proportional representation. This would be most strictly in accord with 'fifty majority in the House of Commons' theory, but it is rendered implausible by the fact that the total number of peers who were members of the Government was substantially less than twenty (when Asquith formed his Government in 1908, he gave office to only thirteen peers, including the Household appointments).

In urging this he committed himself to the following magnificently bland statement. 'We must, in the first place,' he wrote, 'remember that we are ourselves convinced House of Lords reformers, and that the House of Lords itself took up the question long before the conference was dreamed of.'[2] But it is nevertheless clear that his main reason for stressing reform at the conference was tactical; and a subject approached in this spirit from the Unionist side, and bristling with inherent difficulties for both sides, was not likely to be one on which progress could be made. Yet without progress here common ground on the composition of joint sittings was almost impossible to find. We must therefore agree, not with Mr. Ensor, but with Asquith's biographers when they wrote that 'no agreement could be reached … in what numbers respectively the two Houses should be represented at the joint sittings'.[j]

The problem of constitutional or 'organic' legislation raised still greater difficulties. The Unionists wanted bills which fell within this category and which had twice been rejected by the House of Lords to be submitted to a referendum. Trouble here arose both over the definition of 'organic' bills and over the inherent dislike of the Liberal representatives, and particularly of the Prime Minister, for such an innovation as a plebiscite. Sir Harold Nicolson has commented that 'the very word "referendum" would cause his (Asquith's) usually tolerant features to

---

[2] Balfour, who was the recipient of the memorandum in which this sentence occurs and who was less addicted to self-deceit than most men, must have found it somewhat difficult to reconcile with the exchange of views which had passed between himself and Lansdowne at the time of the previous election, or with his own opinion, as relayed by Austen Chamberlain, at the Shadow Cabinet in March *(see* pp. 143–4 *supra)*.

writhe into an expression of contemptuous disgust'[3][iii] There is, indeed, no indication that the Government side was ever prepared to introduce this innovation. What they were prepared to do was entirely to exempt bills on certain subjects, which should be listed individually rather than left to arise out of the definition of a category, from the operation of the Parliament Act. The House of Lords would retain all its existing powers over such measures. Suggested for inclusion in the list were matters relating to the Crown or the Protestant Succession, or a bill to amend the Parliament Act itself.

Such a list did not satisfy the Unionists (although Lansdowne, at least, believed that it was necessary to proceed by an extension of this method rather than by the general definition of 'organic' changes). They did not suspect the Government of wishing to abolish the Crown, or to change the Protestant Succession, or even, once its passage was secured, to amend the Parliament Bill. What they were interested in was Home Rule. This was a practical issue, and their dominant interest at the conference was to prevent the easing of its passage.

The Government was prepared to make some concession on this point. The Chancellor of the Exchequer proposed that, in the case of the next Home Rule Bill and of that one only, a first

---

[3] The referendum was not universally popular on the Unionist side either. F. E. Smith included the following passage in a letter to Austen Chamberlain dated October 21: 'Personally I hate the referendum. We should win matters which don't much matter like the licensing question or education on its sectarian side. But if the referendum once comes it will spread and in the great predatory appeals of the future the Tory Party will always be beaten. Imagine a referendum upon the last Budget!' (Birkenhead: *Frederick Edwin, Earl of Birkenhead* vol. 1, p. 207.)

rejection by the Lords should be followed by an immediate general election. If the Government won, the bill would be proceeded with as ordinary legislation. If it lost, resignation would of course follow, but the next Liberal Government would not be prevented from proceeding with Home Rule under the ordinary provisions of the Parliament Act. This was not enough for the Unionists. Balfour was able to argue with some tren- chance that 'we could not make ourselves responsible for a scheme which seemed to imply that, since the people had on three separate occasions expressed their hostility to Home Rule, it was high time to withdraw the subject from their cognizance and to hand it over to the unfettered discretion of the House of Commons and the joint sitting'.[k] 'High time' may have been an exaggerated phrase for a contingency which was most unlikely to arise within seven or eight years, but the compromise Liberal suggestion did lay the Government open, as tends to be the way with compromise suggestions, to a charge of some illogicality. Balfour suggested that, had the Government been willing to subject Home Rule to permanent special treatment, agreement might have been possible.

It was clear, however, that the Liberal representatives could go no further without estranging their supporters. Indeed, as early as October 14, Asquith had written to the King in the following terms:

'Mr. Asquith regrets to say that the prospect of agreement is not so favourable as it appeared to be at the beginning of the week.... The point of divergence which has been reached is the question whether organic and constitutional changes (such e.g. as Home Rule, the franchise, redistribution) should be exempted from the procedure of joint sessions ...; and should ... be submitted to a popular *referendum ad hoc.*

'The representatives of the Opposition insist on this distinction; the representatives of the Government are opposed to it, not only on its merits, but because they know it would be quite impossible to induce the Liberal Party to agree to it.'[*l*]

After this letter was written the concession on Home Rule which has been mentioned was made. It therefore became doubly impossible further to give way, and when the concession was not accepted there was no alternative but for the conference to recognise its failure and break up. The question arises to how far the two sides were genuinely seeking an agreement and where the blame for failure to reach one must primarily lie. It cannot be adequately dealt with in simple generalisations about Liberals on the one hand and Unionists on the other, but must rather be answered individually for the principal participants.

There can be little doubt that Asquith wanted an agreement. Austen Chamberlain, 'to the end of his life', in the words of his biographer, '... could never make up his mind whether the Prime Minister really wanted a compromise or was merely playing for time';[*m*] but Austen, despite his political experience and his generous temperament, was capable of singular acts of incomprehension. Balfour, too, believed a story that the Master of Elibank had declared 'the Government and his Party ... so determined not to have an election till after the Coronation that they will keep the conference going till next year'.[*n*] But all the direct evidence was the other way. Asquith incurred some substantial unpopularity by commencing the conference.[4] He ignored it throughout the course of the negotiations. He himself vigorously abstained from making any controversial public speeches. He advanced substantial and even dangerous concessions. He was continually optimistic. His temperament and the difficulties in which he would otherwise be involved with the King united to make him eager for a settlement. The summing up of his biographers is a fair one. 'No one had better reasons for desiring a settlement than Asquith,' they say, 'but there came a point at which he felt constrained to say that he could not justify to his supporters the concessions which he was asked to make, if the machinery for settlement between the two Houses was not to apply to the questions in which they were most interested.'[6]

Balfour was also anxious to be reasonable. He always saw the other side's case with a dangerous ease. He was just as eager as Asquith not to impede the work of the conference by provocative outside speeches.[5] He sought to narrow the

---

[4] An indication of this is given by the almost apologetic speech which Augustine Birrell thought it necessary to deliver to his constituents at Bristol on June 24, '... do not be agitated,' he said, 'there is no need to be agitated.... It is obviously the duty of any persons engaged in any such task as this not to invent compromises but to discover agreement; and then, if discovery is not made, or if it is unsatisfactory, I assure you all, the most enthusiastic politician amongst you, that you will find yourselves relegated to your former positions, with all your rights preserved and able to fight as hard, and I hope as vigorously, with as much good sense and as much information as before, when the time comes.'

[5] He went to the almost fantastic length of writing to Austen Chamberlain asking advice as to whether he should speak in public at all. 'Of course,' he

154

differences, and on the day of the failure of the conference he inspired the Prime Minister to write of his attitude in the following terms: 'We all agree that A.J.B. is head and shoulders above his colleagues. I had a rather intimate talk with him before the conference this morning. He is very pessimistic about the future, and evidently sees nothing for himself but chagrin and a possible private life.'[p]

Yet, despite his 'head and shoulders' superiority, Balfour did not dominate the Unionist side of the conference. It was Lansdowne who filled this role. He was indefatigable in analysing proposals and putting his views upon them on paper, and it is not merely due to the greater thoroughness of his biographer[6] that his attitude during the conference is known to us in much greater detail than is that of Balfour.

Lansdowne's dominance did not assist agreement. He was throughout both stubborn and pessimistic. As early as the end of July he was writing 'supposing … that *per impossible* we were to arrive at an agreement',[q] and by September he was still more resolved on failure. Mr. Ensor is almost certainly right in attributing Lansdowne's negative approach to the fact that 'his interest in tariff reform remained tepid (while) his views about Ireland remained narrowly obstinate, being those of a Southern Irish landlord who had never forgotten the Land League'.[r] Many others in the Unionist Party would have been prepared to agree

said, 'I should make not the most distant allusion to the "constitutional question" but, even with this limitation, I hesitate....' (quoted by Petrie, *op. cit.*, vol. 1, p. 255.)

[6] Nevertheless, Mrs. Dugdale's feat of filling two large volumes with information about Balfour, while leaving so many of his most interesting letters and statements to be quoted by other people, is remarkable.

to some form of federal Home Rule in order to clear the decks for tariff reform. Such views were put forward in the *Observer* by J. L. Garvin,[7] in a series of letters to *The Times* by Austen Chamberlain's friend F. S. Oliver,[8] and by Alfred Lyttelton[9] in private correspondence with Balfour. F. E. Smith gave characteristically sweeping expression to them when he wrote, in a letter, 'Nor does it seem to me logical to submit the tremendous domestic problems of the future to joint session and reserve federal Home Rule—a dead quarrel for which neither the country nor the party cares a damn outside of Ulster and Liverpool.'[5] Austen Chamberlain, who was the recipient of this letter, did not dissent greatly from its views and was even more at one with those of Garvin and Oliver. He was able to discover that his father had been in favour of federal devolution before Mr. Gladstone's 'mischievous and destructive scheme', and that was good enough for him.

Lansdowne was uninfluenced. He had been stubbornly obscurantist on Ireland in 1880 when he was a young man, and he remained so in 1910 when he was an old man. He was throughout quite prepared to see the conference fail rather than agree to a solution which would make easier any form of Home Rule. Cawdor supported him, and Austen Chamberlain, while markedly more moderate on a number of points, was not at his strongest on a complicated constitutional issue and put up little resistance. Indeed, when the end was near and the King was

---

[7] 1868–1947. Editor of the *Observer*, 1908–42.

[8] 1864–1934. He wrote the letters under the pseudonym of *Pacificus*.

[9] 1857–1913. Liberal Unionist member for Leamington, 1895–1906 and for St. George's, Hanover Square, 1906–13. Secretary of State for the Colonies, 1903–5.

appealing for forbearance on both sides, Austen wrote with some truculence that 'we cannot sacrifice the constitution in the vain hope of sparing the Throne'.[1]

The remaining member of the conference whose views were distinct and of the highest importance was Lloyd George. It might be thought that he, like Austen Chamberlain in this respect if in so few others, would not have dominated on detailed constitutional points. Mrs. Asquith records that when, at the conclusion of the conference, a complicated state paper was drawn up by the Cabinet and presented to the King, she asked her husband which of his colleagues had contributed most. After being assured that 'all Winston's suggestions had been discounted', she asked 'What about X——?' (and the identity of 'X' in Mrs. Asquith's memoirs is never in doubt), and was answered that 'it was not his *"genre"* as he was useless upon paper'.[2] But all the sources of information of what passed at the conference itself go to show that Lloyd George played a vital role. He was in the centre of the stage and so full of fertile suggestions that Unionist memoranda for, and recollections of, the conference refer continually to the Chancellor of the Exchequer's proposals or to Mr. Lloyd George's objections. But mainly to the former, for there can be no doubt that throughout this period he was desperately anxious to reach a compromise with the Opposition. 'That the Chancellor of the Exchequer was sincerely desirous of an agreement he (Austen Chamberlain never doubted,' Sir Charles Petrie wrote[3] immediately after recording Austen's more doubtful view of Asquith on this point.

What Lloyd George wanted, indeed, was not a limited agreement covering the points in dispute at the conference, but a coalition Government, with an agreed programme on all the major issues of the day. He sought this, not by hints and intermediaries, but by a peculiarly straightforward method,[10] and perhaps for this reason his proposals, outside a quite small circle, remained a well-kept secret for a number of years.

On August 17 he addressed from Criccieth a long memorandum. He began by stressing the number of problems awaiting solution, and the urgency of dealing with them which was imposed upon the nation by the rise of foreign competitors. Yet none of these problems could be effectively dealt with 'without incurring temporary unpopularity'. In an evenly balanced political situation no party could afford this, and so the true interests of the country suffered. Furthermore, there was a tendency for the extremist tail of each party to wag the dog of the moderate elements: 'As a rule the advanced sections of a party, being propagandist, are the most active, the best organised, the most resolute, and therefore the most irresistible.' Joint action would make it unnecessary to pay 'too much attention to the formulae and projects of rival faddists'. An additional argument was provided by Lloyd George's belief that neither party commanded the services of more than 'half a dozen first-rate men'. Other posts had to be filled with politicians of very limited ability. Coalition would obviously help to repair this deficiency.

What were the urgent questions which would justify the calling into existence of this 'Ministry of All the Talents', and what were the lines upon which it was to deal with them? The Chancellor of the Exchequer was fairly specific in his delineation of the

---

[10] In the sense that he was frank in his dealings with other leading politicians, not in the sense that he informed the electorate of what he was doing, of course.

issues, but less so in his proposals. He listed twelve points. First came matters of social reform. Housing was to be improved, some method of curbing excessive drinking was to be devised, the Poor Law was to be overhauled and recast, and a system of insurance, directed more against the 'accidents of life' than against the foreseeable difficulty of old age, was to be developed. Under only one heading within this group of subjects did Lloyd George go beyond the expression of aspirations. This heading was 'unemployment', but the subject dealt with was not its prevention (which the Chancellor apparently regarded as impossible) but the mitigation of its effects by state insurance. This, however, would have to be done in the teeth of opposition from the industrial offices, and, more importantly, from their multitudinous army of agents and collectors. These agents could not be bought out, because the money involved in paying compensation would 'crush the scheme and destroy its usefulness'. They could not be incorporated in the new arrangement, because this would make impossible a great lowering of the costs of collection. Yet 'they visit every house, they are indefatigable, they are often very intelligent, and a Government which attempted to take over their work without first of all securing the co-operation of the other party would inevitably fail in its undertaking'. The insurance agents had apparently driven large nails into the coffin of the party system.

Then came a series of headings dealing with wider subjects. 'National Reorganisation' demanded the settlement of the denominational issue in education policy on a non-party basis, and a great extension of technical instruction. 'National Defence' involved the closer scrutiny of service spending in some directions and the deliberate encouragement of greater outlay in others. A system of compulsory selective service, following the Swiss model, should be sympathetically investigated. Local government reform was necessary, and 'the various problems connected with state assistance to trade and commerce could be enquired into with some approach to intelligent and judicial impartiality....' It was hinted that tariff reform and transport reorganisation (possibly involving the nationalisation of the railways) were suitable subjects for investigation in this way. The land should be more efficiently farmed and this involved both parties turning their backs on the dangerously short-sighted policy of encouraging smallholdings. Big farms, adequate capital, and intelligent management were more sensible if less immediately popular items for an agricultural programme. "Imperial Problems" was an interesting section only because it included the problem of Ireland—the other points here were trite. 'In this connection the settlement of the Irish question would come up for consideration,' Lloyd George cautiously began. 'The advantages of a non-party treatment of this vexed problem are obvious. Parties might deal with it without being subject to the embarrassing dictation of extreme partisans, whether from *(sic)* Nationalists or Orangemen.'

On foreign policy, his last point, the Chancellor of the Exchequer was rotund rather than penetrating. 'Such a Government,' he wrote, 'representing as it would, not a fragment but the whole nation, would undoubtedly enhance the prestige of this country abroad.' That was the end of the memorandum.

There is some conflict of evidence as to what Lloyd George did with it. F. E. Smith's biographer says that Mr. Churchill and Smith were used as intermediaries by the Chancellor, and that Balfour first heard of the proposals from Smith, and Asquith from Mr. Churchill.ᵂ *The Times*, in its obituary of Balfour, published on March 20, 1930, makes no mention of communication through Mr. Churchill or Smith, but speaks of an 'intrigue' and of 'Mr. Asquith being excluded'. This is explicitly denied by Asquith's biographers. 'It may be stated with confidence,' they write, 'that Asquith believed himself to be fully informed of all that was going on, and he was certainly aware that Mr. Lloyd George was conferring with Mr. Balfour'.[x] They do not, however, confirm Sir Harold Nicolson's belief that the memorandum was shown to Balfour by Asquith himself, after he had received it from Lloyd George and discussed it with five more of his Cabinet colleagues.[y] This view cannot be reconciled with Sir Charles Petrie's statement[z] that Balfour did not at first realise that the Prime Minister was privy to the proceedings, but it is probably nearer to the truth than the others which have been mentioned. The consensus of opinion is that no approach was made to Balfour without the approval of the Prime Minister and the knowledge of Crewe, Grey, Haldane, and Mr. Churchill. Smith and Mr. Churchill were certainly eager skirmishers for coalition, but the second Lord Birkenhead is too flattering in the roles which he ascribes to them.

When the proposal reached Balfour, by whatever method it had come, he thought it worthy of the closest consideration. In Lloyd George's own words, he 'was by no means hostile; in fact he went a long way towards indicating that personally he regarded the proposal with a considerable measure of approval. He was not, however, certain of the reception which would be accorded to it by his party.'[aa] This he endeavoured to ascertain by consulting some of his colleagues. The other Unionist members of the Constitutional Conference were brought in, and so, amongst others, were Bonar Law, Akers-Douglas, and Gerald

Balfour.[11] F. E. Smith, although informed by Lloyd George, was not directly consulted by the leader of his party.

All this took time—the negotiations were still in progress at the end of October—and during this period some of the proposals were given a sharper edge. Attention strayed from the more original and constructive parts of Lloyd George's plan and became concentrated upon a series of straightforward and mutually compensating party bargains. The Unionists were to get a stronger Navy, compulsory military training (which they had never publicly advocated, but which they were not thereby inhibited from regarding as a great prize), and (possibly) tariff reform. In return they were to allow the Liberals to proceed with Home Rule (although under the much less offensive guise of federal devolution), to agree to a compromise solution of the denominational question in education which would probably be nearer to Liberal desires than to their own, and (although there was no mention of this in Lloyd George's memorandum) to envisage Welsh Church Disestablishment. An agreed solution to the House of Lords question, along the lines discussed within the conference, was necessary as a prerequisite to the wider agreement, of course.

The provisional horse-trading, so far as the more eager advocates of coalition were concerned at any rate, went further than this. It extended to the allocation of offices. Asquith was to remain Prime Minister, but was to meet the fate which he had tried to thrust upon Campbell-Bannerman in 1905. He was to

---

[11] 1853–1945. Succeeded his brother as 2nd Earl Balfour, 1930. Conservative member for Leeds, Central, 1885–1906. Chief Secretary for Ireland, 1895–1900. President of the Board of Trade, 1900–5. President of the Local Government Board, 1905.

go to the Lords and leave the leadership in the Commons to Balfour, who would also be Chairman of the Committee of Imperial Defence. Lansdowne was to have the Foreign Office, Mr. Churchill the War Office, and Austen Chamberlain the Admiralty. Lloyd George, although he at one stage offered, inevitably rather rhetorically, to retire if this would ease Unionist difficulties,*bb* was to remain at the Exchequer. For the rest the offices were to be divided on a strictly equal basis between the two parties.

All this came to nothing, for Balfour, despite his initially favourable response and the gloomy fears of Unionist foolishness which he expressed both to Asquith and to Lord Esher*cc* at about this time, eventually killed the plan. Most of the leaders whom he consulted inclined towards acceptance (although it is most difficult to believe that Lansdowne, who remained aloof from this whole negotiation, was not an exception). But Akers-Douglas, Balfour's former Chief Whip, told him that the views of the rank and file of the party would be quite different. They would not stand for such a wholesale compromise of principle and such a sudden *rapprochement* with men against whom they had worked up a quite unusual degree of personal bitterness. This appears to have been decisive with Balfour. He was obsessed at the time (in so far as so detached a mind can ever be said to suffer from an obsession) with what he regarded as the bad example of Peel,[12] and he was determined not to split his party on the issue. Eighteen

---

[12] 'I cannot become another Robert Peel in my party,' he said to Lloyd George (*War Memoirs*, vol. 1, p. 38). 'But his (Balfour's) "stalwarts" and his young wreckers are opposed to him, and he does not fancy the role of Sir Robert Peel,' Lord Esher recorded on November 9 (*Journals and letters*, vol. III, p. 30). 'Yet there was much nobility in the Peel of 1846,' Esher added.

years later, discussing with his biographer these negotiations, he stressed the relevance of the Peel precedent.

> 'My own remark about Peel,' Mrs. Dugdale records him as saying, 'that was the point. I should say it now and may well have said it then. Peel twice committed what seems to me the unforgivable sin. He gave away a principle on which he had come into power—and mind you, neither time had an unforeseen factor come into the case. He simply betrayed his party.'[dd]

Furthermore, Balfour claimed on this occasion that neither at the time nor in retrospect was he greatly attracted by Lloyd George's plan on its merits. And his comment on the Chancellor of the Exchequer's personal attitude was sharp:

> 'Now isn't that like Lloyd George. Principles mean nothing to him—never have. His mind doesn't work that way. It's both his strength and his weakness. He says to himself at any given moment: "Come on now—we've all been squabbling too long, let's find a reasonable way out of the difficulty"—but such solutions are quite impossible for people who don't share his outlook on political principles—the great things.'[ee]

But there were undoubtedly some of Balfour's followers whose minds and principles were just as flexible in 1910 as were those of Lloyd George. F. E. Smith was the outstanding example. He put his thoughts with great frankness into two letters to Austen Chamberlain, one of which concluded with the urgent but fortunately unheeded instruction: 'Please burn this.'

Smith looked at political groupings with all the unprejudiced realism of a Talleyrand considering possible alliances. And he was convinced that acceptance of the Lloyd George offer would strengthen the right and weaken the left.

> 'I am absolutely satisfied of L.G.'s honesty and sincerity,' he wrote. 'He has been taught much by office and is sick of being wagged by a Little England tail. But if he proved in a year or two *difficile* or turbulent, where is he and where are we? He is done and has sold the pass. We should still be a united party with the exception of our Orangemen: and they can't stay out long. What allies can they find?'[ff]

Later, in his second letter, Smith took an even stronger view of the weakness of Lloyd George's position.

> 'I am tempted to say of him,' he rather surprisingly wrote, *'quem Deus vult perdere prius dementat*. It seems to me that he is done for ever unless he gradually inclines to our side in all the things that permanently count.'[gg]

Smith also saw that a coalition would greatly build up the powers of resistance to economic change and weaken the position of the left outside the Liberal Party as well as within it:

> 'A great sigh of relief would go up over the whole of business England if a strong and stable Government were formed. … Furthermore such a Government could (1) say to Redmond: thus far and no further, which Asquith standing alone cannot; and (2) absolutely refuse reversal of the Osborne judgment, which Asquith standing alone cannot.'[hh]

165

Here, leaving aside the reference to the Irish question, we catch a foretaste of the spirit of the post-1918 coalition. A strong businessman's Government, a firm front to labour, and compromise on the traditional 'political' disputes was to be the recipe which prevailed then even if it failed in 1910. And the response which Lloyd George's proposals evoked from different politicians in 1910 presaged to a remarkable degree the attitude which they were to take up in 1921 and 1922. The enthusiasm of Lloyd George himself and of F. E. Smith was, as we have seen, undoubted. Mr. Churchill was equally eager. It was a scheme after his own heart.

Austen Chamberlain, to whom Smith's letters had been addressed, had a less mercurial mind. Unlike Smith and Churchill, he was a little shocked, although not without a touch of pleasure, at the sudden boldness of the plan. 'What a world we live in, and how the public would stare if they could look into our minds and our letter-bags,' he wrote. But he also appreciated the solid advantages which might accrue from it:

'We equally recognise the vast importance of the results which Lloyd George holds out to us. To place the Navy on a thoroughly satisfactory basis, to establish a system of national service for defence, to grant at once preference to the Colonies on the duties immediately available, and to enquire, not with a view to delay but with a view to action at the earliest possible moment, what further duties it is desirable to impose in the interests of the nation and the Empire—these are objects which silence all considerations of personal comfort and all individual preferences or antipathies. And in saying this please understand that I am as assured as you are yourself that Lloyd George has made

166

this proposal in perfect good faith and without any unavowed or unavowable *arrière pensée.* [ii]

Despite one or two detailed objections, he was moving steadily towards a position of firm support for the plan.

Here, then, lined up behind the Chancellor of the Exchequer in 1910 (even if, in some cases, eager to push as well as to follow), were the three men—Birkenhead (as Smith had then become), Churchill, and Chamberlain who in 1922 remained loyal to the coalition to the end and paid the penalty of brief periods in the political wilderness; none of them was a member of the Bonar Law-Baldwin Government.

Asquith, equally presaging the future, was always cool towards the Lloyd George plan. It is true that he did not dismiss it out of hand, nor seek to discourage Lloyd George from making what he could of it. But the latter's statement that 'Mr. Asquith regarded the proposal with considerable favour ...' [ii] is almost certainly too strong. Asquith's own biographers write in quite a different tone:

'For himself,' they say, 'he was wholly sceptical about any coalition being possible which would have effected the desired objects of settling the House of Lords question and carrying the Home Rule Bill and other controversial measures by consent, and he would certainly not have been willing to pay the price (compulsory military service, imperial preference, etc.) which, according to rumours current at the time, the Tory leaders would have required for their connivance. He thought the ground treacherous and dangerous for both parties, but with his accustomed tolerance, he was willing to let those who thought otherwise try their hand; and he watched the progress of the business to its inevitable conclusion with a certain detached amusement.'[kk]

On an issue of this sort Asquith's essential conservatism made him a better radical than Lloyd George. He was a great man for guiding the plough to which he had set his hand, rather than for searching the horizon for some new task. In consequence he was much less willing to abandon the struggles to which he had grown accustomed—Home Rule, the battle with the Lords and the defence of free trade—in return for the excitement of a fresh twist to the political kaleidoscope. Confronted with a new issue, Asquith's instinctive reaction to it would have been far more conservative than would Lloyd George's. Confronted with an old one, he could be far more stubbornly radical.

The breakdown of the coalition negotiations, coming as it did just before the breakdown of discussions on the narrower point within the Constitutional Conference, reinforced the feeling amongst leading politicians that progress by compromise and secret conclave was impossible. The next round would have to be fought out in public.

This was instantly appreciated by Mrs. Asquith when, on November 10, she received a telegram from her husband announcing that all the talks were over. With a very full sense of the duties of a Prime Minister's wife, she reacted, in her own words, as follows: 'It was clear to me that there was nothing for it but for us to have another General Election as quickly as possible before the discontent of our party could become vocal. I sent our Chief Whip—the Master of Elibank—a telegram to this effect, and another to Henry, who had gone to Sandringham to see the King.'[ll]

Fortunately the Chief Whip had no conflicting orders to try to obey, for the Cabinet took roughly the same view as did Mrs. Asquith. But a dissolution raised some delicate problems. It necessarily required the King's consent, and, in the view of the Government, on this occasion it required also to be preceded by some Royal guarantee that, if the Liberal Party were again returned, the Parliament Bill would pass into law. These were not obtained without difficult constitutional negotiation.

X

The King and then the People

On Novemberc 10, the day of the breakdown of the Constitutional Conference, Asquith did not go to Sandringham to see the King, as the quotation from his wife's autobiography at the end of the last chapter suggests. He held a Cabinet in London, at which it was decided, with some doubters, that the correct course was to dissolve at once and to get the election over before Christmas.[1] It was only on the following day

---

[1] It is suggested by his biographer that this decision was almost entirely due to the advice of the Master of Elibank. 'Alick, as Chief Whip, and in charge of the Party organization,' writes Colonel A. C. Murray (*Master and Brother,* p. 59), 'had always been firmly of the opinion that if the Conference failed the Government should immediately appeal to the country, and although, to begin with, the Cabinet was against him, his view ultimately prevailed.' 'Ultimately,' at least, seems to be the wrong word, for the Cabinet decision in favour of an immediate election was made on the first occasion on which a decision could have been taken.

that he travelled to Norfolk, not, in his own words, 'to tender any definite advice, but to survey the new situation created by the failure of the conference, as it presents itself at the moment to His Majesty's Ministers....'[a]

As part of the survey he informed the King of the decision to seek an early dissolution, said that if this were followed by another Government victory the issue with the House of Lords would have to be put to a conclusion, and, while pointing out that it would be theoretically possible for this to be done by the Crown either withholding writs of summons or exercising the prerogative of creation, stressed that there were precedents for the latter course but not for the former. He added that he had no doubt that the *threat* of creation would alone be sufficient to bring about an agreement.

The King, however, was so pleased with one aspect of this audience that he could hardly notice anything else about it. 'He asked me,' he wrote in his notebook after the Prime Minister had gone, 'for *no guarantees*.'[b] '(Mr. Asquith) did not ask for anything from the King,' Sir Arthur Bigge[2] confirmed in a minute written the same night: *'no promises, no guarantees during this Parliament.'*[c]

Neither the King nor his private secretary understood that this was merely a preliminary discussion, intended to show the way the mind of the Cabinet was moving, and that exact advice would follow later. It was, indeed, an example of Asquith's over-delicate

---

[2] 1849–1931. Assistant private secretary to Queen Victoria, 1880–95, and principal private secretary, 1895–1901. Private secretary to George V as Duke of York and Prince of Wales, 1901–10, joint private secretary (with Lord Knollys) to him as King from 1910–13, and principal private secretary from 1913–31. Created Lord Stamfordham, 1911.

method of approach to the King on the constitutional issue. 'Unaccustomed as he (King George) was to ambiguous phraseology he was totally unable to interpret Mr. Asquith's enigmas,' Sir Harold Nicolson has written.[d] A more direct, even if more brusque, approach would have been better understood. It might have avoided the very delicate situation which arose three days later, when Lord Knollys came up from Sandringham to Downing Street and discovered that the Prime Minister's intentions had become more definite. 'What he now advocates,' Knollys wrote to the King, 'is that you should give guarantees at once for the next Parliament.' The King's response was to instruct Bigge to telegraph to Vaughan Nash, Asquith's private secretary, in the following terms: 'His Majesty regrets that it would be impossible for him to give contingent guarantees and he reminds Mr. Asquith of his promise not to seek for any during the present Parliament.'[e] This message was despatched and received on the same morning (November 15) that the Cabinet was giving final approval to a minute to the King, formally outlining 'the advice which they feel it their duty to tender to His Majesty', of which the key paragraph read:

'His Majesty's Ministers cannot, however, take the responsibility of advising a dissolution, unless they may understand that, in the event of the policy of the Government being approved by an adequate majority[3] in the new House of

---

[3] A rather vague phrase, it may be thought, and one which departed from the salutary principle that in parliamentary affairs a majority is a majority, and a bill carried by one vote is just as effectively law as one carried by 250. But Crewe, speaking in the Vote of Censure debate nine months later, indicated that it was intended to be more than a phrase. 'The question

Commons, His Majesty will be ready to exercise his constitutional powers (which may involve the prerogative of creating peers), if needed to secure that effect should be given to the decision of the country.'[7]

The minute added the suggestion that the understanding should not be made public unless and until the actual occasion should arise.

The King and his Ministers were rapidly moving into positions of direct conflict. And the situation was not made easier by the fact that the Sovereign was receiving directly contradictory advice from his two private secretaries. Lord Knollys, in London, was for accepting the wishes of the Cabinet. 'I feel certain that you can safely and constitutionally accept what the Cabinet propose,' he wrote in a letter accompanying the Government minute, 'and I venture to urge you strongly to do so.'[8] He had the advantage, in the King's eyes, of greater experience of the constitutional issue, having served King Edward VII and seen the difficulty develop from the beginning.

Bigge, at Sandringham, had the advantage both of being with the King at the time and of having been his own private secretary, not for a few months as was the case with Knollys, but for nearly ten years. He was passionately, almost violently, opposed to the King giving way. He summarised his views in a document prepared for His Majesty:

---

whether at any time the advice to "create peers" should be given,' he said, 'must necessarily depend for one thing upon the adequacy of the majority with which we were returned to the House of Commons... Fortunately the question of interpretation never arose.

'The King's position is: he cannot give contingent guarantees. For by so doing he becomes a partisan and is placing a powerful weapon in the hands of the Irish and Socialists who, assured of the abolition of the veto of the House of Lords, would hold before their electors the certainty of ultimate Home Rule and the carrying out of their Socialist programme.[4] The Unionists would declare His Majesty was favouring the Government and placing them (the Unionists) at a disadvantage before their constituencies. Indeed it is questionable whether His Majesty would be acting constitutionally. It is not His Majesty's duty to save the Prime Minister from the mistake of his incautious words on the 14th of April.'[h]

On the proposal for secrecy, Bigge was still more vehement.

'Is this straight?' he asked the King. 'Is it English? Is it not moreover childish?'

The issue which Bigge did not face was what was to happen if the King accepted his advice and ignored that of his Ministers and of Knollys. In these circumstances Asquith would certainly have resigned. The King must then have sent for Balfour. To have refused the advice of one Prime Minister and sent for another would have been a dangerous enough proceeding at the best of times, but unless it was known that Balfour would accept the commission it would have been merely silly. The King, with a great loss of face, might have found himself back where he

---

[4] Exactly why there should be constitutional danger in parties indicating that if the electorate voted for them their policies might be carried into effect is not clear.

started—with Asquith, and with no possible alternative.

It fell to Knollys to give the decisive advice on this point (he had got the King up to London by November 16 for an audience to Asquith and Crewe that afternoon). In Sir Harold Nicolson's words, 'Lord Knollys assured him that Mr. Balfour would in any event decline to form an administration.'[i] This was curiously firm advice, for it was far from certain that Balfour would not agree to form a Government, and no one had better reason to know this than Lord Knollys. On April 29 he had been present at a secret meeting at Lambeth Palace, convened by the Archbishop of Canterbury and attended also by Balfour and Lord Esher.[5] His own record of the meeting says, 'Mr. Balfour made it quite clear that he would be prepared to form a Government to prevent the King being put in the position contemplated by the. demand for the creation of peers.'[j] Knollys communicated the substance of this talk to King Edward on the day before his death, but did not subsequently pass the information on to King George. This was not perhaps surprising, for it may well be that no occasion to do so arose, either at the time of the change of reign or in the following months. But what is remarkable is that when specifically asked about the point in November, Knollys should have given advice based on facts directly contrary to those which he had recorded in a minute six and a half months previously.

The decisive nature of this advice cannot be doubted. The King gave way to the Cabinet's demand at this interview with

---

[5] 1852–1930. Reginald Baliol Brett. Succeeded his father as 2nd Viscount Esher, 1899. Liberal member for Penryn and Falmouth, 1880–85. Subsequently became a Liberal Unionist. Friend and confidant of King Edward VII and King George V.

Asquith and Crewe on the afternoon of November 16.[6] That night he wrote his own version of what had transpired:

> 'After a long talk' he recorded, 'I agreed most reluctantly to give the Cabinet a secret understanding that in the event of the Government being returned with a majority at the General Election, I should use my Prerogative to make Peers if asked for. I disliked having to do this very much, but agreed that this was the only alternative to the Cabinet resigning, *which at this moment would be disastrous* (my italics). Francis (Knollys) strongly urged me to take this course and I think his advice is generally very sound. I only trust and pray he is right this time.'[k]

Asquith, speaking of the occasion in the House of Commons nine months later,[7] used the following carefully chosen words: 'His Majesty, after careful consideration of all the circumstances past and present, and after discussing the matter in all its bearings with myself and my noble friend and colleague, Lord Crewe, *felt that he had no alternative but to assent to the advice of the Cabinet.*' (my italics.)

The implication of both statements is that, had he thought Balfour's attitude to be different, the King might have shifted his

---

[6] Asquith was a good deal criticised for having taken Crewe to the interview, 'as if,' it was said, 'he needed a witness of what passed'. (*See* Spender and Asquith, *op. cit.,* vol. I, p. 297*n*.) More characteristically he had made a hurried appearance at the wedding of a Unionist politician—Mr. L. S. Amery —before proceeding to what he described as 'the most important political occasion in my life'.

[7] In the Vote of Censure debate, August 7, 1911.

own position. And this is borne out by a piece of subsequent history related by Sir Harold Nicolson. Knollys gave up his appointment in 1913, the King finding the arrangement of joint private secretaries unsatisfactory. A few months afterwards King George saw for the first time the minute of the meeting of April 29, and dictated the following short note upon it: 'It was not until late in the year 1913 that the foregoing letters and memoranda came into my possession. The knowledge of their contents would, undoubtedly, have had an important bearing and influence with regard to Mr. Asquith's request for guarantees on November 16, 1910.'[1]

Sir Harold Nicolson thinks that Lord Knollys, despite what it is difficult to regard as other than a deliberate act of concealment, was substantially right in the information he gave the King, because Balfour had changed his mind by November. The evidence he cites in support of this is a letter from Balfour to Lansdowne, dated December 27. In this letter Balfour wrote: 'I do not believe, however, as at present advised, that it would be fair to the King to suggest that he will better his position by attempting, under present circumstances, to change his Government.' [m] But this is no evidence at all. By December 27 the second 1910 election had occurred and confirmed the result of the first. It was therefore obvious, and this point is made by Balfour elsewhere in the letter, that a third dissolution was unthinkable. In November, as in April, the situation was quite different. A second election seemed inevitable, and the point at issue was whether it should be fought with a majority Liberal Government in office, choosing the ground to confirm its position, or with a minority Unionist Government, choosing the ground to achieve a majority. By the end of December a change of Government was possible only if the new Government could carry on with the existing Parliament, and this the Unionists manifestly could not do.

This does not mean that Balfour was certainly still willing to form a Government in November. Indeed his increasing apprehension of the political future makes it quite likely that he was less ready for a rash venture then than he had been in April. But it does mean that we have no evidence that this was so, and that it is improbable that Lord Knollys had any either. What Knollys appears therefore to have done was not merely to have suppressed a piece of information because a better piece came to hand and he did not wish to confuse the King, but to suppress the best piece which he had because he was so convinced that the King should accept the advice of the Cabinet that he was unwilling to advance any facts which might turn his mind the other way.

Knollys was confident of the rightness of his own view, and he made no attempt to minimise the part which he had played. He proudly told Mrs. Asquith that, after her husband had left the Palace on the afternoon of November 16, the King had turned to him and said, 'Is this the advice that you would have given my father?' and that he had replied, 'Yes, Sir; and your father would have taken it'.[8n] For his services at this time, even if his methods

---

[8] In fact there is no evidence that King Edward had made up his mind what to do if and when the Cabinet demanded the exercise of the prerogative. He certainly approached the matter with distaste, and during his last visit to Biarritz was toying with the compromise idea of ennobling only the eldest sons of Liberal peers and thus rendering the damage to the House of Lords merely temporary (Nicolson, *op. cit.,* p. 129). But his death saved him from the difficulty of decision. Perhaps because he knew this, Sir Arthur Bigge was particularly incensed at Knollys introducing King Edward into the controversy. 'This quoting what a dead person would do is to me most unfair, if not improper, especially to the King, who has such a

were somewhat unorthodox, the nation and the institution of constitutional monarchy owe Knollys a deep debt of gratitude. But it was not a debt which was recognised by King George. Immediately after the decision was made he felt a sense of relief, and in the following week Lord Esher found him 'proud of his strict adherence to the lines of the constitution ... (and) also perfectly calm'.[o] But resentment soon set in. Eleven months later, again in a conversation with Esher, he was saying that 'what he especially resented was the promise extracted from him in November that he would tell "no one"'[9p] Nor did he quickly forget the issue. His attitude when the minute of the Lambeth Palace meeting came to light has already been noted; and for the longer term we have Sir Harold Nicolson's testimony that 'King George remained convinced thereafter that in this, the first political crisis of his reign, he had not been accorded either the confidence or the consideration to which he was entitled.'[q]

What was the danger from which Lord Knollys saved the King? Partly because of the secrecy which enveloped the result as well as the course of the negotiations with Asquith and Crewe it was widely misunderstood. An observer with as many ears to the ground as Sir Almeric Fitzroy,[10] for example, who fully realised that there was a crisis afoot, believed that it arose because the King was making difficulties about the grant of a dissolution of 'a Parliament of (Ministers') own choosing, in which so far

---

high opinion of his father's judgment. But might I not equally have urged that 1 was perfectly certain Queen Victoria would have done what I advised?' (Nicolson, *op. cit*, pp. 138–9.)

[9] This part of the arrangement, of course, was inserted against the convenience of the Liberal Cabinet, in an attempt to ease the position of the King.

[10] 1851–1935. Clerk to the Privy Council, 1898–1923.

they have not met With a rebuff in either House and during the existence of which they have not lost a seat...." Even Lord Esher, who was better informed to the extent of knowing most of what transpired at the meeting of November 16, believed that the difficulty until that day had been the King's refusal of a dissolution to Asquith. Furthermore, he saw the dangers of a change of Government in these terms: 'Obviously Arthur Balfour could only form a Government either if the Liberal moderates supported him, which was not to be thought of, or if he in his turn were granted a dissolution. The King therefore would have been in the position of according to a Tory Prime Minister what a few days before he had refused to a Radical.'⁵

This passage, although it puts succinctly the danger which would always confront a Sovereign who refused a dissolution to a majority Prime Minister,[11] was not on the point. King George never contemplated refusing Asquith's request for a dissolution. From first to last there is nothing in the King's own writings, in those of his private secretaries, or in the Cabinet memoranda to suggest that there was any difficulty on this issue. The most that the King did, on the occasion of Asquith's visit to Sandringham, was to suggest 'that the veto resolutions should first (i.e. before a dissolution) be sent up to the House of Lords',' To this condition, his biographers say, Asquith readily complied, and there was therefore little to the matter, less perhaps than the King implied whenche told Lansdowne two months later that 'it was owing to him that we had been allowed to have the Parliament Bill in the

---

[11] As late as 1950, Lord Simon was rash enough, in a letter to *The Times*, to suggest that this would be a constitutionally proper course for King George VI to take.

House of Lords at all'.¹¹ Furthermore, there was no suggestion in the part of the Cabinet memorandum of November 15 which touched on this—'The House of Lords to have the opportunity, if they demand it, at the same time, but not so as to postpone the date of dissolution, to discuss the Government resolutions'—that the Government had to be peculiarly submissive here in order to obtain a general election at all.

Simply by granting a dissolution to Balfour the King would not therefore have been treating him differently from the way in which he treated Asquith. But he would, none the less, have been accused, and justly accused, of favouritism and of unconstitutional behaviour. He would have changed his Government because the advice of the incoming Prime Minister was more congenial to him personally than was that of the outgoing Prime Minister; and he would have precipitated an election in which a principal issue was bound to be the known fact that one party enjoyed his favour and the other did not. He would have been making himself far more of a partisan than by taking the course which he did and which Sir Arthur Bigge feared would produce exactly this result. The consequences of such an action, in the explosive atmosphere of pre-1914 England, might have been far reaching, and the narrowness of the margin by which Lord Knollys prevented their being set in train cannot be doubted.

Parliament reassembled, after the long recess, on November 15. An early dissolution was known to be contemplated, but no statement could be made until the negotiations with the King were complete. Asquith therefore moved the adjourment and promised to give more information three days later. The House of Lords could not so easily be made to wait upon the Government's convenience. Lansdowne announced that on the following day he would move a resolution inviting the

181

Government immediately to submit the Parliament Bill; and when this had been moved, and accepted by Crewe (although with a rather bad grace and accompanied by the statement that the Government would accept no amendments), Rosebery gave notice that he now intended to proceed at once with the two more detailed resolutions of reform which he had tabled in April after the success of his three more general ones, but which had not been debated because of the death of King Edward and the subsequent truce.

He brought them forward on November 17, and they were disposed of after half a day's debate—the first being carried without a division, and the second abandoned by Rosebery himself on the curious ground that it 'went too far into detail'. The terms of the resolutions were these:

'(1) That in future the House of Lords shall consist of Lords of Parliament: *(a)* chosen by the whole body of hereditary peers from amongst themselves, and by nomination by the Crown; *(b)* sitting by virtue of offices and of qualifications held by them; *(c)* chosen from outside. (2) That the term of tenure for all Lords of Parliament shall be the same, except in the case of those who sit *ex officio,* who would sit so long as they held the office for which they sit.'

The main interest of the debate was provided by Lansdowne's speech, in which he gave his view that a half of the reformed House might be hereditary peers, and that he would like those selected to be 'familiar with country life, familiar with the management of landed property' rather than 'veterans with a distinguished record, who have arrived at a time of life when they would look naturally for repose'.

On the next day—Friday the eighteenth—the Government statements were made in both Houses. The dissolution was announced for November 28, certain parts only of the postponed Budget (of 1910) were to be proceeded with before then, and (as a counter to the Osborne judgment) the Government, if it won the election, was to propose the payment of members of Parliament in the next session. On the whole there was good temper.

'I heard Asquith and A.J.B. yesterday afternoon,' Esher wrote on the following day. 'The House was crowded. Asquith very concise and dignified. Arthur extremely mild and unaggressive. No reference in either speech to highly controversial things. Lansdowne, on the other hand, showed some bitterness.'[w]

After these announcements interest quickly began to move to the constituencies, although the proceedings in the House of Lords during the following week were of considerable importance. The motion for the second reading of the Parliament Bill came up on the Monday. Lansdowne, who spoke second, claimed that with no amendments allowed the debate was unreal. He would therefore move its postponement in order to bring forward, later in the week, proposals of his own in the form of resolutions. This he did on the Wednesday. The resolutions did little more than re-state the case which the Unionists had made within the Constitutional Conference. They implied a 'reduced and reconstituted' House of Lords, although they gave no information as to its composition, and they stated that, provided a joint committee of both Houses with the Speaker exercising only a casting vote, and not the Speaker alone, determined what was and what was not a money bill, the House of Lords would abandon its right of rejection in this field; that where a difference between the two Houses on other bills arose and persisted for a year it should be settled by a joint sitting, unless the bill related 'to a matter of great gravity and had not been adequately submitted to the judgment of the people', in which case it should be put to a referendum.

After a full debate the resolutions were carried without a division, but also, of course, without the support of the Government peers. It cannot be pretended that they were not greatly disliked by many Unionists. The almost impossible position into which the Tory Party had manoeuvred itself was making many converts of convenience to reform. '... (The debate's) most remarkable feature,' wrote Lord Newton, 'was the enthusiasm shown for drastic reform by some of those who had previously deprecated any action of this nature as inopportune and ill-advised.'* But even this simulated enthusiasm was far from universal. There were many who agreed with Lord Esher[12] that Lansdowne's proposals constituted more of a break in the English constitutional tradition than did the Government plan for limiting the veto. And so indeed they did. To reconstitute the House of Lords, to distinguish between different bills according to the highly subjective test of their importance, to introduce the entirely novel device of the joint sitting, and, in Asquith's words, to substitute 'a plebiscite' for 'parliamentary government', all as a result of no more than six months of far from calm thought, was fairly hard going for a Conservative Party. But in constitutional matters and

---

[12] He expressed these views in a memorandum prepared for the King. (See *Journals and Letters*, III, pp. 30–3.)

where its own influence is at stake, the Tories can sometimes be a party not of conservation but of restless innovation.

The election campaign was generally agreed to have been a dull one. 'The general election (of December, 1910),' wrote Sir Sidney Low in the *Fortnightly* for January, 1911, 'was the most apathetic within living memory.' The issues were inevitably rather stale, although Home Rule played a larger part than in January, and the electorate was bored with being asked to vote again so quickly. Over one in six, indeed, of those who had previously voted declined to do so, and the total poll fell by more than a million votes. There were some shafts of interest, however. Lloyd George turned with vigour from the moderation of his coalition proposals to the immoderation of his platform manner, and at Mile End, at the beginning of the campaign, he gave what was almost a second edition of his Limehouse speech. He described the Lords (according, it may be thought, an unduly ancient lineage to most members of the peerage) as 'descended partly from plunderers who came over with William the Conqueror and partly from plunderers of the poor at the Reformation', and contrasted their good fortune with that of a man he had seen in Dartmoor who, he claimed, had been sentenced to thirteen years' penal servitude for stealing 2s. from a church box when drunk. 'An aristocracy,' he added, 'is like cheese; the older it is the higher it becomes.'

In this speech Lloyd George also delivered a *riposte* to a Unionist line of attack which was given great prominence throughout the campaign. Redmond and three other Nationalist members had spent the recess touring Canada and the United States and collecting dollars for the Home Rule cause. A very respectable list of subscribers, including the name of Sir Wilfrid Laurier, the Canadian Prime Minister of the day, gave them a total of £40,000. But the respectability of its sources did not prevent the Unionist press from denouncing the menace of this dollar fund. Even Balfour joined in the attack, when, in his Nottingham speech of November 17, he announced that 'the Government were going to destroy the constitution at the will of American subscribers'. The issue showed every sign of developing into the major Tory stunt of the campaign. Lloyd George attacked it as such, and related it to the other 'bogeys' which the Unionists had created for previous elections. 'But since when,' he asked, 'has the British aristocracy despised American dollars? They have underpinned many a tottering noble house.' It was an effective thrust, sufficiently so at any rate to provoke the Duke of Marlborough,[13] who, the *Annual Register* assures us,[z] had entertained the Chancellor of the Exchequer at Blenheim, 'publicly to denounce his reference to American heiresses'.

In their different ways the Liberal leaders pursued the campaign. Mr. Churchill began firmly by writing a public letter to the chairman of his election committee announcing that 'The Liberals had long claimed equal political rights. They were now going to take them.'[aa] But he then missed a great opportunity by declining Bonar Law's offer that they should fight each other in North-West Manchester (where Mr. Churchill had been defeated at a bye-election in 1908, but which had again become Liberal at the first 1910 general election), the loser to remain out of the next Parliament. The seat stayed in Liberal hands. Sir Edward Grey argued strongly against the referendum—'a pig in a poke'— and Lord Morley broke a Nestorian silence to ridicule 'the appeal

---

[13] 1871–1934. 9th Duke. In 1895 he had married Consuelo Vanderbilt of New York, his father having previously married, late in life, a rich American as his second wife.

to moderate men by a Unionist Party which had destroyed the House of Lords and were destroying the parliamentary system'.[bb]

To a greater extent than at the previous election, however, Asquith dominated the Government campaign. From his Hull speech on November 25, with its famous and sustained satire of the peers' sudden eagerness to reform themselves,[14] through to the end he rained a series of hammer blows on to the Opposition case. 'He spoke in all parts of the country,' his biographers tell us, 'expounding with rare force and dignity what he believed to be the true constitutional doctrine, employing raillery and satire, when they served his purpose, but most carefully refraining from all violence of language and mob-oratory.'[cc]

---

[14] 'Ah, gentlemen, what a change eleven short months have wrought!' this passage began. 'This ancient and picturesque structure has been condemned by its own inmates as unsafe. The parricidal pickaxes are already at work, and constitutional jerry-builders are hurrying from every quarter with new plans. Dr. Johnson once said of a celebrated criminal, who after his condemnation showed literary activity, "Depend upon it, Sir, when a man is going to be hanged in a fortnight it concentrates his mind wonderfully." The activity recently displayed by the House of Lords in providing itself with a successor is surely a miracle of this kind of mental concentration. In a single sitting, not unduly prolonged, the venerable institution, which has withstood the storm and stress of ages, was transformed—in principle, of course; some of the details are still withheld—into a brand new modern Senate.... The motive for this feverish exhibition of destructive and constructive ardour is not far to seek. The Tory Party were determined at all hazards not to face another General Election with the incubus of the House of Lords on their back. There must be something to put in its place, something—it did not matter for the moment very much what—but something which could be called a Second Chamber, with a coat, however thin, of democratic varnish.' (Spender and Asquith, *op. cit.*, vol. 1, pp. 299–300.)

On the Unionist side the chief excitement was provided by Balfour's partial retreat from tariff reform. As soon as the election became imminent he was strongly urged by some supporters of his party to do this.

'The editor of the *Express*, Buckle,[15] Norton-Griffiths,[16] M.P. for Wednesbury, some others, and Garvin—Garvin of all men!' Austen Chamberlain wrote on November 13, '… had all been in quick succession to tell Balfour that we could not win with the food duties, that he must —not indeed abandon them altogether—but announce that if returned to power now he would not impose any new food duty without yet annother appeal to the country.'[dd]

In addition, the Liberals naturally enough made great play with the point that if the Unionists believed in a referendum before a change as constitutionally important as Home Rule was effected, they should also wish it to precede a change so economically important as tariff reform. On November 29 the Prime Minister put out a direct challenge in a speech before an audience of 8,000 in the railway sheds at Reading. The same night it was unexpectedly answered by Balfour at the Albert Hall. After consultation only with Lansdowne (no one else was quickly available) he announced that, provided there were no technical difficulties which he had not yet had time to consider, 'he had not the slightest objection to submit(ting) the principles of tariff reform to a referendum'.[ee] 'That's won the election!' cried an

---

[15] 1854–1935. Editor of *The Times*, 1884–1912, and biographer of Disraeli.
[16] 1871–1930. Sir John Norton-Griffiths. Member for Wednesbury, 1910–18 and Wandsworth, Central, 1918–24.

eager listener, and the whole audience rose to its feet to cheer the pronouncement with due reverence.

Elsewhere it was received with less enthusiasm. Austen Chamberlain said he 'felt the decision like a slap in the face', and later, when the end of the election campaign found him unwell, described his real complaint as 'referendum sickness'; [ff] the *Morning Post* urged tariff reform candidates to take no notice of their leader; and whatever else Balfour's retreat did, it did not win the election. Whether it made any appreciable difference to the result is open to question. Mr. R. C. K. Ensor refers without argument to 'a shelving of Chamberlainism which won him (Balfour) back some Lancashire seats';[gg] but Austen, impressed by Unionist defeats at Cheltenham ('where the moderate man with a small fixed income is supposed to abound') and Lincoln (where there was a distinct Unionist Free Trade organisation) and by the fact that the only Opposition candidate in Manchester to increase his poll was one who repudiated Balfour, was convinced that the insignificance of Unionist opposition to tariff reform had been exposed. In fact eight Lancashire seats which had been held by the Government parties earlier in the year swung over to the Unionists, but as five of them were away from predominantly cotton areas, where tariff reform might have been expected to be electorally most dangerous, and as two Lancashire seats changed hands the other way, there is no very strong evidence to support Mr. Ensor's view.

Nevertheless the main pattern of the results was provided by Unionist gains in Lancashire offset by Liberal gains in London.[17] In the 'Nonconformist fringe', also, there was a slight recession

---

[17] A list of the surprisingly large number of seats which changed hands at this election is given in appendix c.

from Liberalism, four seats in the West Country, two in Wales and one in Scotland changing over to the Unionists. The net result of these and other changes was to reduce the Unionists by one and the Liberals by three, but to increase the Nationalists and the Labour Party by two each. The Government became marginally stronger vis-à-vis the Opposition and marginally weaker vis-à-vis the more independent parts of its own majority. But these slight changes were totally insignificant compared with the broad confirmation of the result of the previous January which the election gave. The Liberal Government achieved the distinction, unique since 1832, of winning three successive general elections. In Mr. Ensor's words: 'Nothing could in its way have been more decisive. Any further election was out of the question.... The people regarded the issue as settled, and only wanted the dispute wound up as quickly as possible.'[hh] Their wants had still to wait some little time before they could be satisfied.

XI

The Peers Persist

When the dust had settled, after Christmas, there could be
no doubt that the Government had secured a 'sufficient
majority' within the meaning of the November arrangement
with the King. Augustine Birrell spoke of 'the sudden emergence
of a certainty', and Asquith's biographers, who quote this
remark, say that it 'struck the popular imagination'.[a] But it did
not strike the Unionist leaders. Asquith had assumed, during the
negotiations in November, that the King's promise could always
remain secret. If the Government were defeated at the polls, the
matter would not arise. If it won, the peers would surely accept
the verdict to the extent of allowing the Parliament Bill through
without forcing the use of the prerogative. In this chain of
reasoning he over-estimated the ability of Lansdowne to see
ahead and to map out a firm course, and he under-estimated
Balfour's growing weariness with emotional or stupid followers.

The trouble began early in the New Year. Lord Esher and
Lord Knollys dined with Balfour at the Marlborough Club on

January 10 and passed on to the King a whole series of very sensible remarks from this source.

> 'Mr. Balfour therefore holds,' wrote Esher, 'that the King should now assume from his general knowledge of the state of affairs that no alternative government is at this moment possible, and that being the case, His Majesty could not well ultimately refuse to comply with Mr. Asquith's demand, should it be made, for a promise to create peers.... Mr. Balfour ... went on to say that he was sure that it would be the strong desire of Mr. Asquith, Mr. Lloyd George, and Lord Crewe to safeguard as far as possible the position of the King, and to ease the situation for him as far as they could do so having regard for the exigencies of their party. He feels sure that no public disclosure would be made of the so-called guarantee, and so far as he and his own party leaders are concerned the Government would not be questioned on the point.'[b]

From this analysis a Unionist policy of retreat under protest seemed to follow quite automatically. But from Lord Lansdowne, whom later in January he thought he would like to see personally for a discussion of the Unionist position, the King obtained a rather different view. Asquith at first objected to this suggested audience and then, when the King persisted, reluctantly agreed. In 1909, before the Lord's rejection of the Budget, the Prime Minister had taken the initiative in advising the King to see the Opposition leaders, but on this latter occasion, when the King's own actions were to be central to the next phase of the constitutional struggle, Asquith thought that it would be difficult to draw a line between 'desiring knowledge' and 'seeking advice'. He went so far as to draw up a formal minute for the King on the point.

> 'The part to be played by the Crown in such a situation as now exists has happily been settled by the accumulated traditions and the unbroken practice of more than seventy years. It is to act upon the advice of the Ministers who for the time being possess the confidence of the House of Commons, whether that advice does or does not conform to the private and personal judgment of the Sovereign. ... It follows that it is not the function of a Constitutional Sovereign to act as arbiter or mediator between rival parties and policies; still less to take advice from the leaders of both sides, with the view to forming a conclusion of his own.'

The disputed audience took place at Windsor on January 29. Lansdowne showed himself unconvinced that the prerogative would if necessary be used, or that his task was to extricate his forces from a lost battle.

> 'It (the creation of peers),' he wrote in his note of the conversation, 'was a step which I felt sure H.M. would be reluctant to take, and his Ministers not less reluctant to advise; and I thought it not unfair to say that, up to a certain point, we should be justified in bearing this fact in mind when considering whether it was desirable to offer resistance to the Government proposals.'

Later in the interview he showed that he had no desire to see the dispersal of the fog in which he was enveloped:

'I thought it would be most unwise for any of those concerned, either H.M.G. or the Opposition, or, if I might be permitted to say so, H.M. himself, at this moment to commit themselves finally to any particular line of action, or above all to allow it to become known that they had so committed themselves.'

This distaste for decision arose primarily out of Lansdowne's refusal fully to accept the finality of the election result. He realised that it made an immediate change of Government, necessarily involving another appeal to the country, out of the question. But he clung to the hope that if a conclusion could be postponed, the dispute might be shifted on to slightly different ground and a Unionist claim for yet a third election given some plausibility.

'It might, however, happen, that as the situation developed, the issue might undergo a change,' he told the King. 'For example, supposing an amendment to be carried for the purpose of safeguarding the Constitution against a violent change during the time which, if the Bill became law, would pass before a reformed House of Lords could be called into existence, a new issue of the kind which I contemplated might arise. Was it conceivable that H.M.'s advisers would desire that he should create 500 peers for the purpose of resisting such a proposal?'[d]

Asquith had realised that this pitfall might be dug for him and was determined not to fall into it. Combined with his own understanding of the position, the promises which he had secured from the King in November gave him adequate protection against its dangers. The arrangement was, not that the Government should merely be protected against an outright rejection by the peers of the Parliament Bill, but that, provided an adequate victory at the election was secured, the King would use the prerogative if necessary to get the bill through in the form which the Government desired. Lansdowne was therefore clutching at what was hardly even a straw. But he preferred to do this rather than give a firm order to retreat. His tactic in consequence became one of delay. If the issue was brought to a head immediately his position was hopeless. He had to try to give it time to change, and this attempt was the motive behind most of his actions between January and July. The difficulty was that while he was delaying many of his followers were busily and ostentatiously digging themselves into positions from which retreat was impossible.

The new Parliament was opened by the King on February 6, and the Parliament Bill—in exactly the same form that it had been presented in the previous Parliament—was taken immediately after the Address. It was read a first time on February 22, by a vote of 351 to 227. The Unionist leaders in the Lords replied with the only delaying manoeuvre of which they could think. They decided to press on further with a scheme for reform. Lord Newton has described how 'the party wire-pullers became extremely active, and much pressure was exerted to induce the House of Lords to introduce a Reform Bill at the earliest opportunity. The Whips were very insistent that a Bill should be brought in at once, and in their zeal went so far as to urge that a bad Bill was better than nothing, and that unless something was done promptly the party would be completely smashed.'

This approach did not command the unanimous support of the anti-Government forces. Those who were opposed to any change were naturally hostile, but so was such an eager reformer as Rosebery. He thought that it was fatal for an Opposition to commit itself to the details of a bill. That might attract the attack away from the proposals of the Government. The best course would be for Lansdowne and his followers to reaffirm their general position by another series of resolutions. This was not far from Lansdowne's own view, but he allowed himself to be swayed by the balance of opinion as expressed through his post-bag and by the insistent energy of Curzon. He accordingly gave notice, on the day of the Parliament Bill's first reading in the Commons, of his intention to introduce a House of Lords Reform Bill.

After this expression of intention, however, no further progress was made for some time. Lansdowne was seriously ill for most of March. But the mere announcement that a bill was in preparation set off a babel of Tory tongues, each proclaiming a different plan for the composition of the new Second Chamber. Some, like the Duke of Bedford, wanted a wholly elective senate, but most wanted a more conservative arrangement. A hundred Unionist members met at the House of Commons on February 28 to plan a campaign, but in the absence of an agreement as to what they should campaign for the meeting broke up unsatisfactorily. The Opposition was manifestly less united than was the Government.

The second reading of the Parliament Bill occupied the four nights from February 27 to March 2. The debate followed a largely familiar pattern. The Unionists denounced the Government for forcing through a constitutional revolution at the behest of the Irish Party (although, as George Lansbury pointed out, during the dinner hour on the first night only one Unionist was present in the chamber, trying to prevent this dire consequence, and he was speaking), and Government speakers denounced the Opposition for refusing to accept the clearly expressed verdict of the electorate. The most notable features of the debate were Haldane's last major speech in the Commons[1] and a duel between Balfour and Asquith, with the Prime Minister, on this occasion, very much in the ascendant. The leader of the Opposition claimed that 'for practical men it was folly to abandon the hereditary principle, which was accepted by the great majority of mankind, and in the case of the Monarchy was invaluable as the bond of Empire'. Then, in a typically Balfourian passage, 'he admitted that Liberal legislation did not get fair play, but granting that a kind of sporting equality between parties should be the goal of their ambitions, surely this was no reason for allowing all Governments to have an uncontrolled license'. He wanted a constitutional change because the House of Lords was at present not strong enough to carry out its func-tion. Later he became less typically Balfourian, denounced Ministers passionately, and created a scene by accusing them of having imposed their proposals on the country by fraud.

Asquith replied that 'the House now knew that the real motive of the Tories in taking up Second Chamber reform was to strengthen it *(sic)* against the representatives of the people.... The Opposition schemes would all perpetuate a Second Chamber in which one political party would be predominant.' He poured scorn on Balfour's use of the hereditary argument. 'The Monarchy was doubtless strong, but where was the Veto of the Crown?' He scoffed at the 'constitution mongers', who were then hastily at work behind closed doors. Balfour wished the Government to hold its hand until these hasty improvisers had

---

[1] He was created a viscount at the end of March.

completed their task. 'It was not for that that the electors had sent them (the Government) there. Their first and paramount duty was to pass the Bill.'[g] After the closure and the defeat of a Unionist amendment, the bill was read a second time by 368 to 243.

On the same night Balfour of Burleigh introduced into the House of Lords his Reference to the People Bill. This provided that whenever there was a disagreement between the two Houses, the measure in dispute, on the demand of either House, should be submitted to a referendum. Even when both Houses were agreed upon a measure, 200 members of the House of Commons acting together could demand a similar submission. This was a wildly far-reaching proposal which would have made impossible any continuity of Government policy. As Crewe rightly noted, it would have been a greater departure from existing constitutional practice than either the Parliament Bill or a measure abolishing the House of Lords. This did not prevent the straw-clutching Unionists from looking upon it with some favour. Selborne[2] declared that his party greatly preferred a general use of the referendum to 'Single-Chamber tyranny'.

The bill was given a first reading. But when it came up for second reading, three weeks later, the Unionist leadership had returned to the more cautious hands of Lansdowne, who while deploying a number of arguments in favour of the referendum, which, he held, 'had become indispensable', thought that the bill went further than he was prepared to go at the time, and asked Lord Balfour not to press it. After Cromer had given strong

---

[2] 1859–1942. William Waldegrave Palmer. 2nd Earl of Selborne. First Lord of the Admiralty, 1900–5. High Commissioner in South Africa, 1905–10. President of the Board of Agriculture, 1915–16.

support to the measure on the entertaining ground that it would involve each party in one unsuccessful referendum and one unsuccessful general election within eighteen months, purging the Liberals of Home Rule and the Unionists of tariff reform, the request was complied with. The debate was adjourned, and was never resumed.

Meanwhile some progress had been made with the more serious official Unionist proposals. Selborne unfolded a few details in a series of speeches in the middle of March. A combination of the methods of indirect election, selection by the hereditary peers, qualification by office, and nomination by the Government might effect what he called 'a moderate reform'. The two Houses might then attempt to settle differences by informal conferences. If these failed they might sit and vote together. In certain cases a joint committee, presided over by the Speaker and made up in accordance with the relative strength of the parties in the two Houses, could order the submission of bills to a referendum. A number of points remained very vague.

On March 28, Lansdowne announced his intention of moving an Address to the Crown to deal with the difficulty that his Bill would limit the prerogative in so far as it related to the creation of peers and to the issue of writs of summons to existing peers. Royal consent would therefore be necessary in advance.[3] Three days later he moved his motion, quoting a number of precedents for the course. Lord Morley, for the Government,[4] rather

---

[3] This point has again arisen recently (1952) in connection with Lord Simon's bill for the creation of life peerages.

[4] On March 3, Lord Crewe had collapsed and become seriously ill while attending the dinner at Claridge's Hotel which it was then the custom for the Lord President to give annually in connection with the 'pricking' of the

typically added a few precedents which Lord Lansdowne had omitted and announced that His Majesty's Ministers, while retaining their full freedom of action, had no wish to impede discussion of a reform bill and would accede to the motion. Rosebery, very difficult to please, lugubriously observed that he 'had hoped, rather than expected, that the Government would refuse its concurrence', and the matter was then disposed of.

The bill itself did not come up until well after Easter. Lansdowne presented it for first reading on May 8. Its provisions were very close to the plans which had been outlined by Curzon in February and by Selborne in March, although more detail was given. The reconstituted House was to be limited to about 350 members, for no hereditary peer (except for Princes of the Blood) was to be summoned unless he were a 'Lord of Parliament' as defined by the bill. Of these Lords of Parliament, 100 were to be elected by the whole body of hereditary peers from amongst such of their numbers as held or had held certain scheduled offices: ex-Ministers, former Viceroys, Governors, High Commissioners, and Ambassadors and others Heads of Mission were qualified; so were Privy Councillors, members of the Army Council or the Board of Admiralty, captains in the Navy and colonels in the Army, and permanent heads of Government departments. On the territorial side, Lords Lieutenant of counties, chairmen of county councils or sessions and Lord Mayors or Provosts of cities were included.

Sheriffs. Apart from a brief appearance in the Vote of Censure debate in August, he subsequently took no further part in the constitutional struggle. Morley temporarily took his place both as Secretary of State for India and as leader of the House of Lords, assuming a new importance in relation to the Parliament Bill.

Another 120 were to be indirectly elected on a regional basis. The members of Parliament for the region would constitute the electoral colleges. The third main group of Lords of Parliament were to be another 100 appointed by the Government of the day, in strict proportion to the strength of the parties in the House of Commons. In addition there were to be seven Lords Spiritual (the two archbishops and five bishops elected by the Episcopate), together with sixteen peers who had held high judicial office. These law lords would sit for life and the two archbishops would sit so long as they held their sees. The other Lords of Parliament, including the five bishops, were to be elected for periods of twelve years, with a quarter of each category retiring every third year.

The other main provisions of the bill limited the right of creation of new hereditary peerages (except for those conferred upon past or present holders of Cabinet office) to a maximum of five a year, and freed hereditary peers who did not become Lords of Parliament from their ineligibility for membership of the House of Commons.

Perhaps the most interesting comment on the bill was supplied by Lansdowne himself in his speech of introduction. He calculated that under the conditions then existing (i.e. a Government majority of 126 in the Commons) the new House would have a Unionist majority of eighteen, 'which', he added complacently, 'was not too large for purposes of revision and delay'.[i] Furthermore, it should be noted, the initial bias of the new chamber against a Liberal Government would be less than that which might be expected to develop in the future. The Unionist majority of eighteen would be produced despite the fact that the Lords of Parliament nominated by the Government and chosen by the electoral colleges would, to begin with, all reflect the existing balance of parties in the Commons. At subsequent periods of radical Government substantial proportions of the representatives of these two categories would not reflect the then existing balance of parties, but would be a 'hangover' from the balance of parties, probably less favourable to the left, which had existed three or six or nine years before. With a similar Liberal majority in the Commons, a Unionist majority in the reconstituted Upper House of substantially more than eighteen was therefore likely in the future.

Despite the fact that no real sacrifice of power by the Unionist Party was therefore envisaged, the bill was not greeted with acclaim by many of its members. 'These proposals,' Lord Newton has written, 'which really amounted almost to a sentence of death upon the most ancient Legislative Chamber in the world, were received by a crowded and attentive House in a dignified if frigid silence, and the pallid and wasted appearance of the speaker, who had but lately recovered from a severe illness, seemed to accentuate the general gloom,'[j] The *Morning Post* took up an attitude of clear-cut hostility. But neither this lead nor widespread grumbling amongst what were coming to be called the 'backwoods' peers produced any revolt which was both widespread and determined. Lansdowne was able to proceed to a second reading a week later. On this occasion a number of Unionist peers, including the Dukes of Somerset and Marlborough and Lords Bathurst, Willoughby de Broke, Raglan, Saltoun, and Killanin opposed the bill in their speeches, but, except for Bathurst, did not continue their opposition when the question was put; and even he did not persist to the extent of causing a division to be called. Haldane was able fairly to sum up the tone of the debate as 'sombre acquiescence punctuated every now and then by cries of pain'.[k]

The tension had been taken out of the debate by an earlier Government speaker. Morley had declared on the first day that the Parliament Bill would apply to a reformed House of Lords as to the existing one, and that declaration made Lansdowne's manoeuvre purposeless. There was no point in trimming the privileges of the hereditary peers if a less emasculated Second Chamber was not to be the result. When, therefore, the second reading was secured with Government supporters proclaiming their indifference by walking out of the House—it was the end of the road. Nothing further was heard of the bill.

During the spring the Parliament Bill had completed its progress through the Commons. It had been a keenly contested progress, with more than 900 amendments tabled. Seventy of them were in the names of Government backbenchers, and the remainder from the Opposition. After a number of late sittings and a free use of the 'kangaroo closure', the committee stage was disposed of in ten days. The Government made a few minor concessions, accepting amongst others amendments to exclude all private bills from the category of money bills and to postpone the start of the two-year period necessary before a measure could pass over the veto of the Lords from the date of the introduction of the bill to the date of second reading; but the great majority of amendments were resisted and the bill retained substantially its original form. Government majorities were adequate throughout, although Sir Henry Dalziel led 137 dissidents into the lobby in favour of reducing the period of delay from three sessions to two, and the Labour Party voted against the preamble on the ground that abolition or a further curtailment of powers was preferable to reform.

The Unionist amendments mostly followed well-worn lines of argument, although some of them showed a startling willingness to embrace any constitutional novelty which would serve the interests of the party. Sir Frederick Banbury[5] proposed that the Royal Assent should no longer be automatically given upon the advice of the Government, but that the whole Privy Council should be empowered to advise the Crown on such matters; and J. F. Hope[6] wished a special tribunal, composed of judges and former colonial Governors, to be interposed between the King and his Ministers for this purpose. Sir Alfred Cripps[7] proposed that only measures passed by both Houses should be referred to as Acts of Parliament and that those passing under the new procedure should be given some different, inferior title. Arthur Griffith-Boscawen[8] and Lord Hugh Cecil wished the House ot Commons to introduce secret voting on the third reading ot money bills in order to safeguard members against what they regarded as the illicit pressure of the party caucus. It was not very clear whether he regarded this pressure as equally undesirable on both sides, and whether Arthur Balfour felt himself to some extent under fire. In any event, although Balfour had

---

[5] 1850–1936. Member for Peckham, 1892–1906, and for the City of London, 1906–24. Created 1st Lord Banbury, 1924.

[6] 1870–1948. Member for Sheffield, Brightside, 1900–6, and Sheffield, Central, 1908–29. Chairman of Committees and Deputy Speaker, 1921-February, 1924, and December, 1924–29. Created 1st Lord Rankeillour, 1932.

[7] 1852–1941. Charles Alfred Cripps. Created 1st Lord Parmoor, 1914. Conservative member for Stroud, 1895–1900, Stretford division of Lancashire, 1901–6, and Wycombe, 1910–14. Later joined the Labour Party and was Lord President of the Council in 1924 and 1929–31.

[8] 1865–1946. Member for Tonbridge, 1892–1906, Dudley, 1910–21, and Taunton, 1921–23. Minister of Agriculture, 1921–22. Minister of Health, 1922–23.

supported the other innovations, he found this one a little too novel for his taste and left its support in the lobby to an unofficial band of Unionists.

Proceedings on the report stage were governed by a timetable resolution which limited the number of days available to three. The course taken by the debates on these days made it seem unlikely that many undeployed arguments were cut out by the restriction.

Third reading, limited to one day, took place on May 15. F. E. Smith moved the rejection, and Asquith made the early speech for the Government. He replied to the suggestion that a constitutional revolution was being forced through against the will of the people by remarking that 'I am unable to discover a murmur of protest or tittle of remonstrance, though I am made conscious occasionally of a yawn of weariness over the unduly prolonged discussion....'[l] Mr. Churchill wound up for the Government and was in an aggressively radical, post-Tonypandy mood. He pronounced himself 'almost aghast at the Government's moderation. The powers left to the House of Lords,' he thought, 'would be formidable and even menacing.... The Bill made a moderate but definite advance towards political equality. It was territory conquered by the masses from the classes; and when they had placed it on the statute book, without condition or alteration, it would be time to discuss the further steps to be taken.'[m] Fortified by this somewhat truculent benediction, the bill completed its passage through the Commons with a vote of 362 to 241 and passed on to the less friendly atmosphere of the House of Lords.

There it came up for second reading on May 23. Midleton, speaking for the Unionist Front Bench, indicated on the first day that the intention was to allow it through at that stage but to propose sweeping amendments in committee. Thereafter the three-day debate followed a familiar course, with the regular speakers making the regular points. Public attention was elsewhere. In so far as it was directed towards any political issues, it was temporarily upon the National Insurance Bill, which Lloyd George had just launched, and the Trade Union Bill,[9] designed partly to undo the effect of the Osborne judgment. But to an increasing extent the Coronation and associated festivities were thrusting all party political questions into the background. It was a summer of great heat and of fevered and lavish gaiety. And despite the intense personal animosities which the constitutional struggle had provoked, the great social gatherings were still able to bring together the leading contestants in a way that, a year or two later, the bitterness of the Ulster quarrel made impossible. One of the most flamboyant of these gatherings was the fancy dress ball which Lord Winterton and F. E. Smith gave at Claridge's on May 24. Mr. Asquith and Mr. Balfour were both present, but in costumes no more exciting than ordinary evening dress. Mr. Churchill was also disapppointingly conservative, with a red Venetian cloak and a domino his only concessions to the occasion. The Speaker of the House of Commons, however, in full Arab regalia, showed that high political rank was no bar to full participation in the evening. Mr. Waldorf Astor,[10] then a

---

[9] It was in the debate on the second reading of this bill, on May 30, that Mr. Churchill, whose radicalism reached its apogee during this summer, made his famous and much-criticised comment that 'while the courts were eminently fair between man and man, where class issues and party issues were involved they did not command the same degree of confidence'. (*Annual Register,* 1911, p. 132.)

[10] 879–1952. Member for Plymouth, 1910–19. Succeeded his father as 2nd Viscount Astor, 1919.

Unionist Member of Parliament, attracted the most notice by appearing in a peer's robes of state and bearing above his coronet a placard with the figures '499' on one side and the legend 'still one more vacancy' on the other. A political joke was still possible in mixed political company. A few mornings later, however, the levity of this evoked a vigorous letter of protest to *The Times*, appearing under the signature of 'A Peer'.

The Coronation itself took place on June 22. It was a cool and showery day in the midst of a blazing summer, and perhaps for this reason the crowds were not so large as had been anticipated. It was the last great gathering in London of the representatives of monarchical Europe, but this was not to be known either by those who came to watch or by those who stayed away. Indeed, contemporary reports that, as the procession passed, the most cordial welcomes were given to the representatives of Germany, the United States, and France" showed that the shadow of future events was not interfering with the catholicity of the British public.

The only echo of the bitter political struggle came from the stands reserved for members of Parliament and their families and friends. From these the Chancellor of the Exchequer received a somewhat mixed reception as he made his way to the Abbey. But for those who were not more interested in the Clapham Common murder and other sensations of the day the political issues were never far below the surface. As if to act as a reminder of the comparative turbulence of the times a widespread seamen's strike persisted throughout the festivities; and the politicians were all busy calculating the best positions from which they could resume the constitutional battle. The Opposition hoped that the period of national rejoicing might have created a new atmosphere and a new set of circumstances in which they could ignore the verdict of the previous December. Even so neutrally conformist a source as the *Annual Register* commented: 'It may be that the keener Unionist politicians expected the sentiments roused by the Coronation ceremonies to tell in their favour with the electorate.'[9] But their hopes in this respect were doomed to disappointment. Neither the bye-elections which had taken place earlier in the year nor those which followed in July (the combination of the Coronation honours and of a number of unseatings on petition[11] produced quite a spate) showed any trend against the Government. When the battle was rejoined, it was an early conclusion, and not the opening of a new phase upon new ground, which was to follow.

Amendments to the Parliament Bill were placed upon the paper of the House of Lords on June 26, and the committee stage began on June 28. It took the form of a six-day massacre of the Government's proposals and the virtual substitution of the scheme which the Unionist leaders had unsuccessfully urged upon the constitutional conference. A joint committee of both

---

[11] The Nationalist members for Louth, North, and Cork, East, the Unionist members for Hull, Central, and the Liberal members for Cheltenham and West Ham, North, all met this fate. The last of these was C. F. G. Masterman, then Under-Secretary at the Home Office and electorally most unfortunate of politicians. He found another seat at Bethnal Green, lost it when forced to seek re-election by his promotion to the Cabinet three years later, and then proceeded to lose in quick succession two further bye-elections in formerly Liberal seats. After this he ceased to try, and did not re-enter the House of Commons until 1923. In addition to these successful election petitions, there were unsuccessful ones against the Unionist members for West Bromwich, Nottingham, East, and Exeter. At the conclusion of the hearing in the last case the Liberal appellant 'publicly denounced the judges at the railway station'.

Houses and not the Speaker alone was to determine what was and what was not a money bill, and this committee was to be given the instruction of a further amendment which very narrowly defined such bills. Clause Two, dealing with general legislation, was altered so that any measure which *(a)* affected the existence of the Monarchy or the Protestant Succession, *(b)* established a National Parliament or Council in any of the three kingdoms, or *(c)* was considered by the joint committee to raise an issue of great gravity upon which the opinion of the country had not been fully ascertained, fell outside its scope. Such measures were to be submitted to a referendum. This amendment was described by Morley as 'tearing up the bill'.

Despite this and despite the complaint of one Unionist peer, Montagu of Beaulieu, that another amendment was 'contrary to the spirit in which a second reading had been given to the bill', the Opposition suffered from no lack of support in the division lobby. Cromer's amendment to substitute the joint committee for the Speaker was carried by 183 to 44 and Lansdowne's amendment to introduce the referendum by 253 to 40. On the latter occasion no less than twenty-seven of the peers voting in the minority were Campbell-Bannerman or Asquith creations— a different situation from that which had prevailed at the time of the great Reform Bill, when the holders of the older peerages had been somewhat more liberal than the new creations. Indeed Lansdowne's difficulties were with his more extreme and not with his more moderate followers. Lord Willoughby de Broke, a young peer who had come into sudden prominence as an organiser of the die-hards, moved and carried to a division an amendment to make a general election *and* a referendum necessary in the case of all measures which came under Clause Two of the bill. Eighteen peers voted with him, but the Opposition leaders, finding this proposal rather strong meat even for their stomachs, went into the other lobby and helped to produce a majority vote of ninety. This division, it was suggested, showed the lines of the coming Unionist split. This is not entirely true, for although those who voted for the amendment were all for resistance *à outrance*, others who subsequently joined and even led them in this defiance were nearer to Lansdowne's point of view at this stage. Thus Lord Willoughby also expressed grave misgivings about Lansdowne's official 'referendum' amendment, but Lord Salisbury, who was later to add the weight of the whole Cecil faction to the die-hards, spoke strongly in its favour.[12]

But whatever the state of internal Unionist Party relations the salient feature of the committee stage (and the position was in no way retracted at the report stage, which took place on July 13) was that the House of Lords had declined to accept the verdict of the second 1910 general election and had thrown down an unmistakable challenge to the Government. The bill which the House of Commons had passed had been changed out of all recognition.

---

[12] It is recorded, however, that the effect of the noble Marquess's speech on this occasion was 'rather marred by the passing of an aeroplane'. It must either have been a very short speech or a very slow aeroplane.

XII

The Disunion of the Unionists

Confronted with this challenge the Cabinet sent a minute to the King declaring that the 'contingency' referred to in the November negotiations had arisen, and that Ministers would expect the King to act in accordance with the undertaking he had then given. The minute was dated July 14 and was couched in very firm language:

'The Amendments made in the House of Lords to the Parliament Bill are destructive of its principle and purpose,' it ran, 'both in regard to finance and to general legislation. There is hardly one of them which, in its present form, the Government could advise the House of Commons, or the majority of the House of Commons could be persuaded, to accept. The Bill might just as well have been rejected on Second Reading. It follows that if, without any preliminary conference and arrangement, the Lords' Amendments are in due course submitted to the House of Commons, they

211

will be rejected *en bloc* by that House, and a complete conflict between the two Houses will be created. Parliament having been twice dissolved during the last eighteen months, and the future relations between the two Houses having been at both Elections a dominant issue, a third Dissolution is wholly out of the question. Hence, in the contingency contemplated, it will be the duty of Ministers to advise the Crown to exercise its Prerogative so as to get rid of the deadlock and secure the passing of the Bill. In such circumstances Ministers cannot entertain any doubt that the Sovereign would feel it to be his Constitutional duty to accept their advice.'[a]

Asquith's biographers inform us that three days later the King indicated that he would accept this advice. It appears, however, from Sir Harold Nicolson's life of King George V[b] that when, a few days afterwards, the question arose of the exact stage at which the prerogative should be exercised, a slightly different interpretation of this agreement was given by the King on the one hand and his Ministers on the other. The King indicated by means of a letter from Lord Knollys to the Prime Minister that he was unwilling to agree to a creation before the Lords had been given an opportunity to pronounce on the Commons' rejection of their amendments, and that, in any event, he feared that an *en bloc* rejection by the Commons would be likely to provoke the peers to more determined resistance. The difference was resolved by the Cabinet deferring to the King on both issues. It is difficult to believe that when it came to the point, even without the King's remonstrance, Asquith would have forced a creation until the last possible moment.

More important, however, was the question of making known

to the Opposition the Sovereign's general view of his constitutional duty. The Government had observed most carefully the arrangement as to secrecy which had been reached in November. But this arrangement, designed to protect the King, had become an embarrassment to him and made him feel guilty of dissimulation in his dealings with the Unionist leaders. Furthermore, so long as the King's undertaking was not known, an increasing number of peers were liable to commit themselves to positions of resistance from which they could not retreat. Balfour, as his conversation with Lord Esher at the beginning of January made clear, had long envisaged both that the Government would if necessary invoke the prerogative and that the King would accede to such a course. But there is little evidence that he convinced even so close a colleague as Lansdowne that this would be the course of events. Certainly Lansdowne's action between January and the beginning of July gave no indication that he recognised the strength of the Government's hand. Curzon, also, remained defiant for some time because he believed that defiance would triumph. 'Even after the Election (of December 1910),' his biographer has written, 'he had spoken derisively at a private luncheon of Unionist candidates and M.P.'s of any such proceedings (a wholesale creation of peers), and had advised his audience—somewhat incautiously as it turned out—to fight in the last ditch and let them make their peers if they dared.'

Other peers, less close to the hub of affairs than either Lansdowne or Curzon, found it still easier to build upon false premises. 'Early in July,' we are informed by Sir Harold Nicolson, 'Lord Derby,[1] and subsequently Lord Midleton, had

---

[1] 1865–1948. Edward George Villiers Stanley, 17th Earl of Derby. Conservative member for Westinghouse, 1892–1906. Succeeded to

warned the King that a large number of Unionists remained convinced that the Government were bluffing and that the Prime Minister would hesitate, when it came to the moment, to invoke the Royal Prerogative.'[d] Their excuses for such convictions thereafter diminished rapidly, although some Unionists did not change their minds as a result. On July 7, Balfour received private information of what had passed between the King and his Ministers in November.[2] The Shadow Cabinet was immediately summoned to a meeting at his house in Carlton Gardens. The other Unionist leaders were informed of the knowledge which Balfour had acquired, and, in the words of his biographer: 'There for the first time surrender by the House of Lords was discussed as practical politics.' It was not discussed in an atmosphere of general agreement. It was noted at the time, Mrs. Dugdale informs us, that 'there was a distinct division of opinion among those present, but the majority decided that it would be imprudent to resist the menace of the creation of peers'.[e]

A week or so later the Chancellor of the Exchequer, acting as the agent of the Prime Minister, saw Balfour and Lansdowne by arrangement and confirmed the information which they had acquired on July 7. He further informed them, it being still five days before the Cabinet received the King's remonstrance on this point, that the intention was to proceed to a creation before

---

earldom, 1908. Secretary of State for War, 1916–18 and 1922–24. H.M. Ambassador in Paris, 1918–20.

[2] Probably from Lord Knollys; although, in view of the terms of Esher's letter to the King of the same date (*Journal and Letters*, III, pp. 54–6), it is difficult to believe that he did not make the position quite clear at his meeting with Balfour on July 5.

the bill was sent back to the Lords. This was to avoid any risk that the bill might be lost between the two Houses.

This warning was delivered on Tuesday, July 18. Two days later the bill came up for third reading in the Lords. Here the split within the Unionist Party came more into the open. For some time previously a number of Unionist peers, amongst whom Willoughby de Broke was the most active, had been organising together. As early as June II Lord Willoughby was able to write to Lord Halsbury that 'at a Meeting of Peers recently held it was resolved "to adhere to such amendments as may be carried in Committee of the House of Lords on the Parliament Bill which would have the effect of securing to the Second Chamber the powers at present exercised by the House of Lords, notwithstanding the possible creation of Peers, or the dissolution of Parliament"'.[1] On July 6 a further meeting was held at Lord Halsbury's house in Ennismore Gardens, and this was followed by another and more important gathering there on July 12. This last meeting, attended by thirty-one peers,[3] resulted in Halsbury writing to Lansdowne, informing him of the meeting and of the common resolve of those present to act along the lines laid down in Willoughby de Broke's earlier letter. Willoughby was still able to refer to this activity as 'strengthening Lord Lansdowne's hands', but it is difficult to believe that Halsbury, who had attended the Shadow Cabinet held on July 7 and had expressed

---

[3] The Dukes of Somerset, Bedford, Northumberland, and Sutherland, the Marquesses of Salisbury and Abergavenny, the Earls of Lauderdale, Amherst, Portsmouth, Halsbury, Cathcart, Kinnoull, Sondes, Lovelace, Minto, Lindsey, Scarbrough, Selborne, Bathurst, and Londesborough, and Lords Ampthill, Vaux, Ebury, Vivian, Bateman, Abinger, Wynford, Hatherton, Raglan, Lovat, and Willoughby de Broke.

beforehand his intention of asking some pertinent questions of his leaders, did not believe by this stage that there was more of defiance than of support in his behaviour.

After this meeting and the despatch of Halsbury's letter to Lansdowne, Willoughby continued to canvass hard for support. Two days later he had brought the number of signatories to fifty-three, and a day after this to sixty. 'And I shall get I trust quite eighty before the day,' he wrote to Halsbury. Evidence that this trust was not misplaced came as early as July 20, the day of the third reading, when almost exactly this number of Unionist peers assembled at Grosvenor House[4] in the morning and pledged themselves not to surrender. But there was still no open split in the party; Lansdowne himself, in his behaviour on the committee stage, had given no hint of retreat. That evening, however, the fissure became a little more obvious. Halsbury delivered a violent speech and committed himself and his followers to an insistence upon the Lords' amendments at all costs. Lansdowne, on the other hand, cautiously announced that the Opposition would not be prepared to withdraw some of their amendments 'as long as they were free agents'. He was at last beginning to deal with facts and not with fantasies.

Despite this clear difference of emphasis, the bill was let through in its new form without a division, and the fissure was not therefore as deep at this stage as it might have been. Lansdowne had told Newton that he expected a 'revolt',[g] and it had been Halsbury's original intention to provoke one, a course from which he was dissuaded by the reluctance of Salisbury and Selborne to desert their leader so soon.[h] Next morning the

---

[4] The London home of the Duke of Westminster.

dispute was continued at a meeting of the Shadow Cabinet. For this and for a general meeting of Unionist peers which took place at Lansdowne House in the afternoon, Balfour and Lansdowne had fortified themselves with a written statement of the Government's intentions from Asquith. This took the form of identical letters written in the following terms to each of the two Unionist leaders:

10, Downing St.,
July 20, 1911

Dear { Mr. Balfour
Lord Lansdowne,

I think it courteous and right, before any public decisions are announced, to let you know how we regard the political situation.

When the Parliament Bill in the form which it has now assumed returns to the House of Commons, we shall be compelled to ask the House to disagree with the Lords' amendments.

In the circumstances, should the necessity arise, the Government will advise the King to exercise his Prerogative to secure the passing into Law of the Bill in substantially the same form in which it left the House of Commons, and His Majesty has been pleased to signify that he will consider it his duty to accept and act on that advice.

Yours sincerely,
H. H. Asquith[i]

The possibility of such an official communication had been discussed at the meeting between Lloyd George and the Unionist leaders on July 18. It was thought that an announcement of the

217

Government's intentions in this form rather than in the form of a public statement by the Prime Minister in the House of Commons might be less provocative to the peers. This view was further pressed by Lansdowne when Lord Knollys had called upon him on the evening of July 19. Lansdowne's alternative plan that the King himself should write, through his Private Secretary, was rejected as inappropriate, but it was at the suggestion of the Palace that the Prime Minister's letters were despatched.

These letters may have reduced the provocative effect of the statement which Asquith subsequently made in the House of Commons (although, in view of the scene which then took place,[5] this is difficult to believe), but they did nothing to ease the tensions of the Unionist meetings on July 21. The 'rebels' had already held a 10.30 meeting at Grosvenor House before those of their number who were summoned left for Carlton Gardens to attend the 11.30 Shadow Cabinet. Here a vote was taken, and what might previously have been disguised as a normal difference of opinion, natural to the successful functioning of any committee, became a dispute of climacteric importance, with every man forced to declare his position, with old loyalties broken and with new animosities aroused. Mrs. Dugdale, quoting from the diary which was kept at the time by J. S. Sandars, Balfour's secretary, gives the alignment. In favour of resistance were Lords Selborne, Halsbury, and Salisbury, Austen Chamberlain (who, it need hardly be added, spoke for his father as well as himself), F. E. Smith, George Wyndham,[6]

---

[5] *See* pp. 230–2 *infra.*

[6] 1863–1913. Conservative member for Dover, 1889–1913. Private Secretary to A.J. Balfour, 1887–92. Chief Secretary for Ireland, 1900–5.

who greatly felt the rift with Balfour, Edward Carson, and Balcarres,[7] the Chief Whip. On the other side were Balfour and Lansdowne; Curzon, Midleton, Londonderry,[8] Derby, and Ashbourne[9] amongst the peers; and Bonar Law, Walter Long, Alfred Lyttelton, Henry Chaplin,[10] Robert Finlay,[11] and Steel-Maitland[12] in the House of Commons. Akers-Douglas made it clear that he sympathised with the resisters, but voted with the majority out of loyalty to Balfour a strong indication of the

---

[7] 1871–1940. Conservative member for Chorley, 1895–1913. Chief Opposition Whip, 1906–13, when he succeeded his father as 27th Earl of Crawford. Lord Privy Seal, 1916–18, and holder of various other offices, 1918–22.

[8] 1852–1915. 6th Marquess. Unionist member for Down, 1878–84. Lord Lieutenant of Ireland, 1886–89. Postmaster-General, 1900–2. President of the Board of Education and Lord President of the Council (from 1903), 1902–5.

[9] 1837 1913. Edward Gibson. Created 1st Lord Ashbourne, 1885. Conservative member for Dublin University, 1875–85. Attorney-General for Ireland, 1877–80. Lord Chancellor for Ireland, 1885–86, 1886–92 and 1895–1905.

[10] 1841–1923. Created 1st Viscount Chaplin, 1916. Conservative member for Mid-Lincolnshire, 1868–1906, and for Wimbledon, 1907–16. Chancellor of the Duchy of Lancaster, 1885–86. President of the Board of Agriculture, 1889–92, and of the Local Government Board, 1895–1900.

[11] 1842–1929. Created 1st Lord Finlay of Nairn, 1916 (Viscount, 1919). Liberal Unionist member for Inverness Burghs, 1885–92 and 1895–1906, and for Edinburgh and St. Andrew's Universities, 1910–16. Solicitor-General, 1895–1900. Attorney-General, 1900–5. Lord Chancellor, 1916–18.

[12] 1876–1935. Unionist member for Birmingham, East, 1910–18, Birmingham, Erdington, 1918–29, and Tamworth, 1929–35. Minister of Labour, 1924–29. Attended Shadow Cabinet in 1911 as chairman of the Unionist Party Organisation.

depth of feeling which separated the two factions.

Lansdowne then returned to his house to meet the Unionist peers, about 200 of whom attended. He took a note of the proceedings, which his biographer thinks was intended for the information of the King. As a description of a meeting at which his own leadership was put to its greatest test, Lansdowne's memorandum is frighteningly indifferent and detached in tone. His opening speech stressed the impropriety of not allowing the Lords to reconsider the bill after the Commons' deletion of the original amendments of the Upper House, and then came very near to striking a balance between the arguments for resistance and those against. 'Lord Lansdowne allowed it to be seen,' he summarised his concluding passage, 'that in his view the more prudent course might be to allow the Bill to pass....' He did not, however, ask the peers present to arrive at any decision, and advised them, on the contrary, to await the statement which would be made by the Prime Minister on Monday. He then went on to describe how Selborne, 'in a speech of great force and earnestness', had urged resistance; how similar views 'were expressed by Lord Halsbury with great vigour, by the Duke of Bedford, Lord Salisbury, and Lord Willoughby de Broke, and in more cautious terms by the Duke of Norfolk'; how St. Aldwyn, 'in a speech which produced a deep impression', argued that the deliberate judgment of the country would be against a policy of 'dying in the last ditch'; and how Curzon 'spoke with much ability in the same sense'. He summed up by saying: 'Lord Lansdowne is inclined to think that a majority of the peers present were in favour of the view which he expressed, but a large number not only differed but acutely resented the suggestion that they should desist until they were beaten in the House by H.M. Government aided by a reinforcement of Radical peers.... The peers referred to will, in Lord Lansdowne's opinion, certainly not recede from their attitude.'^{j} No vote was taken at the meeting, but other estimates put the number of 'ditchers'[13] present at fifty; the remaining 150, however, were less firmly attached to Lord Lansdowne's point of view than the minority were to Lord Halsbury's.

In part this was because enthusiasm for moderate courses is always difficult to arouse. In part, too, it was because the 'non-die-hard' peers had been given no strong lead. It is difficult to disagree with the comment on the meeting of Lord Newton, who combined sympathy for Lansdowne with an informed but comparatively unprejudiced judgment of the issue.

'The impression left upon me at this meeting,' he wrote, 'was that—for once in a way—Lord Lansdowne showed some slight deficiency in the art of leadership. He had personally made up his mind as to the course which should be followed, however unpalatable it might be to some of his followers, and it seemed, therefore, that he ought to have spoken with greater decision, and to have intimated that he would resign if his advice was not followed. Instead of doing so, he appeared to invite expressions of opinion, and the opportunity was at once seized by Lord Halsbury, Lord Selborne, Lord Salisbury, the Duke of Norfolk, and Lord Willoughby de Broke to raise the standard of revolt...'^{k}

---

[13] Those in favour of resistance became known at this time as 'die-hards' or 'ditchers', both words being derived from the phrase 'dying in the last ditch'. *Per contra,* the moderates became known as 'hedgers', or, as the hysteria of some of their opponents increased *(see,* for example, pp. 266–7, *infra),* by more uncomplimentary names.

For his weakness on this occasion Lansdowne paid a heavy price in the ensuing weeks.

After the meeting both sides, undeterred either by its being ate on a Friday afternoon or by the shade thermometer having reached ninety degrees, set themselves to a rapid work of organisation. On the official side difficulties arose out of the lukewarmness of Lansdowne, who was still disinclined to exert pressure on any peer, and the defection of the two Unionist whips—Lord Waldegrave and Viscount Churchill. These difficulties were swept away by the energy and determinaton of Lord Curzon. As has been seen, he was vigorously in favour of the utmost resistance a few months before. Once convinced that the threat of creation was a real one, he changed his position and advocated his new views with as much enthusiasm as he had shown for his old ones. Almost alone in the Unionist Party he stood out during this period as evidence against the truth of the lines of Yeats:

> 'The best lack all conviction,
> And the worst are full of passionate intensity.'

They could be applied only too appropriately to others upon that stage.

What were Curzon's motives? Some supplied harsh judgments: '… it was all snobbishness on Curzon's part', said George Wyndham. 'He could not bear to see his Order contaminated by the new creation.' But on another occasion Wyndham himself delivered another judgment which, by implication, was far kinder. 'He is a fool,' he said, 'for he might have been the next Prime Minister.'[1] And to accuse a man as ambitious as Curzon of throwing away his chances is almost to compliment him. In fact,

Curzon saw more clearly than most that further resistance could achieve nothing and would do great harm to the House of Lords, the Unionist Party, and the Monarchy; and he had no patience with those who were too stupid or too opinionated to see this. But he also believed, unlike Balfour, that he could make his views triumph over theirs. He had the intellectual arrogance and the conviction of personal rightness without which it is difficult for moderate men to achieve the force to be effective.

The loyalist peers moved from Lansdowne House to a further meeting at Curzon's home in Carlton House Terrace. Here a small committee was set up, which thereafter met daily under Curzon's lead. It was known that the voices of prominent members of the House of Lords, like the Archbishop of Canterbury, Rosebery, St. Aldwyn, Midleton, and Cromer, would be on Lansdowne's side, but the problem was to make contact with the 'backwoodsmen', the men who rarely came to Westminster, but who might be expected for the critical vote. This was approached from two angles. In the first place they were to be given as clear a lead as could be extracted from Balfour and Lansdowne. In addition they were to be canvassed by Curzon and his organisation.

Balfour was the first problem. His views were broadly sound, but they had to be given greater force and greater publicity. To this end, Curzon, Walter Long, and Henry Chaplin believed that a full party meeting might help, and pressed Balfour to summon one. The 'ditchers' were working closely with sympathisers in the House of Commons and it was therefore desirable for the moderates to rally their own supporters in the Lower House. Balfour refused, on the characteristic ground that such gatherings at a period of crisis always did more harm than good. Indeed he went further and restricted his opportunity for public pronouncement by cancelling a meeting which he was due to address in the City of London during the following week. On the Saturday, however, he wrote a paper for circulation to the other members of the Shadow Cabinet. This is so typically a Balfourian production, and sums up with such engaging frankness his views at the time, that it is worth giving in full, even though, at the insistence of one or two of his close colleagues, it never saw the light of contemporary day:

'I am sorry to trouble my colleagues with any further observations on the Constitutional crisis; but I find that some who were present at the meeeting at my house on Friday last have formed a wrong impression of my position.

'Put briefly, that position is as follows. I regard the policy which its advocates call "fighting to the last" as essentially theatrical, though not on that account necessarily wrong. It does nothing, it can do nothing; it is not even intended to do anything except advertise the situation. The object of those who advocate it is to make people realise what (it is assumed) they will not realise otherwise, namely, the fact that we are the victims of a revolution.

'Their policy may be a wise one, but there is nothing heroic about it; and all military metaphors which liken the action of the "fighting" Peers to Leonidas at Thermopylae seem to me purely for Music Hall consumption.

'I grant that the Music Hall attitude of mind is too widespread to be negligible. By all means play up to it, if the performance is not too expensive. If the creation of X peers pleases the multitude, and conveys the impression that the Lords are "game to the end", I raise no objection to it, *provided it does not swamp the House of Lords.* All my criticism yesterday was directed against the policy of so profoundly modifying the constitution of the Second Chamber that it would become, with regard to some important measures, a mere annexe to the present House of Commons.

'From this point of view the creation of fifty or 100 new Peers is a matter of indifference.

'Let me add two further observations. I regard the importance attached to the particular shape in which the House of Lords are to display their impotence in the face of the King's declaration, as a misfortune. The attention of the country should be directed not to these empty manoeuvres, but to the absolute necessity of stemming the revolutionary tide, by making such abuse of Ministerial power impossible in the future.

A.J.B.'[m]

This was dreadful. It was calculated to enflame the die-hards, discourage the moderates, and leave everyone convinced that the leader of the party regarded its crisis of decision as a foolish irrelevancy. So, at least, Lansdowne and Curzon thought. They were also greatly disturbed lest it became known that Balfour contemplated a limited creation with equanimity. This would destroy the whole basis of the Curzon campaign, for the resisters, who were great optimists in their own favour, would never believe that they were risking a full creation. Balfour therefore agreed to suppress the memorandum and the ideas contained in it.

His next excursion was somewhat more helpful to the moderates. On Monday, July 24, Lansdowne wrote to every peer taking the Unionist whip who was not already pledged, to express his own view that submission was the better course and to ask upon what support he could count. 'It is of the utmost importance that I should be made aware of the views of those Peers who usually act with us,' the letter concluded, 'and I should therefore be grateful if your Lordship would, with the least possible delay, let me know whether you are prepared to support me in the course which I feel it my duty to recommend.'[o] To follow this up, Balfour was persuaded, again by Curzon, to write a letter of support on the following day and to publish it. This took the form, to quote Lord Newton, of 'a reply to a perplexed peer who required advice, and I learnt, to my surprise, that I had been selected as the imaginary correspondent'.[o] In it, Balfour committed himself quite firmly to Lansdowne and his course of action. 'I agree with the advice Lord Lansdowne has given to his friends,' he wrote; 'with Lord Lansdowne I stand; with Lord Lansdowne I am ready, if need be, to fall.'[p] But he put forward this unequivocal declaration much more upon the grounds of loyalty and the need to preserve a united party than because it was overwhelmingly the better course. Indeed he repeated, in slightly less provoking a form, some of the arguments of his suppressed memorandum. The impression conveyed was that there was not a great deal to choose between the two alternative courses, but that, Lansdowne having decided in favour of one of them, it was much better to stick to him. Nevertheless, this letter aroused strong objection from Austen Chamberlain, who had assumed all the touchiness of a rebel. But some of his complaints were well founded.

'I have read your letter with pain and more than pain.' he wrote. 'I think we have deserved better treatment at your hands. ... I have discussed this matter with you in council of your colleagues and in conversation. Nothing that you have said on any of these occasions has prepared me for the line you have now taken up or given me a hint of your intention to treat this as a question of confidence in the leadership of either yourself or Lansdowne. On the contrary, you have repeatedly stated that this was a question which must be decided by each individual for himself. The crisis at which we have now arrived has been visible for a year past. We have frequently discussed it. Yet till this morning you had given no lead....' [q]

Balfour replied that no issue of disloyalty to himself arose (it is almost impossible to imagine a letter of political disagreement to which he would not have returned this slightly weary answer), and with a *tu quoque* to the charge, which Chamberlain also made, that he had denounced the 'ditchers' rather than answered their arguments. This interchange of letters is interesting as an indication both of the personal irritation which had developed between the two sides and of the conviction that Balfour had shown no leadership which existed in the mind of even so naturally loyal a man as Austen Chamberlain.

Lansdowne's letter was something, and so was Balfour's, but Curzon did not allow matters to rest there. He published a most cogent statement of his own position in *The Times* on July 24. He kept careful watch of the replies which came in to Lansdowne's letter (more than 200 peers indicated in writing that they would abstain; about fifty replied that they would vote with Halsbury). And he wrote individually to many peers, couching his letters in far more persuasive terms than Lansdowne had felt able to employ.

'Any vote that you can give now,' he argued (ineffectively, as it transpired) to Lord Roberts on July 30, 'can either produce no effect or drive into the Government lobby some self-sacrificing and conscientious Unionist Peer who will go so far as to vote for the Government sooner than see the peers created. That would be a lamentable result and we desire that no one should be placed in so invidious a position.'ᵣ

On the rebel side the campaign was carried on with at least equal determination and, in most cases, much greater enthusiasm. Immediately after the Lansdowne House meeting a committee was formed with Halsbury as chairman and F. E. Smith and Willoughby de Broke as joint secretaries. The offices were deliberately shared between the two Houses, and in the next few weeks the die-hard members in the House of Lords worked far more closely with their sympathisers in the House of Commons than did their opposite numbers in the 'hedgers' camp. Austen Chamberlain, George Wyndham, F. E. Smith, and Lord Hugh Cecil were as violent in their attachment to the cause of the Upper House as was any peer.

Willoughby organised a meeting at Grosvenor House[14] on the Sunday afternoon and wrote to inform Halsbury, who had taken to his bed for the week-end, that they were to be at least sixty strong there, with another forty absent adherents. There was probably a meeting of the committee on the same day too, for on the following day a scene which was both organised and without recent precedent took place in the House of Commons. Asquith was to outline the Government's intentions on the motion to consider the Lord's amendments. He was cheered by

---

[14] This had become the headquarters of the die-hard movement.

crowds in the streets as he drove with his wife in an open motor car from Downing Street, and he was cheered by his own back-benchers as he walked up the floor of the House of Commons. But as soon as he rose to speak he was greeted by a roar of interruption. 'Divide, divide,' was the dominant shout, but interspersed with it were cries of 'Traitor', 'Let Redmond speak', 'American dollars', and 'Who killed the King?' For half an hour the Prime Minister stood at the box, unable to make any full sentence heard to the House, and unable to fill more than a staccato half-column of Hansard. F. E. Smith and Lord Hugh Cecil were manifestly the leaders (Will Crooks, the Labour Member for Woolwich, proclaimed that 'many a man has been certified insane for less than the noble Lord has done this afternoon'), but there were many others who took a full part. In a moment of comparative calm, Sir Edward Carson attempted to move the adjournment of the debate. Balfour sat unruffled in his place throughout these proceedings. He took no part in the scene, but he did not make any attempt to restrain his followers.

At last Asquith gave up. With a remark about 'declining to degrade himself further', he sat down. Balfour followed and was heard in silence throughout his speech. He had begun with a very mild implied rebuke to those who had perpetrated the scene, but made no further reference to it. Then Sir Edward Grey rose. He had been subjected to a perhaps understandably hysterical note passed down from the Ladies' Gallery by Mrs. Asquith, but it is not clear whether or not this was the decisive cause of his intervention. 'They will listen to you,' the note had run, 'so for God's sake defend him from the cats and the cads!' This Grey made some attempt to do, and his performance satisfied Mrs. Asquith at least.

'Arthur Balfour followed,' she wrote in her diary, 'and when Grey rose to speak the silence was formidable. Always the most distinguished figure in the House, he stood for a moment white and silent, and looked at the enemy: "If arguments are not to be listened to from the Prime Minister there is not one of us who will attempt to take his place," he said, and sat down in an echo of cheers. … I met Edward Grey for a moment afterwards alone, and, when I pressed my lips to his hands, his eyes filled with tears.'[s]

In Hansard,[t] however, the firm and clear-cut statement which Mr. Asquith recorded was lost in a column of repetitive, diffuse and inconclusive sentences. The speaker appeared to know neither what to say nor when to sit down. Perhaps in the actual performance Grey's widely acclaimed gifts of character shone through and gave dignity to his intervention.

When Grey had finished F. E. Smith rose and attempted to carry on the debate. Not unreasonably, the Government back-benchers who had listened in silence to Balfour decided that this was too much. Uproar again developed, and after five minutes the Speaker suspended the sitting on the ground that a state of 'grave disorder' had arisen. Standing Order 21, under which he did this, had not previously been invoked since 1893, and a prec-edent for the refusal of a hearing to a Prime Minister could not be found without a much longer research.

The incident aroused great resentment, and not only amongst normal supporters of the Government. Even Lord Halsbury, we are informed by his biographer, took exception to the scene, 'for it was as alien from his principles as it was temporarily damag-ing to his cause'.[u] *The Times, Daily Telegraph,* and some leading Unionist papers in the provinces delivered stern rebukes to the ringleaders,[15] and a number of Opposition members of Parliament, led by Sir Alfred Cripps and Colonel Lockwood,[16] sent a letter of apology to the Prime Minister. But the bitterness could not easily be undone, especially as those who had provoked the incident were in no way repentant. 'The ugliest feature,' Mr. Churchill had accurately reported to the King, 'was the absence of any real passion or spontaneous feeling. It was a squalid, frigid, organised attempt to insult the Prime Minister.'

Nevertheless, the die-hard movement as a whole was animated by a good deal of passion and some hysteria. The following extract from the diary of Wilfrid Scawen Blunt[17] for July 25 gives a fascinating picture of the atmosphere of Boy Scout enthusiasm and breathless extremism in which much of the planning of the 'ditchers' was carried on:

'In the evening just before dinner, I looked in at 44 Belgrave Square and found George Wyndham there with F. E. Smith and Bendor;[18] all three much excited. "Here you see the conspirators," said George. For some time past George has

---

[15] The general alignment of the Unionist press at the time was that *The Times, Daily Telegraph, Scotsman, Yorkshire Post,* and *Birmingham Daily Post* (showing surprising independence of the Chamberlain influence) favoured submission, while the *Observer, Morning Post, Standard, Globe, Pall Mall Gazette,* and *Manchester Courier* called for resistance. The subsequent casualty rate has been noticeably higher amongst die-hard papers.

[16] 1847–1928. Member for Epping, 1892–1917. Created 1st Lord Lambourne, 1917.

[17] 1840–1922. Conservative candidate for Camberwell, 1885. Liberal candidate for Kidderminster, 1886. Poet, landowner, traveller, and breeder of Arab horses.

[18] The Duke of Westminster, George Wyndham's stepson.

been organising a revolt against Lansdowne and Arthur Balfour's management of the Tory Party in the matter of the Veto Bill, and yesterday they brought matters to a head by making a violent scene in the House of Commons and refusing to let Asquith speak. Hugh Cecil and F. E. Smith are the leaders of the revolt with George, Bendor has turned Grosvenor House into an office, where they hold their meetings, and they are to give a banquet to old Halsbury tomorrow as the saviour of the Constitution. They are all in the highest possible spirits at the commotion they have caused and consider they have forced Balfour's hand.... The two others did not stay many minutes, and when they were gone George talked it over with me, promising an absolutely full account of it when the crisis should be over, but he had given his word of honour not to reveal certain things at present. Nevertheless, I gather from him that they suspect Arthur Balfour of having been all through in secret collusion with Asquith, and that perhaps now Arthur is in secret collusion against Asquith with them. It appears that just before the last election in January *(sic)* Asquith got the King to promise to create a sufficient number of peers to pass the Veto Bill, which the King promised, thinking the electors would go more against Asquith than they did. The King does not at all want to create the peers, neither does Asquith, though the King is in favour of Home Rule for Ireland. They hope the peers will give in without that necessity, and have been looking all along for a compromise, but the extremists on both sides will have none of it, and now George says the country is in revolt, meaning the Tories in the constituencies. "If we had given in without a fight there would have been an end of the Tory Party." George thinks they have saved that at least. They are ready for actual armed resistance, or rather, they would like that. They have chosen old Halsbury for their nominal leader because of his great age (eighty-eight),[19] otherwise there would have been jealousies. All the best men of their party are with them, including Austen Chamberlain, whom they did not expect. The only one who has disappointed them has been George Curzon…. George (Wyndham) thinks war with Germany quite possible,' the entry rather inconsequently concluded, 'and he wants it.'[w]

This willingness to put the issue to the test of violence did not find expression only in the private conversations of such an emotionally unstable character as George Wyndham. It also appeared in a letter which Willoughby de Broke wrote to Halsbury on July 28. 'Anyhow,' he concluded a passage suggesting that the right to sit of the 'puppet peers' should be challenged, 'I put it to you that even if Lord Lansdowne opposes it, we shall at least have accepted Midleton's challenge, and put ourselves right in the sense that we have used every weapon save personal violence. I should not be adverse to using even that!'[x] Willoughby's opinion on this point gained sufficient currency for Lansdowne in his final crisis speech on the House of Lords to feel it necessary to raise the matter and deliver a rebuke. 'My noble friend will think me a very pusillanimous person,' he said, 'but I confess that I prefer Parliamentary methods.'[y] It was a beginning to that Tory taste for violent resistance to disliked measures which was later to spread much wider in the party.

---

[19] In fact he was eighty-seven.

More immediately the 'ditchers' were concerned with counteracting the effects of Curzon's canvassing and displaying their own strength. On the Tuesday a circular letter was sent out under the signatures of Halsbury, Selborne, Salisbury, Mayo, Lovat, and Willoughby de Broke. Perhaps because of the greater difficulty of drafting by a committee, perhaps because of a simple difference of intellectual power,[20] it was far less lucid than was Lansdowne's appeal to the uncommitted peers, Balfour's letter to Newton, or Curzon's to *The Times*, to all of which it was intended as a reply. 'Should a General Election take place,' it argued with a never wearying determination to demand another chance, 'the Electors would for the first time have the opportunity of deciding between the alternative policies of reconstitution and revolution, and of expressing an opinion of the attempt to rob them of their constitutional right to give the final decision on grave national issues'. The crux of the advice given was as follows: 'We do not believe that the credit of the Peerage can be as much injured by the number of new Peers which may be created, as it would be degraded by our failure to be faithful to our trust.'[z]

The display of strength took the form of the Halsbury Banquet, which was referred to in the extract from Blunt's diary. This was organised with great speed. The idea appears to have originated during the week-end. On Monday the following notice was sent out:

---

[20] Halsbury must be the only Lord Chancellor to have been placed in the Fourth Class at Oxford (after quite hard work), and none of his fellow signatories, from Salisbury (who was one of the less distinguished heads of his family) to the fox-hunting Willoughby, had much mental prowess.

Carlton Club, Pall Mall, S.W.

July 24, 1911

HALSBURY BANQUET

Dear Sir,

Viscount Wolmer, M.P., and Mr. Harold Smith, M.P., will be at the House of Commons tomorrow, Tuesday, with tickets for the Halsbury Banquet on Wednesday. Tickets can also be obtained by application to Mr. F. E. Smith at Grosvenor House by telegram or letter.

Austen Chamberlain

Edward Carson

F. E. Smith

George Wyndham [aa]

During the Tuesday applications for tickets poured in, and on the Wednesday evening 600 guests sat down to dinner at the Hotel Cecil.[21] Selborne presided, and the other speakers were Halsbury himself, Wyndham, Milner, Salisbury, Austen Chamberlain, Carson, and F. E. Smith. A letter from Joseph Chamberlain was read. It was an occasion for unrestrained demagogy, and little of interest emerges from most of the speeches. Austen Chamberlain's was to some extent an excep-

---

[21] According to W. S. Blunt, however, only forty peers were present, and to some extent the dinner was therefore a discouragement to those who were organising the die-hards. (*My Diaries,* p. 772.)

tion.[22] He was, by virtue of his position in the Unionist hierarchy, the most responsible politician present, and he gave it as his considered opinion that the Government threats were still not to be taken seriously.

'They have been playing and they are playing a game of gigantic bluff,' he said. 'They do not wish to create peers. Those peers will be an embarrassment to them in their creation and when they are created, and they have sought to believe themselves, and have induced others to believe, that no peers would need to be created. Even now the bluff continues, and in spite of the letter of the Prime Minister which tells us what the King's undertaking is, it is sought to intimidate us by the idea that the pledges go far beyond any Mr. Asquith has pretended to have asked, still less to have received, and that the House of Lords will be swamped by these new creations because one hundred or two hundred peers are found to follow Lord Halsbury's lead. I say that is bluff, and fraudulent bluff.'[bb]

Nothing would make the 'ditchers' look squarely in the face the consequences of their own actions. They persisted in believing that the only danger was that of a creation which would balance the number by which their own adherents exceeded

---

[22] In that it contained something of interest, not that it was lacking in demagogy. He spoke of a 'revolution, nurtured in lies, promoted by fraud, and only to be achieved by violence'. 'The Prime Minister and his colleagues,' he added, 'have tricked the Opposition … entrapped the Crown, and … deceived the people.'

those of the Government,[23] and that—a curious logical position for such a self-righteous band—they could count upon enough Unionists abstaining with Lansdowne to make this number tolerably small.

At the end of the evening the enthusiasm for Halsbury and the cause he had come to represent was such that the banqueters wished to draw him in triumph from the Strand to his house in Kensington. The plan was abandoned only because his family feared the effect of the excitement upon his health. The fact that it was ever put forward shows how uphill must have been Lord Lansdowne's struggle for the cause of dull reason.

Thereafter the revolt against the official leadership became still less restrained. Any suggestion that their movement was directed against Balfour and Lansdowne or was designed to deprive them of their positions was scouted by the rebels; but such denials are common form with political dissidents, and did not prevent the 'ditchers' from assuming most of the features of what would today be called a party within a party. 'We have our meetings now not at Lansdowne House,' Halsbury wrote to his

---

[23] Some of the responsibility for this widespread impression seems to rest with the King. When he saw Lansdowne on July 24, he said that both himself and his Ministers were anxious to avoid a large creation. He added that the Prime Minister would be satisfied with a majority of one for the bill, which was a slightly ambiguous remark in the context. (See Newton, op. cit., p. 425.) Furthermore, Austen Chamberlain's letter to Balfour of July 26 refers to the King having informed Salisbury that his promise extended only to the smallest creation necessary to pass the Bill, and to his determination not to allow a wider use of the prerogative. Chamberlain took this as firm evidence against the risk of a large creation, and argued accordingly to Balfour (see Petrie, op. cit., vol. I, p. 284.) Later, however, His Majesty took positive steps to counteract this impression (infra, p. 259).

237

daughter at the beginning of August, 'but at Lord Leith's[24] and the Duke of Westminster's, and we have our Whips. I enclose a specimen.'[cc] Nor was the importance of a separate propaganda appeal neglected. Special public meetings were organised at the Chelsea and St. Pancras Town Halls and at some places in the provinces; Halsbury and others attended and made appropriately defiant speeches. It was a deep and bitter schism, with both sides publicly proclaiming their respect for the motives and characters of the leaders of the other group, but with great hostility and unpleasantness present behind the scenes.

What were the lines along which the Unionists split so sharply? Almost all the obvious and attractive generalisations fail to give an answer. With a substantial part of the die-hard leadership provided by the Cecils, and with men like Bonar Law and Alfred Lyttelton firmly faithful to Lansdowne, it was hardly a case of the protectionists demanding resistance and those who were luke-warm on this issue urging submission; in any event the tariff question was much less in the forefront of politics than it had been in the immediately preceding years. Nor did the split occur clearly along any of the lines dividing the different economic interests which made up the Unionist party. With seven or eight dukes the 'ditchers' were rich in magnates, but they did not sweep the board in this category—how could they with Lansdowne leading the 'moderates'?—as the anti-Home-Rulers had done in 1886. The country gentlemen were even less decisively on the side of resistance. Wyndham, as we have seen, was a violent 'ditcher', but he was far less typical than was Walter

---

[24] 1847–1925. Alexander John Forbes-Leith. Scottish landowner, created 1st Lord Leith of Fyvie, 1905.

Long, who combined a general tendency to complain about his leaders with, on this occasion, an almost aggressive loyalty to their policies. Furthermore, the Chamberlains with their Birmingham business background (largely honorary in Austen's case) might be on one side, but Bonar Law with the Glasgow business background was on the other.

Little help is given by considering the issue—Home Rule—which had dominated so much of the constitutional struggle. The fear that the Parliament Bill would make this a certainty may have made Sir Edward Carson a die-hard, but if so, why did it leave Lansdowne, whose political life had been largely shaped by his narrow and obstinate views on Ireland, or the Ulster landowner Londonderry, on the other side?

Was the split not perhaps a simple division between the clever and the stupid, with those who could think ahead leading the 'hedgers' and those whose mental processes were closer to those of bulls charging gates on the other side? This would be an entertaining theory and one containing a grain of truth, but not much more. On the die-hard there was no one, except perhaps for Milner, who did not understand English politics, of the mental calibre of Balfour, Curzon, or Lansdowne. The talent of the 'ditchers' was largely forensic, and clever, successful lawyers, as there are many examples to show, can be sparingly endowed with general intellectual equipment. But Carson and F. E. Smith, at least, were not fools, and Smith possessed a very cool head. Too much cannot therefore be explained away in this manner.

What then was the quality, the distinguishing quality, common to all the 'ditchers'? It was that they were tired of the existing leadership of their party. Some of them had specific policy grievances, like Austen Chamberlain, who had spent the early part of the year suffering from 'referendum sickness'. Others, like F. E. Smith, were made more hostile by cool personal treatment.[25] Others, again, like George Wyndham, combined great personal affection for Balfour with mounting impatience at the loss of three successive general elections to the wretched radicals. It was inconceivable that rightminded Englishmen could award three successive victories to such a band of sophists and disrupters. It must be the Unionists' own fault; the leadership must be to blame.

And everyone, whether or not they had particular grievances, and in whatever direction they wished to be led, felt the need for a firmer hand on the reins. It was not so much that Balfour was pusillanimous as that he was indifferent. It was not so much that Lansdowne was wrong as that he could not make up his own mind what was right until it was too late to influence the minds of many others. The crisis was therefore in the fullest sense of the phrase a crisis of leadership. The revolt grew out of the

---

[25] The political honours in the Coronation List, as is the custom, stretched beyond party, and Asquith proposed that Smith should be elevated to the Privy Council. Balfour protested, ostensibly on the ground that he regarded Coronation honours as a reward for past services, and wished the decoration to go to Hayes Fisher. He informed Smith of his views, in a flattering letter which was obviously intended to suggest that the latter should decline Asquith's offer. To this invitation Smith firmly declined to respond, and in due course the honour was bestowed. The question then arose as to whether the recipient should sit on the Front Opposition Bench. Balfour refrained from offering a direct invitation. 'By the way,' he wrote, 'are you proposing to sit on our bench?' And Smith stayed where he was. Later, when Bonar Law assumed the leadership, a pressing invitation was extended and Smith quickly responded. (*See* Birkenhead, *op. cit.*, vol. I, pp. 213–16.)

successive defeats to which the party had been led, it was fed upon indecision at the top in the spring and early summer, and its real purpose, however much its perpetrators might protest, was to put new men at the head of the Unionist Party. Balfour himself fully appreciated how much his conduct was directly under fire, and in the end ceased to be indifferent to this aspect of the matter at least.

'Politics have been to me quite unusually odious,' he was to write from Paris to Lady Elcho on August 10. 'I am not going into the subject, but I have, as a matter of fact, felt the situation more acutely than any in my public life —I mean from the personal point of view. As you know I am very easy-going, and not given to brooding over my wrongs. But last Friday and Saturday I could think of nothing else: a thing which has not happened to me since I was unjustly "complained of" at Eton more than forty years ago! On Saturday the cloud lifted; yet it *has* not, and perhaps *will* not disappear until recent events are things barely remembered....'[dd]

It was a deep and unpleasant quarrel which could so ruffle Arthur Balfour.

XIII

The Issue Resolved

Confronted with this gaping split in their party, the Unionists' leaders did what politicians in trouble have often done. They tried to bring together their own followers by launching a strong attack upon the other side. They tabled votes of censure in the two Houses. Both were in substantially the same terms, the exact form of that in the Commons being: 'That the advice given to His Majesty by His Majesty's Ministers whereby they obtained from His Majesty a pledge that a sufficient number of peers would be created to pass the Parliament Bill in the shape in which it left this House is a gross violation of Constitutional liberty, whereby, among many other evil consequences, the people will be precluded from again pronouncing upon the policy of Home Rule.'

This motion was moved by Balfour on August 7. It was a delicate subject, but it did not call forth one of his most effective speeches. This may have been partly because the Unionists were uncertain of the gravamen of their charge against the Government. Was it that it was in itself wrong to advise the use of the prerogative to force through a keenly disputed measure, more especially as the points at immediate issue had arisen since the last general election? This was an argument which Balfour and his supporters (as well as Curzon and the others who spoke in the Lords on the following day) used strongly. But they also relied to a great extent upon the view that Asquith's greatest sin was that he demanded and obtained a hypothetical undertaking from the King, so that the Crown was committed before the Bill had even received a second reading in the Commons, and long before the final form of the dispute could be envisaged. This has since developed into a criticism that it was wrong for Asquith to seek any advance understanding because he should not have doubted that the King would accept the advice of his Ministers when the moment came. This, says Lord Halsbury's biographer, was the real infamy of the Government.[a] But it is a view which is manifestly incompatible with the first line of attack. Asquith could hardly be expected to be certain that the King would behave in a way which almost the whole Unionist Party professed to believe was unconstitutional. Some of Balfour's unease therefore came from the attempt to ride two rather ill-matched horses.

In part, too, it arose from the difficulty of developing the attack without criticising the conduct of the King. Unlike Lord Hugh Cecil, who on the following day made no attempt to disguise his disapproval of the Sovereign's behaviour, Balfour avoided this pitfall, but only at the expense of some remarks about King George which, while sympathetic, were by implication far from complimentary. Advantage, he said, had been taken of 'a sovereign who had only just come to the throne, and who, from the very nature of the case, had not and could not have behind him that long personal experience of public affairs which some of his great predecessors had'. Of a man of forty-six, who had been Heir Apparent for a decade before his accession, these were slighting words to use; they were also nonsensical, for there is a strong likelihood that King Edward VII would have acted exactly as did King George V, and a probability that Queen Victoria would have done so too.

Asquith made a more notable reply, which included an impressive passage on his relations with the King:

'I am accustomed, as Lord Grey in his day was accustomed, to be accused of breach of the Constitution and even of treachery to the Crown. I confess, as I have said before, that I am not in the least sensitive to this cheap and ill-informed vituperation. It has been my privilege, almost now I think unique, to serve in close and confidential relations three successive British Sovereigns. My conscience tells me that in that capacity, many and great as have been my failures and shortcomings, I have consistently striven to uphold the dignity and just privileges of the Crown. But I hold my office, not only by favour of the Crown, but by the confidence of the people, and I should be guilty indeed of treason if in this supreme moment of a great struggle I were to betray their trust.'[b]

The King, however, was more sensitive to 'cheap and ill-informed vituperation' than was his Prime Minister. He spoke to Lord Morley on the subject on the morning of August 8 and pronounced himself much concerned at the criticism to which he had been subjected in the Commons. He was also worried, he further told Lord Morley, at the language which was probably used in private at the Carlton Club about his actions, at the large number of unfriendly anonymous letters which he was receiving, and at the charge of having betrayed the Irish 'loyalists'. On the first point Morley returned a sharp answer. It was better, he said, to run the risk of criticism in the Carlton Club than 'to be denounced from every platform as the enemy of the people'.[c]

But the King's anxieties were not to be easily dismissed. He had just been reading the previous day's censure debate in the Commons (the Council after which he spoke to Morley had been held up from 11.0 to 11.30 in order that he might complete this task) and he did not feel that Asquith had gone quite far enough in exonerating the Crown from responsibility. As a result of this complaint, according to Sir Almeric Fitzroy, it was arranged at the last moment that Crewe, who had not attended the House of Lords for several months, should intervene in the censure debate there that afternoon and go a little further than Asquith had done. His qualification to speak was that he had participated in the November conversations. Speaking under great strain and with painful slowness[1] he described the King's attitude in November in the following terms: 'His Majesty faced the contingency and entertained the suggestion (of a creation) as a possible one with natural, and if I may be permitted to use the phrase, in my opinion with legitimate reluctance.'[d]

This phrase, while awakening a wave of undesirable speculation amongst Unionists who wished still to believe that the Government was bluffing, did not satisfy the King. His Majesty

---

[1] As soon as his speech was concluded he returned to Crewe House and took no part in the division at the end of the debate; but he was present again for the decisive vote two nights later.

wished even further stress to be laid upon the reluctance with which he had agreed, and he expressed this wish in a letter which Knollys wrote to Asquith's secretary, Vaughan Nash, on August 9. But the Prime Minister was resolved to go no further. Indeed a note of asperity enters his biographers' description of his reactions to the King's request. He thought that his own statement: 'The King was pleased to inform me that he felt that he had no alternative but to accept the advice of the Cabinet,' was both accurate and adequate. 'To be led into public discussions about the feelings and motives of the King or his views about the policy of the Government, would, in Asquith's opinion, be even less in the interests of the King than of the Government.... Nothing would ever have induced him to use any language which could have been construed as an admission that he had "coerced the King".'*e*

On other points Asquith had shown a great respect for the views of the King. By August 4 it had become known to the Opposition that there was to be no creation of peers before the Lords had again had an opportunity of pronouncing on the bill, and this substantial retreat from the position Ministers had taken up at the time of Lloyd George's interview with the Unionist leaders on July 18 was motivated principally by the King's wish. There was little enough other reason for it. If the Lords proved recalcitrant, it meant the loss of the bill to the Government and the need to begin again in the next session. If they proved submissive, it meant that the Government would get its bill but that it would still have to wait more than two years for Home Rule and Welsh Disestablishment, whereas a creation of peers would have made both these measures possible within a year. If the character of most of the leading members of the Cabinet constituted a strong *a priori* refutation of the Unionist view that the Government was bent on revolution, their extreme reluctance to take the step, advantageous from their own point of view, of swamping the House of Lords constituted powerful empirical disproof of that interpretation. It was not that the Cabinet were not ready for creation should the necessity be forced upon them, or that they could not find a large body of men who would serve their purposes while far from disgracing the House of Lords. Amongst Asquith's papers was discovered a list of 249 gentlemen whom he proposed to approach, as prospective Liberal peers, should the necessity be forced upon him. It cannot be assumed that all of those included would have accepted the offer, but the existence of the list is an indication of the advanced stage of the Government's preparations, and the nature of it shows that no lowering of the intellectual calibre of the House of Lords, and little enough of its social composition, would have been involved. Twenty of those listed were the sons of peers, forty-eight of them were baronets, and fifty-nine knights. Twenty-three were Privy Councillors and nineteen members of Parliament. Many of them were later to be elevated to the peerage in the ordinary course of events. Amongst figures of note whose names were listed may be mentioned Thomas Hardy, James Barrie, Bertrand Russell, and Gilbert Murray. Sir Thomas Lipton and Sir Abe Bailey come perhaps in a somewhat different category, while General Baden-Powell, General Sir Ian Hamilton, and the Lord Mayor of London of the day were unexpected inclusions.

The Prime Minister, even if unprepared for a creation of the size envisaged in Mr. Churchill's somewhat oracular pronouncement at the end of the censure debate,[2] was obviously in earnest

---

[2] 'Why should we shrink from the creation of 400 or 500 Peers?' the Home Secretary had asked in a much-to-be quoted sentence.

about, and ready for, a very substantial creation. But he was sufficiently loath to act that he made no attempt to override the King's desire to give the Lords another chance, even though there was no firm evidence to suggest that this would not mean the loss of the bill. Curzon's efforts had increased to 320 the number of those who were prepared to abstain with Lansdowne, and a list containing these names was published at the end of the first week in August. Morley had also been active on behalf of the Government. He sent out an interrogative whip to all the nominally Liberal peers, and received firm promises of support from eighty, which was a better result than had been expected. But it was not in itself good enough. The die-hards were not at this stage divulging their strength, and Lansdowne declined to place his information at the disposal of the Government in order to help them determine what this strength might be. Halsbury would obviously not muster all the peers not listed by either Lansdowne or Morley—had he done so he would have got more than 200—but he was known to be increasing his strength from day to day. 'Backwoodsmen' were often difficult to communicate with, but they were likely, if present, to support Halsbury; and the fact that numbers of peers who had not previously bothered to do so were engaged each day in taking the oath indicated a large attendance of the little known. On July 31, Morley, having gone carefully through the list of peers, came to the conclusion that a creation could not possibly be avoided without Unionist votes for the Government, and that at least forty of these would be necessary. By August 3, however, when the answers to his whip had come in, he was more hopeful and thought that the Government might scrape by under its own steam. On the following day Selborne wrote to Halsbury giving a slightly different version of the Government estimate, which he had obtained by a very circuitous route. 'So the Government are going to risk it on Wednesday without any creation of Peers,' he wrote. 'Lovat tells me that Newton told him that he knew as a fact that the Government are relying on the Bishops for their majority! Can you take any measure to put a spoke in that wheel?' he added.⸍

Fortunately Curzon was also taking measures to put a spoke in the wheels of Lords Halsbury and Selborne. He realised at least as clearly as did Morley the dangers of the position at the end of July and he set in train a series of private enquiries as to how many Unionists might be prepared to vote for the Government. This action, taken against the wish of Lansdowne, produced an encouraging result. Curzon himself, as a member of the Unionist Shadow Cabinet, did not feel entitled to go beyond the official party attitude, and St. Aldwyn, who is given by Newton as one of the most prominent of those who were willing to vote, either never took up or did not maintain this position; but about forty others indicated that they would go into the lobby against Halsbury. Notable amongst these were Cromer (who was in fact prevented from voting by illness), Minto, Camperdown, Desart, and Fortescue. Despite close personal relations between Curzon and Morley, there is no evidence that this information was passed to the Government.

The plan for an immediate creation had been abandoned, and the Cabinet had decided to defer to the King's suggestion and not reject the Lords' amendments *en bloc;* without immediate creation the Cabinet itself was no doubt attracted to this suggestion on its own merits, for the goodwill of the moderate Unionists became of paramount importance. Consequently the amendments had to be dealt with *seriatim.* This was done on August 8, the day of the censure debate in the Lords. Mr. Churchill was in charge, for Asquith had lost his voice, but the attitude of the Government was quite conciliatory. The amendment excluding from the scope of the bill any measure which would extend beyond five years the duration of a Parliament was accepted, and a concession was also offered on Cromer's amendment to Clause One. The Speaker, in determining what was a money bill, should take into consultation the Chairman of Ways and Means and the Chairman of the Public Accounts Committee, the latter being by firm tradition a member of the Opposition. The exact form of this concession did not commend itself to the House, however, and after debate a change which substituted two members of the Chairman's Panel, nominated by the Committee of Selection, was put forward by J. F. Hope and accepted by the Government. The motion for disagreeing with the Lords' other amendments was carried by a majority of 106.

The most notable feature of the day's debate was a speech of startling violence and bitterness delivered by Lord Hugh Cecil. He announced that he would be glad to see Asquith punished for high treason by the criminal law, and declared that, if peers were to be created, the more completely the constitution were broken, the better it would be for the Unionist Party. 'The Home Rule issue,' he continued ... 'would be decided in Belfast. There might be secession and a separate body might be organised to collect taxes. These might be regarded as empty threats: so had disorder in the House. He looked back on it with satisfaction; it showed that the Government could not silence the Opposition.'[g]

On the following day, Wednesday, August 9, the Lords, meeting specially for this purpose at ten o'clock in the morning, received the Commons' amendments. Having ordered them to be printed the House then adjourned until half past four in the afternoon. There was then to begin a two-day debate which was the final encounter of the long played-out constitutional struggle. Unlike most of the other phases of the struggle it assumed something of the air of drama. The debate itself was almost unique amongst major parliamentary occasions of the past eighty years in that the result was not known beforehand. There had been no last-minute developments to turn the tide decisively one way or the other. Lord Morley had been able to muster only sixty-eight Liberals to oppose Curzon's motion of censure, and this might have slightly encouraged the die-hards. But then it was thought that he was reserving his major whipping effort for two nights later. Lord Salisbury, on the other hand, had secured 120 guests for the supper party at Arlington House which he gave to 'ditcher' peers after the division on the Tuesday. But this was not widely known; and, in any event, these signs of Liberal weakness and of die-hard strength were just as likely to swell the number of Unionists preparing to vote in the Government lobby as to produce any other result. The debate therefore opened in a penumbra of doubt. All that was certain was that, for once in a way, speeches would count, and that every vote was important.

Those most vitally affected awaited the result according to their various habits of behaviour. Balfour incurred more criticism by retiring to Paris, on his way to Bad Gastein. He occupied the final day of the crisis, as we have seen, by writing letters of complaint to Lady Elcho from the Ritz. He could bear London no longer. From the suspense he was more immune than most men; it was the bickering which he found tiring. Asquith was also away, although not out of the country. He travelled down to Wallingford on the Wednesday to stay with friends and recover from his laryngitis. From there, on the Thursday, he wrote a laconically matter-of-fact note to his secretary. 'If the vote goes wrong in the H. of L.,' it ran, 'the Cabinet should be summoned for 11.30 Downing Street tomorrow morning and the King asked to postpone his journey till the afternoon. ... If I have satisfactory news this evening I shall come up for Cabinet 12.30. My voice is on the mend but still croaky.'[h] But the King, more agitated by the prospect of the result than either of the two party leaders, and much less at ease with himself than Asquith at least, was too involved to wish to leave London, despite the date and despite the temperature.

This last factor provided another element of drama. It was the hottest weather for seventy years. The whole summer had been torrid, and the previous week exceptionally so. On August 9 the shade temperature over most of England rose to 95°. At South Kensington it was 97° at Greenwich Observatory it was 100°— the highest ever recorded in Great Britain. Roads melted. Railway lines were distended. That evening a serious fire developed at the top of the Carlton Hotel in Pall Mall. In these circumstances the unfettered House of Lords began its final debate.

Morley rose to move that the Commons' reasons for disagreeing to several of the Lords' amendments be now considered. He indicated that he would have preferred to take the amendments *seriatim*, but that in deference to the views of the Opposition he was now moving a motion which would provide for a general debate. There was an understanding that the detailed examination of the Commons' reasons would begin at about dinner time on the following evening.

Morley deployed no arguments and within five minutes he had resumed his seat. Thereafter there was no Government speaker for the whole of the day. From the Liberal backbenches Earl Russell and Lord Ribblesdale[3] were heard, and from the

---

[3] 1854–1925. 4th Lord. Married to Mrs. Asquith's sister.

episcopal bench the Archbishop of York and the Bishop of Winchester. For the rest it was a day of battle between the two sections of the Unionist Party. Lansdowne began it. He dismissed the concessions made by the Commons as of trivial importance and threw in occasional words of strong condemnation of the Government, but almost the whole of his argument, very cogently expressed, was directed against his own dissidents. The safeguards left to the House of Lords under the bill were worth something. But a swamping creation would sweep these safeguards away, and might also confront the next Conservative Government, intent upon undoing the damage, with a delaying radical majority in the Upper House. Furthermore, the effect of a mass creation, not because of the individuals concerned but because of the manner of their ennoblement, would be degrading to the House of Lords, to parliamentary institutions, and to the King. What of the suggestion that a mass creation was not possible? Lansdowne cited a statement which Crewe had made in the censure debate the previous night,[4] interpreted this as implying a very heavy creation, and asked Morley to confirm his

---

[4] ...but this I do feel compelled to say, that if we are to be forced, to my keen personal regret into giving advice which would have the effect of the creation of Peers we cannot pretend that the number to be so created could necessarily be limited by any newspaper list, of which there have been so many seen of late; nor would it necessarily have any reference whatever to any division lists of your Lordships' House which may be seen when the question of the Amendments once more comes before this House. All such lists will have become, if the lamentable necessity arises, altogether irrelevant, and all the various combinations of noble Lords opposite of which we read in our morning newspapers must be assumed to be at an end, because they have reference to an entirely different state of things.' (*Parliamentary Debates, Lords.* Fifth Series, vol. IX, col. 842.)

view. This Morley refused to do, saying that it was too delicate and important a matter to be dealt with by an intervention. Lansdowne concluded by referring to a long constitutional struggle ahead and the undesirability of divided counsels in the Unionist Party. He was followed by Halsbury who showed himself truculently sensitive to the charge of disloyalty, but who added little by way of argument, perhaps because his principal speech had been delivered in the censure debate. The Hansard report of his speech, however, is enlivened by frequent appearances of the splendid archaism 'forsooth!' He had not been born in 1823 for nothing. But on some observers his speech, in juxtaposition with that of Lansdowne, did not create a good impression.

'Lord Lansdowne,' Sir Almeric Fitzroy wrote, 'who always shines in a position of extreme difficulty, acquitted himself of the task he had to perform with the greatest tact, polish, dignity and address, and but for the fact that he appealed to a section of the House impenetrable to reason and proof to the dictates of prudence, his allocution could not have failed of success. It was lamentable to see his calm and dispassionate view of a very critical situation succeeded by a blunt appeal to blind passion, couched in terms of turgid rhetoric and senile violence.'[i]

Dr. Lang of York, who followed, stressing that he spoke only for himself, censured the Government and urged moderation with some force and more unction. Then came Salisbury, who placed upon Crewe's statement an entirely different construction from Lansdowne, again pressed Morley for clarification, and, failing to receive an answer, took this as further evidence that talk of a large creation was not to be taken very seriously. In any event, he somewhat surprisingly argued, if the radicals created 500 peers to serve their purpose, the Conservatives could easily do the same when their time came, so there would be no great disadvantage from their point of view. The other die-hard speakers that day were Willoughby de Broke, Bedford, Marlborough, Ampthill, Denbigh, Scarbrough, and Stanhope. Of these, Willoughby and Ampthill remained sceptical of the threat to create, whilst the two dukes and, to some extent, Stanhope thought that there could be many worse things than even the largest of mass creations. Marlborough said quite bluntly that he would prefer a big reinforcement to the 'purge' which Lansdowne had tried to force upon the House; Bedford believed that creation would advertise the despotic power that the majority in the Commons was arrogating to itself; and Stanhope thought, ingeniously and possibly correctly, that a Government majority in the Lords and the rapid implementation of the principal Liberal measures would result in the break-up of the coalition upon which the Government depended in the Commons. Within the die-hard ranks there was another conflict between the 'autocrats' and the 'democrats'. Some, like Ampthill and Bedford, persisted in the claim that their refusal to accept the will of the Commons was bound up with their determination to give the electorate an endless series of last words. Even on the Parliament Bill they could not admit that it had yet spoken with a decisive voice. Others, like Willoughby—and Halsbury would probably have agreed with him—faced the issue more frankly:

'... I suggest that all these conventions with regard to the Cabinet representing the House of Commons and the House of Commons representing the electors and the electors representing the nation are only applicable to ordinary legislation and become tyrannical if used to push through extraordinary legislation. When they are applied to legislation which is not only extraordinary but in our view absolutely unthinkable and impossible, then we cannot entertain that affection for representative government which we ordinarily extend to it. You may claim majorities if you like in favour of the Parliament Bill at a dozen General Elections, but that will not alter my view and I do not think it will alter the view of Lord Halsbury or those acting with us in this matter.'[j]

That was clear enough.

On the side of submission the Bishop of Winchester combined his moderation with a little more liberal feeling than his brother of York had shown, Lord Russell rebuked the Duke of Bedford and Lord Ampthill[5] for their desertion of the cause with which the name of Russell had once been associated, and Lord Ribblesdale gave the Government rather cooler support than might have been hoped for from the brother-in-law of the Prime Minister. But the speeches of note came from St. Aldwyn and Newton. The former attacked Halsbury's position with great vigour, both because he was convinced that no change of opinion had occurred in the country since the last general election and because he regarded the threat of a large creation as very real. But coupled with this attack upon the die-hards was another equally strong attack on the Government and upon more

---

[5]   Arthur Oliver Vivian Russell. Succeeded in 1884 to the peerage conferred upon Lord Odo Russell, H.M. Ambassador in Berlin in 1881.

surprising ground. In November, St. Aldwyn argued, Ministers should have advised the King to see the leaders of the Opposition, and it should have been suggested to him that in the event of his declining to give the promise asked for by Asquith and Crewe, Balfour and Lansdowne might be willing to form a Government. In failing so to act Ministers had shown neither common generosity nor common honesty in their dealings with the Sovereign. To the extent that this part of his speech increased Unionist feeling against the Government—and it was referred to with much approval by several subsequent die-hard speakers—it was not altogether helpful to Lord Lansdowne's cause.

Lord Newton was less equivocal, although his arguments were probably couched in too astringent a form to win many votes. He expressed himself tired of the constant public statements of profound mutual esteem to the accompaniment of which the two sections of the Unionist Party had assailed each other.

'To me these expressions of mutual esteem and affection are rather beside the point. As military metaphors are so much in vogue, I will say that I rather look upon it in this sort of light—as if a general were to call his principal officers together on the eve of a most important, if not fatal, engagement, and to give them his orders; and those officers were to reply, "Sir, we have the most profound admiration for your character; we respect you as a man, as a husband, and as a father, but as regards your orders we propose to act in a precisely different direction."'[k]

He touched the die-hards on a very raw spot by pointing out that it was only after another election had become clearly out of the question that they had taken up their fighting position. He stressed the very considerable advantage which could accrue to the more advanced sections of the Liberal Party from an actual creation, and warned his hearers against depending upon ridicule to deal with the Government in these circumstances. 'It seems to me highly probable that we shall have the ridicule and that the Government will have the Peers.'

Twenty minutes after midnight Lord Midleton moved the adjournment and the rest of the debate stood over until the following day. During this adjournment there was an important development. At Buckingham Palace it was feared that Lord Crewe's statement that the King had given the November undertaking with 'natural and legitimate reluctance' was encouraging the die-hards to believe that the Government might still be bluffing. Sir Harold Nicolson tells us that Lord Stamfordham, in particular, realised this danger, and that on the morning of Thursday, August 10, after consultation with the King, he wrote to Lord Morley stating that it was imperative to dispel this false idea. 'For this reason,' his letter continued, 'the King authorised me to suggest that some statement might be made by you—to the effect that in the event of the Bill being defeated the King would agree to a creation sufficient to guard against any possible combination of the Opposition by which the measure could again be defeated.'[1] Upon receipt of this letter Morley provided an exact form of words, submitted them to the King, received them back with his 'entire approval', and held his statement ready for the afternoon's debate. This, it seems clear, both from Stamfordham's letter and from a conversation which Sir Almeric Fitzroy held with Morley on the following day, was the true sequence of events, even though Morley suggests in his *Recollections*[m] that the initiative came from himself and not from the Palace. But his account was written well after the event.

Midleton opened on the second day, speaking for those who were with Lansdowne. He set himself to reply to Salisbury's speech of the previous day and showed how much more frightened of the die-hards than of the Government he had become by arguing that, if the division were to go wrong, a very large creation—much more than 200—would be necessary before there would be a certain passage for the bill. He then adduced a new argument, which was alike tactless and of doubtful validity. In the die-hard lobby, it was thought, would be many peers 'who are not, to say the least, of first experience in public affairs'. Perhaps five or ten such men might constitute the majority against the bill. Was it right that men of the sagacity of Lansdowne and Curzon should be overruled in such a way? The purpose of this was difficult to see. It was a form of dialectic which was hardly likely to convince the inexperienced and unsagacious 'backwoodsmen' themselves; and, as the Duke of Northumberland not unreasonably pointed out, the same argument could be applied, *mutatis mutandis,* to any close division in either House. It is not only when party revolts are organised and it is not only in the Upper House that the votes of stupid men count for as much as the votes of anyone else.

When Midleton had finished Rosebery rose and asked if there could not be a reply from the Government at this stage. Morley showed some reluctance to intervene until later—a fact which supports the view that the idea of a statement originated with the Palace and not with himself—but eventually rose, and wrapping a few rather ill-prepared sentences round his agreed statement, delivered a short speech. Most of it was built upon few or no notes, but when he came to the special passage he drew a sheet of writing paper from the pocket of his frock-coat and read carefully. The whole House gave him the closest of attention. 'If the

Bill should be defeated tonight His Majesty would assent—I say this on my full responsibility as the spokesman of the Government—to a creation of Peers sufficient in number to guard against any possible combination of the different Parties in Opposition by which the Parliament Bill might again be exposed a second time to defeat.'[n]

In response to a request from Selborne the statement was read a second time. 'That, I think, is pretty conclusive.' Morley added. And so, on the limited question, did every peer in the House whose mind was capable at that stage or assimilating a new point.

Rosebery came next, on a sudden impulse, he said, and with the intention of speaking for no more than a minute. He put his own gloss on a number of old arguments and urged the Lansdowne policy of submission, but without disclosing whether he himself would abstain or vote for the Government. The speech lasted a quarter of an hour. Milner was then put up to re-state the die-hard case in a form which could be compatible with the certain knowledge that Morley had just given the House. He did so by claiming that those who worked with Lord Halsbury had always taken into full account the possibility of a large creation; but it was necessary not to yield to a threat, however real, because the *threat* of creation was something which could be used again and again, whereas an actual creation would not in practice be possible to repeat. This was not compatible, on either score, with what many of the other die-hards had been saying, but, given the premises, it was a logically coherent argument.

Lord Camperdown followed and introduced a new note into the well-worn discussion. He was the first Unionist peer to announce in the House that he proposed to vote with the Government. As had been anticipated this provoked the Duke of

260

Norfolk to rise and say that he would therefore vote with the diehards. He had been prepared to abstain, but so strongly did he disapprove of Unionist votes for the Government that he would do everything in his power to neutralise their effect. It was thought that the Duke had a number of followers and Lord Halifax, who spoke immediately afterwards, made it certain that he had at least one.

Londonderry spoke in support of Lansdowne and then the Duke of Northumberland delivered the most extreme of diehard speeches. The bill should have been thrown out on second reading, Lansdowne's reform scheme was a great mistake, and the advocacy of the referendum a 'fatal error'. The general election results proved nothing because the electorate had been bribed by the reckless and corrupting financial policies of the Chancellor of the Exchequer. It would have been much better if the House of Lords had not given way in 1832, and it was essential that there should be no repetition of that mistake. He was answered by the new Duke of Devonshire, the nephew of the great Duke. The liberal tradition of the Cavendishes had become too weak for him not to deplore the bill and the behaviour of the Government, but it was still strong enough for him to join issue with the wild obscurantism of Northumberland. 'It is impossible for me,' Devonshire said, 'to regard the opinions and feelings of a large number of my fellow-citizens with the complete indifference which the noble Duke does.'[0] He refuted Milner's point that the threat of the prerogative might again be invoked for Home Rule or Welsh Disestablishment (Morley intervening to support him in dismissing such an idea) and strongly urged abstention with Lansdowne. For Unionist peers to vote in the Government lobby would be a 'repugnant and odious' proceeding, but the responsibility for preventing this was placed firmly on the shoulders of the die-hards.

There were only two more speeches in the general debate, both from die-hards and both of little note. Then, by agreement, the House came to the individual amendments. The first two, dealing with money bills, were disposed of with little debate and no divisions. Morley's motion 'that this House do not insist upon the said Amendment' was in each case accepted. He then moved the same motion in respect of the crucial amendment—Lord Lansdowne's amendment as it had come to be called—which excluded certain categories of bills from the normal operation of Clause Two. Upon this amendment a two-hour debate developed. The speeches were mostly short. The Earls of Meath and Plymouth began by pronouncing themselves on Lord Halsbury's side, the former in a speech of remarkable stupidity. The Archbishop of Canterbury then intervened for one minute to declare himself shocked by the levity or callousness with which some peers appeared to contemplate a wholesale creation and to announce that, contrary to his original intention, he would now vote with the Government. 'There was a ring of leadership in the tone,' Lord Halsbury's biographer wrote.*

Next came Lord St. Levan,[6] with an orthodox die-hard speech distinguished only by a pleasantly *simpliste* description of his

---

[6] When he rose to speak an incident uncommon in the practice of the House of Lords occurred. Lord Heneage, a Unionist 'hedger', rose also. Hansard records that 'As neither noble Lord gave way to the other, there were loud cries of "St. Levan" and "Heneage", but both still continued standing. Halsbury, careful of the interests of his followers, thereupon moved 'That Lord St. Levan be heard'. The Lord Chancellor put the question and there being louder shouts of 'Content' than of 'Not content' it was deemed to be carried. Heneage spoke next. Peers normally arrange amongst themselves the order in which they desire to speak, so that only one rises at a time.

relations with Lansdowne. 'In a kind of way we are not actually resisting Lord Lansdowne,' he said; 'we have followed his lead, only we have gone further. Lord Lansdowne said, "Come on", and we came on so hard and with such good will that we found it impossible to stop.'[q] Lord Heneage, in place of Lord Cromer, who was absent through illness, announced his intention of voting against the die-hards. The division was obviously near, and there then began a contest for the last word. Curzon, who had not previously spoken in the two days of debate, was the first and best justified contestant. He devoted his full effort to averting the catastrophe. His final words were an appeal to the peers 'to be very careful indeed before you register a vote which, whatever may be your emotions at this moment, when you look over it calmly, I do not say tomorrow but a month, three months or six months hence, you may find has wrought irreparable damage to the Constitution of this country, to your own Party, and to the State'.[r] It was for Curzon the final blow in a battle which had drained his great vitality and left him ill and exhausted.

Then, in rapid succession, came the other contestants, Halsbury, Rosebery, and Selborne. Halsbury had been provoked by Curzon but had nothing to add, and Selborne could offer only a few debating points, well below the level of the occasion. But the most unjustifiable intervention was Rosebery's. He offered no leadership. He based his statement on an argument of force only to himself and of no general validity. He had decided, however, to vote in the Government lobby and he could not forbear to tell the House of his great sacrifice and of the pain with which he made it.[7] At last he was down and so was Selborne.

---

[7] Lord Newton (*op. cit.*, p. 429) says that Rosebery concluded this speech by saying that he would never enter the precincts of the House again. In fact

It was a quarter to eleven and the suspense was nearly over. The division could be taken.

Even at this stage no one knew what the result would be. Everything clearly turned on the number of Unionists who would vote with the Government, even though this involved incurring the obloquy of the extremists without the compensation of a blessing from Lord Lansdowne. The bishops also provided an element of doubt, although it seemed highly likely that the majority of them would vote for the bill, following the lead of Dr. Davidson, who, Mrs. Asquith tells us, exerted great pressure on the general mass of peers, being 'cursed and blessed, as he moved from group to group, persuading and pleading with each to abstain'. From the same source we learn that 'some of Lord Murray's (the Master of Elibank) possible Peers watched from the gallery, hoping for rejection'.[5] Others, too, watched, but with different emotions. Lansdowne himself retired from the floor as soon as the division was called, and looked down from the gallery above the Throne. Curzon sat stiff in his place. Stamfordham waited anxiously to receive the news and return with it to the King.

During the division there were a few contradictory indications of the way things were going. Bishops and Unionists were seen entering the Government lobby in good number. But then there was a check to the flow from that lobby while a stream of peers still came from the other. Then again Willoughby de Broke, a teller for the 'Halsburyites', was seen with an anxious, downcast

---

the threat was made, not on this occasion, but at a much earlier stage in the proceedings on the bill; and, in any event, Rosebery was back on the day following the final division, inserting a 'solemn protest' in the book which is kept in the Lords (but rarely used) for this purpose.

face. In all there was no certainty until the Lord Chancellor read the figures. There was a silence of suspense for him to do so. 'Contents, 131; Not contents, 114,' he announced, and the struggle was over. The Government was home by seventeen votes, the die-hards were defeated, and there was to be no creation of peers.

Thirty-seven Unionists and thirteen prelates[8] had given decisive support to Morley's eighty-one Liberals. On the other side, Willoughby, despite the last-minute accession of the Duke of Norfolk's followers and the votes of the Bishops of Peterborough and Worcester, was nine down from the maximum support he had been promised.[9] The weight of argument deployed by the 'hedgers' may have had some effect here.

The division lists show most strikingly how complete had been the desertion of the Whigs. Halsbury had a great vote of magnates—seven dukes with none in the other lobby—and of those who bore famous political titles. Salisbury and Bute, Clarendon and Hardwicke, Lauderdale and Malmesbury were only some of those in this latter category. On the Government side there were many fewer. Chesterfield and Durham had a ring about them, and so perhaps did Spencer and Granville. For

---

[8] Three of these, the Bishops of Hereford, Birmingham, and Chester, supported the bill upon its merits.

[9] This was due to no lack of determination to record what votes were available. Sir Almeric Fitzroy informs us that 'two noble lords', one on either side, were very drunk and voted in that state. One was so bad that for a long time he was kept under supervision in a committee-room, and Lord Ilkeston, who graduated in medicine, was summoned to see him. On his appearance, however, the patient shouted, 'Take the—away; he wants to get two guineas out of me!' He was allowed to go into the division lobby. (*Memoirs,* II, pp. 460–1.)

the rest the list of 'Contents' read more like the *Directory of Directors* or a Lloyd George Honours List. Some of the great families of England were 'ditchers' and more were 'hedgers'. But for the first time in the advance to political democracy in this country there was hardly a patrician who would aid the process.

Immediate reactions to the vote were varied. The die-hards were mostly hysterical. Lady Halsbury refused to shake hands with Lansdowne when she and her husband met him on their way out of the House. There was organised hissing of some of the thirty-seven in the Carlton Club, and a plan for circulating lists of these 'traitors' to all the Unionist Clubs in the United Kingdom was seriously discussed. George Wyndham said 'We were beaten by the Bishops and the Rats', and Lord Robert Cecil suggested that the former category should be excluded from any reformed House of Lords. As for the latter category, the *Globe* expressed the hope that 'no honest man will take any of them by the hand again, that their friends will disown them, their clubs expel them, and that alike in politics and social life they will be made to feel the bitter shame they have brought upon us all'. And the *Observer* maintained the standard of invective by referring to 'the ignoble band, clerical and lay, of Unionist traitors, who had made themselves Redmond's helots'.

At Buckingham Palace the mood was very different.

'At 11.0.' the King wrote in his diary, 'Bigge returned from the House of Lords with the good news that the Parliament Bill had passed with a majority of 17. So the Halsburyites were thank God beaten! It is indeed a great relief to me—I am spared any further humiliation by a creation of peers.... Bigge and Francis have indeed worked hard for this result.'[t]

Next day he left to stay at Bolton Abbey in Yorkshire. While there he wrote of being saved 'from a humiliation which I should never have survived', and received a comforting letter from Lord Esher which spoke of 'the wisdom of Your Majesty's action in not swerving by an inch from the role of a Constitutional Sovereign', and added, 'Queen Victoria could not have done better, and would, I believe, not have done otherwise'.[u]

Elsewhere there were few repetitions of either the fury of the die hards or the extreme relief of the King. The general public remained as unexcited as it had been throughout the long struggle. The Balfourites were dispirited, and the Government, already occupied with Agadir, had no time for self-congratulation before it was plunged into the turmoil of a national railway strike. The sequence of events was a reminder that as the Liberals won their last great victory, purely political questions were becoming increasingly submerged in broader social and economic problems, and August, 1914, was casting its shadow ahead.

XIV

Epilogue

It is tempting to say that, with the Parliament Bill upon the statute book, everything went on much the same as before. But this would not be quite true. The more sweeping constitutional consequences which had been predicted did not, of course, occur. King Edward's view that the bill would mean the 'destruction of the House of Lords' proved quite unfounded. There was a certain falling off in attendance at debates, but the regularity of their appearances at Westminster had never been the most characteristic attribute of their lordships; and in other respects the Upper House continued to discharge much the same functions in much the same way as hitherto. Nor was there any decline in respect for the Lords as expressed through the willingness of outside persons, whether of great or of more limited distinction, to accept peerages. Indeed, in the decades since the Parliament Bill, it has become more than ever appropriate to apply to the House of Lords the words of the old hymn:

'There is room for new creations
In that upper place of bliss.'

Upon the development of the political parties the effect was substantial, although not in the most obvious directions. There was no great unleashing of Liberal power. The radical tide, discouraged by the National Insurance Bill, ebbed heavily in the country. The leaders of the Government were sated by office and lost their taste for its opportunities. They continued with their highly controversial measures, for they could hardly escape from the groove in which their course was set, but they did so without confidence and without hope. And the House of Lords, making full use of the powers remaining to it, ensured that such of these controversial measures as did not founder upon the Government's own incompetence were delayed until they could be submerged in the national unity of 1914. As a result, the Parliament Bill, designed as a prelude, has been left as the last monument of triumphant Liberalism. The concentration of radical purpose which its achievement demanded left the Government and their supporters exhausted but unable to rest. In retrospect, 1911 shines out as the last year of Liberal achievement. Thereafter the seeds of disunity and decay found fertile soil in which to settle.

Upon the Unionist Party the effect of the constitutional dispute was more dramatic. It was to change the leadership and to usher in a new era of violent speech and extra-constitutional action. While Balfour brooded on his wrongs at Bad Gastein during August and September, a permanent Halsbury Club was established and Leo Maxse[1] coined and published the slogan

---

[1] 1864–1932. Editor of the *National Review.*

which became abbreviated into three minatory initials 'B.M.G.' Had Balfour wished to ride out the storm he could no doubt have done so—at the price of personal discomfiture and loss of dignity a party leader is almost irremovable—but he chose otherwise. Recognising the revolt of the 'ditchers' for what it was, an expression of discontent with his leadership, he resigned, without warning but not without premeditation, on November 8. Lansdowne, more guilty but less sensitive, retained his position in the Lords.

Austen Chamberlain and Walter Long were the principal claimants to Balfour's position. But neither of them could command the general support of the party, although it seems likely that Long, despite Balfour's preference for Austen, would have obtained the majority in a straight contest. In the event, however, they both withdrew in favour of a third candidate, the Canadian-born Glasgow ironmaster, Bonar Law, who was then elected unanimously. He had held no office more important than that of Parliamentary Secretary to the Board of Trade, and he had become a Privy Councillor only five months previously. He was a compromise candidate, but not a moderate one. Although not associated with the 'ditcher' revolt, he was as complete a reaction against Balfour as it is possible to imagine. Where Balfour was detached, equivocal, and complex, Law was committed, partisan, and simple. Where Balfour was intellectually preeminent and personally magnetic, Law was pedestrian and unattractive. Where Balfour could always see a large part of his opponent's case, Law could see only the more salient features of his own. As a result, where Balfour hesitated, Law struck, and that was precisely what the Unionist Party of the day wanted. After six years of Opposition and three electoral defeats, they were too bitter and frustrated for Balfourian urbanity, the essential basis of which was a calm and confident expectation of power. With Bonar Law at their head they were no longer troubled with behaviour which was a relic from easier times. In the words of Asquith's biographers, 'he (Law) took an early opportunity of announcing that the era of compliments between politicians was ended'.[a] And with its end, the Unionist Party, enraged rather than discouraged by their defeat over the Parliament Bill, began to move ever faster towards extreme courses and threats of violence.

Since the Parliament Act has been in operation its Clause Two procedure, by which bills may be passed over the veto of the Lords after a delay of two years, has been fully used on three occasions. Its Clause One procedure, by which a money bill may so pass after a delay of a month, has never been used; and, indeed, the practical value of the Clause is not great, for the definition of a money bill, for the purpose of the Parliament Act, is clear but restrictive. Lord Ullswater, who as Mr. Speaker Lowther had first to apply the definition, said that he never had any difficulty in deciding whether to grant or withhold his certificate and that, ironically enough, the Finance Bill of 1909, which was the origin of Clause One, would have been refused its protection.[b] He and his successors took a similar view of many subsequent Finance Bills, so much so that between 1913 and the end of 1937 only twelve out of twenty-nine were considered to be money bills.[c] The others were held by the Speaker of the day to go beyond the 'imposition, repeal, remission, alteration or regulation of taxation'. Bills other than Finance Bills have secured certificates, but they have almost uniformly been measures of minor importance. Between the end of 1937 and the end of 1952 a rather higher proportion of Finance Bills have been afforded the protection of Clause One. Twelve have been certified; seven have gone up to the House of Lords without the Speaker's certificate.[2]

The fact that there has been no repetition of the peers' 1909 behaviour therefore owes more to a change of political climate than to the legal provisions of the Parliament Act. Even when the weak Labour Government of 1929 was in office, the House of Lords accepted the uncertified Finance Bill of 1930 quite as automatically, without a committee stage, as the certified Finance Bill of 1931. Bills dealing with finance have achieved immunity not so much because their lordships' power over some of them have been statutably limited to a delay of one month as because of a general recognition that the peers burned their fingers in interfering with the Budget of 1909.

Two of the three bills which have passed under the Clause Two procedure—the Established Church (Wales) Bill and the Government of Ireland Bill—were introduced by the Asquith Government in the session following that in which the Parliament Act had itself become law. In this same session a Temperance (Scotland) Bill was also introduced, and was so heavily amended by the Lords that the Government preferred to wait until it could be secured under the Parliament Act rather than accept these changes. When it was presented to the Lords for the second time, however, a compromise, reasonably favourable to the Government, was accepted by the Upper House; and the bill became law without the application of the Parliament Bill

---

[2] The following were in the former category: 1938; no. 2 of 1939; nos. 1 and 2 of 1940; 1941; 1943; 1944; 1945; no. 1 of 1946; nos. 1 and 2 of 1948; 1950. The remainder (no. 1 of 1939; 1942; no. 2 of 1946; 1947; 1949; 1951; and 1952) were not certified. I am indebted for this information to Mr. E. A. Fellowes, Clerk-Assistant to the House of Commons.

procedure. A Plural Voting Bill was introduced in 1913 and was rejected by the Lords both in that session and in the following one. The outbreak of war then prevented its being sent up for the third time, and there was therefore no formal invocation of the Parliament Act in this case.

The third bill actually to pass under the Parliament Act procedure was another Parliament Bill, restricting the period of suspensory veto to one year. It was introduced by the Attlee Government in 1947. The Iron and Steel Bill introduced in the session of 1948-49 was also considered a likely candidate for the application of Clause Two procedure—indeed one of the principal reasons for the amending Parliament Bill was to enable the Iron and Steel Bill to pass more quickly over the veto of the Upper House—but in the event a compromise was reached by which the Lords passed the steel measure subject to its operation being delayed until after the general election of 1950. As no earlier date of operation could be secured by use of the suspensory veto procedure there was no difficulty for the Government in the acceptance of this arrangement.

Only on the last of the three occasions on which the Parliament Bill was put to work did the procedure function smoothly. In the case of Welsh Church Disestablishment, the measure, first introduced on April 12, 1912, plodded a long course of three successive journeys through both Houses, consuming a vast amount of parliamentary time before becoming law after the statutory delay in the summer of 1914. But the statutory delay had consumed the whole of the time available for an important and bitterly contested change. The European War was then upon the country and the religious *status quo* in Wales was thought to be so obviously part of the price for national unity that it was unnecessary for the Unionists even to submit a formal demand for payment. The Nonconformists of the Principality, who had asserted their strength and shown their dissatisfaction with the Anglican Establishment in the clearest possible way at successive general elections had to wait until 1920 before a change could be effected. A statutory delay of two years and one month imposed upon a measure which in the opinion of those most intimately concerned was already long overdue extended itself, by using the limited time available for radical change (if the war had not broken out, a general election within the next few months might well have produced much the same result), into an effective delay of almost eight years.

The Home Rule Bill showed up the disadvantages (and dangers) of delay still more clearly. This measure, first introduced a day before the Welsh Church Bill, fell only a little behind it in the course of the three-circuit race. But during this period the questions raised by Home Rule dominated the whole of the political scene, dug a large dent in the 250-year old British tradition of the softening of conflicts, and provided striking support for the view that there are times when almost any swift settlement of an issue is better than a prolongation of controversy. Between April, 1912, and July, 1914, while the House of Lords used to the full its right of delay, a whole series of unprecedented political and constitutional dangers arose. Large-scale private armies were raised and trained, first in the North and later in the South of Ireland. A 'covenant', pledging resistance to an Act of Parliament and threatening the proclamation of an illegal provisional government in a part of the United Kingdom, was signed by more than half a million men and women, headed by a Privy Councillor and former Law Officer of the Crown. The leader of the Opposition, speaking of this threatened revolt, declared that he could imagine 'no length of resistance to which Ulster will go which I shall not be ready to support....' The King was urged to veto the bill when it came up for his assent and to dismiss his Ministers, replacing them by a 'caretaker' Government headed by either Rosebery or Balfour which would hold office during the course of a general election; and he was near to accepting both these pieces of advice. Prominent military servants of the Government, notably Sir Henry Wilson,[3] the Director of Military Operations, engaged in a constant intrigue with the Opposition and with the potential insurgents; largely as a result of misunderstanding, a large number of army officers, stationed at the Curragh, were organised into offering their resignations; and Asquith had himself to take over the War Office in an attempt to retrieve the situation.[4]

In all these ways the constitution showed signs of great strain. Nor did the detailed working of the Parliament Act procedure make it easier to remove any of the causes of friction during the period of delay. It became clear at least as early as the summer of 1913 that some arrangement for the special treatment of Ulster, or of a part of the province, was inevitable. How was this provision to be made? If it was brought forward

---

[3] 1864–1922. Chief of Imperial General Staff, 1918–22. Field-Marshal, 1919. Baronet, 1919. Assassinated in London by Irish terrorists.

[4] The former Secretary of State was J. E. B. Seely. He foolishly gave undertakings to the resigning officers suggesting that they would not be used to enforce the Home Rule Bill. This position could not possibly be accepted by the Government (even Grey wrote: 'I am inwardly boiling with indignation at this stupid prejudiced attempt to dictate policy to us and break us, for that is what it is really; and if it goes on I shall be for taking the hottest election, upon who is to govern the country, that ever has been in our time.' Trevelyan, *Grey of Fallodon,* p. 195.)

as an amendment during the bill's third passage through the Commons it could deprive the bill of the protection of the Parliament Act and cause the Government to start the wearisome process again at the beginning. The alternative was to incorporate the change in a parallel but independent amending bill. This was attempted, and in the third session the Lords were presented with a Government of Ireland (Amendment) Bill before the main measure. But substantial though the concession contained in this amending bill was (six years' exclusion for those districts which, in a plebiscite, expressed a wish for special treatment), the Lords could not resist the temptation further to amend until they had made the compromise measure quite unacceptable to the Government. A Buckingham Palace Conference failed to resolve the deadlock which was thereby created and only the outbreak of war and the suspension of the main bill saved the day. Otherwise the Government would have been faced with the unattractive alternatives of further holding up the main bill until they got their own amending bill under the Parliament Act or of putting into operation a highly controversial measure from some of the features of which they had publicly announced their desire to retreat.

In effect the delaying powers left to the House of Lords under the Parliament Act proved to be still more substantial in the case of the Home Rule Bill than in that of the Welsh Church Disestablishment Bill. Not merely an interval of five times the statutory period, but the Easter Rebellion of 1916, the destruction of the Irish Parliamentary Party, the outbreak of one civil war and the sowing of the seeds of another intervened before different men negotiated a different settlement in 1922. The evil of haste was given a wide berth.

After these excitements, the third measure to pass under the

Parliament Act—the amending Parliament Bill of 1947—had a very quiet passage into law. But it was a much tamed House of Lords which had to deal with it. After 1945 the peers enjoyed the same nominal powers as in the years immediately before 1914, but they did not enjoy the same confidence in their own position in the state. The second Parliament Bill did rather less than keep pace with the change of spirit which had already occurred. It first passed through the House of Commons in the autumn of 1947 and came up for second reading in the Lords at the end of January, 1948. The debate was adjourned in order that the Government might consider an Opposition suggestion for a Constitutional Conference and an attempt at an agreed solution. A few days later the Government announced its willingness to enter into such talks, and the conference was accordingly set up. It was slightly shorter-lived than the conference of 1910, but equally fruitless in its results. A measure of ill-defined agreement was reached on the future composition of the Upper House, but the conflict on powers was not resolved. The Government amended its demand for a maximum delay of twelve months from the date of a bill's first second reading in the Commons to one of nine months from the date of its first third reading, if that should prove to be a longer period. This concession was designed to cover a situation in which a bill had a slow passage through the Lower House. The Opposition, for its part, was prepared to advance as far as twelve months' delay from the first third reading. The difference of three months proved insuperable. It was not as slight as may appear to be the case, for the Government's proposals would have ensured the legislative utility of the fourth session of a radical Parliament, while the Opposition's offer would have confined this inviolability to the first three sessions.

Furthermore, as in 1910, this difference of principle shrouded an intense concern, on both sides, with a particular measure. The nationalisation of the iron and steel industry was as effective a bar to the agreement of Mr. Attlce and Mr. Churchill in 1948 as Home Rule had been to the agreement of Asquith and Balfour thirty-eight years earlier.

Foundering on this rock, the 1948 conference abandoned its work at the end of April. In June the interrupted second reading debate was resumed in the House of Lords, and the bill was rejected by 177 votes to 81. The Government was then confronted with the problem that, if it allowed parliamentary sessions to begin and end at the normal time, the bill would not become law under the processes of the first Parliament Act until a date dangerously near to the statutory end of the Parliament. Its choice of electioneering dates would be seriously impaired. A brief special session was accordingly summoned for September, 1948, during which the bill completed the second of its three rounds. On this occasion it was rejected by the peers by a vote of 204 to 34. The normal 1948-49 session was then extended until December, 1949, and the bill was able to complete its third lap in a leisurely way. It came before the Lords for the last time on November 29, was rejected by no votes to 37, and received the Royal Assent on December 16, the last day of the session and the last sitting day of the Parliament of 1945. This second Parliament Act has not yet been called into operation.

The Constitutional Conference of 1948, as has been noted, was concerned with the composition as well as the powers of the House of Lords. In the former aspect of its work it followed a trail which had been well-worn in the years since 1911. But all those who had trodden it had failed to reach their destination and been forced to retrace their footsteps. The Asquith

Government attempted to honour the terms of the preamble to its Parliament Act by setting up a Cabinet committee to consider reform. But no agreement was reached and no scheme emanated from the Government.[5] The next excursion was made by the Lloyd George Coalition, which appointed the all-party Bryce Conference in 1917. The result of their deliberations on this point was a unanimous suggestion that a majority of the places in a reformed House of Lords should be filled on a non-hereditary basis, but no further agreement. The most popular view in the conference, however, was that the occupants of these non-hereditary seats should be elected by the House of Commons or by a joint committee of both Houses.

In 1922 Lord Peel[6] brought forward a series of official proposals on behalf of the Coalition Government. These provided for a section of the Upper House to be elected by the hereditary peers, another section to be elected from outside,

---

[5] The lines upon which the 'reformers' were working are, however, indicated by some remarks of Haldane, recorded by Esher, in September, 1912. The Lord Chancellor, Grey, and 'a strong section of the Cabinet' wanted an Upper House of 160, a hundred of them to be directly elected by five large constituencies, operating under a system of proportional representation, twenty members to be selected by each of the two principal parties in the Commons, and the remaining twenty to be selected, preferably from Dominion and Colonial statesmen, by the two parties acting together. There was some doubt as to whether the powers of the new House should be those which the House of Lords had enjoyed before, or after, the Parliament Act. (Esher, *op. cit.*, vol. III, p. III.)

[6] 1867–1937. Unionist member for Manchester, South, 1900–6, and Taunton, 1909–12. Succeeded his father as 2nd Viscount Peel, 1912. Secretary of State for India, 1922–24 and 1928–29. First Commissioner of Works, 1924–28. Lord Privy Seal, 1931. Created 1st Earl of Peel, 1929.

and a third to be nominated by the Crown. But the reception was cool or hostile and the plan was not proceeded with. This became a common pattern. It applied to the proposals of Lord Chancellor Cave[7] in 1927, based upon the work of a Cabinet Committee, and to the unofficial plan of Lord Clarendon[8] in the following year. Both of these plans provided for an Upper House of about 350 members, 150 of whom were to be elected by the hereditary peers and 150 nominated by the Crown. Lord Clarendon made it clear that the latter 150 should be nominated in proportion to the strength of the parties in the House of Commons and should serve, unless re-nominated, for one Parliament only.

Lord Salisbury made the next attempt in 1933. He accepted the main outline of the two preceding plans, but left vague the method of choosing the second group of 150. There was a suggestion of indirect election through county councils. An essential part of these proposals was the return to the new Upper House of most of the powers which the House of Lords had lost under the first Parliament Act, and the exclusion for the future of any sudden change in the balance of the new House by the use of the prerogative or other means. As a result, Salisbury's scheme aroused bitter Opposition hostility and did not even secure official Conservative support.

---

[7] 1856–1928. Unionist member for Kingston-on-Thames, 1906–18. Solicitor-General, 1915–16. Home Secretary, 1916–19. Created 1st Viscount, 1918. Lord Chancellor, 1922–24 and 1924–28. Defeated Asquith for Chancellorship of Oxford University, 1925.

[8] b. 1877. 6th Earl. Succeeded his father, 1914. Chief Government Whip in the House of Lords, 1922–25. Governor-General of South Africa, 1931–37. Lord Chamberlain, 1938–52.

A feature of these inter-war reform plans was that, although in this they conflicted with one of the recommendations of the Bryce Conference, they would have left unimpaired the permanent Conservative majority in the Upper House. As such, the proposals naturally failed to interest the other parties. Their primary objection to the House of Lords was that it was partisan, with the fact that it was hereditary and archaic an added but essentially secondary irritant. Reconstruction which did not touch the fundamental point therefore appeared as little more than window-dressing by the Conservative Party.

During the Constitutional Conference of 1948 an attempt was made, in principle, to meet this difficulty. All the party representatives agreed that 'the revised constitution of the House of Lords should be such as to secure as far as practicable that a permanent majority is not assured for any one political party'.[d] As agreement upon powers was not reached, the need to give concrete shape to this principle did not arise; and had it done so it may be surmised that the task would have proved more difficult than the easy statement of approach may have suggested.

As a result of the failure of this conference the preamble of the first Parliament Act has entered upon its fifth decade of non-fulfilment. Nor is it easy to see the conditions for an agreed reform arising in the future. In a broad sense the positions of 1910 are still occupied by the contending parties in the state. The right, attracted by instinct and tradition to the existing hereditary House, contemplates a change only because its attachment to a powerful Second Chamber is still stronger. The left, distrustful of the existing archaism but interested above all in the supremacy of the Commons, sees the relationship between the two Houses, rather than the composition of the second, as the dominant issue, and is unwilling to accept a reform which might increase the prestige of an Upper House still essentially conservative. This is a deadlock which the nation has survived for some years, and the continuance of which it may face with a degree of equanimity.

Appendix A

A comparison between the geographical distribution of Liberal seats in 1906 and Labour seats in 1945

Adirect comparison of constituency with constituency is impossible. Population shifts have changed the character of many divisions and, through the redistribution which they have made necessary, have obliterated many more. The best that can be attempted are 'big city' and regional comparisons. The basis on which they have been made is that, in 1906, 'Liberal' seats are taken to be those in which Liberal, Labour or (in what is now the United Kingdom) Irish Nationalist candidates were elected, on the assumption that, without left-wing opposition, an orthodox Liberal could always have won a division for which a Labour or Nationalist representative was chosen; in 1945, on a similar assumption, 'Labour' seats are taken to be those to which Labour, ILP or Communist but not Liberal candidates were elected. These assumptions give for 1906, 438 out of 592, or 74%, of the seats in what is now the United Kingdom to the Liberal Party, and, for 1945, 402 out of a total of 640 seats, or 63%, to the Labour Party. In estimating the relative importance to the two parties of different areas this disparity between their absolute strengths over the country as a whole must be taken into account.

The drawing of satisfactory regional boundaries is not easy. A straightforward acceptance of those normally used for administrative purposes would amalgamate too many occupationally and socially disparate areas, and thus obscure important differences of political affiliation. The method employed has been to treat separately the County of London and eight other large cities; to amalgamate the East Midland towns of Nottingham, Leicester and Derby into one unit, the Lancashire parliamentary boroughs (other than Liverpool, Manchester and Salford) into another, the Yorkshire parliamentary boroughs (other than Leeds and Sheffield) into a third, and the Scottish burghs and districts (other than Edinburgh and Glasgow) into a fourth; and to divide the rest of the country into counties or small groups of similar counties. It has produced some clumsiness, but it has endeavoured to avoid the marriage of areas which are obviously incongruous.

The results of the comparison are given in the following table:

CITY OR REGION	1906		1945	
	Total no. of seats	No. held by Govt.	Total no. of seats	No. held by Govt.
County of London	62	42	62	49
Glasgow	7	5	15	10
Birmingham	7	0	13	10
Liverpool	9	3	11	8
Manchester and Salford	9	9	13	12
Sheffield	5	2	7	5
Leeds	5	5	6	5
Edinburgh	4	3	5	3

CITY OR REGION	1906		1945	
	Total no. of seats	No. held by Govt.	Total no. of seats	No. held by Govt.
Bristol	4	3	5	4
Nottingham, Leicester and Derby	7	7	9	9
Yorkshire Parliamentary Boroughs, excluding Leeds and Sheffield	14	11	16	16
Lancashire Parliamentary Boroughs, excluding Liverpool, Manchester and Salford	18	16	28	22
Scottish Burghs and Districts, excluding Edinburgh and Glasgow	20	17	13	10
Lancashire County divisions	23	16	18	11
Yorkshire County divisions	26	21	26	16
Durham and Northumberland	24	21	30	27
Potteries and Black Country[1], excluding Birmingham	21	17	21	20
Cheshire	11	11	13	4
Cumberland and Westmorland	8	7	6	3
Derbyshire, Nottinghamshire and Leicestershire County divisions	15	13	16	13

[1] Borough and County divisions of Staffordshire and parts of Warwickshire and Worcestershire.

CITY OR REGION	1906		1945	
	Total no. of seats	No. held by Govt.	Total no. of seats	No. held by Govt.
Herefordshire, Shropshire and Worcestershire (excluding part included in Black Country)	14	5	10	2
Lincolnshire and Rutland	11	7	10	3
Northamptonshire and Warwickshire (excluding Birmingham and part included in Black Country)	12	11	12	7
East Anglia[1]	27	24	18	12
Oxfordshire, Buckinghamshire, Bedfordshire, Hertfordshire and Berkshire	18	13	20	10
Middlesex, Essex and Kent	34	19	66	47
Surrey, Sussex and Hampshire	27	14	38	8
West Country[2]	46	38	38	11
Industrial Wales[3]	17	17	24	22
Rural Wales[4]	13	13	11	3

[1] Norfolk, Suffolk, Cambridgeshire and Huntingdonshire.
[2] Gloucestershire (excluding Bristol), Somerset, Wiltshire, Dorset, Devon and Cornwall.
[3] The counties of Monmouth, Glamorgan and Carmarthen.
[4] The remainder of Wales.

CITY OR REGION	1906		1945	
	Total no. of seats	No. held by Govt.	Total no. of seats	No. held by Govt.
Highland County divisions of Scotland[1]	15	15	14	1
Lowland County divisions of Scotland[2]	24	20	24	17
Six Counties of Northern Ireland	25	10	12	3
The Universities[3]	7	0	12	0

[1] Defined not in a strict racial sense but so as to include everything north of the northern boundary of Argyll and Perthshire.

[2] The remaining counties of Scotland.

[3] Excluding, for 1906, the two Dublin seats.

The results show that in the big towns, particularly Birmingham,[4] Liverpool and Sheffield, and the purely industrial areas, such as the North-East coast region, the Potteries and the Black Country, the strength of the Labour Party in 1945 was, on the whole, appreciably greater than that of the Liberal Party in 1906. The same was true of the Home Counties of Middlesex, Kent and Essex, those in which, between the wars, there was a great development of modern factories and working-class housing estates. In other industrial areas—South Wales, the Lancashire boroughs and the Scottish burghs—the absolute strength of the Liberal

---

[4] Joseph Chamberlain's 1906 achievement here, where he maintained all seven seats intact against the Liberal onslaught, is one of the most remarkable electoral feats in the history of British polotics.

Party was rather greater than that of the Labour Party, and the relative strengths of the two parties about the same. In more mixed areas, containing nevertheless a substantial mining or industrial ingredient, such as the county divisions of Nottingham, Leicester and Derby, and of Lancashire, Yorkshire, and the Lowland counties of Scotland, the same proposition is broadly true, although the Liberal preponderance was here a little greater. The largely agricultural region of East Anglia is also in this category.

In the South of England generally, excluding the large towns, both the Government of 1906 and that of 1945 were relatively weak, but the Labour Party was a great deal weaker than the Liberals had been. These tendencies are shown most strongly in the border counties of Hereford, Worcester and Shropshire, and in the residential counties of Surrey, Sussex and Hampshire. But the West Country breaks this pattern. Here the Liberals were overwhelmingly strong and the Labour Party equally strikingly weak. This was one of four regions where the differences between the 1906 and the 1945 results were so great as to make the one almost the converse of the other. The other three were Cheshire, the Highland counties of Scotland, and the rural parts of Wales. In the case of Cheshire, where the difference was in any case less great than in the other three, the discrepancy is at least partly to be explained by the growth of 'commuting' areas for Liverpool and Manchester which took place between the two elections. Its results look less odd if considered in conjunction with those of Liverpool. The other three areas have many features in common. They none of them have any substantial industry, they are all made up of scattered rural communities, and they all have relatively declining populations; two of them are strongly Nonconformist, and two of them are part of the 'Celtic fringe'.

The collectivism of modern left-wing politics has not appealed to them as did the more purely political aspects of Liberalism, and the Labour Party has so far decisively failed to succeed to their strong radical tradition.

The general conclusion must be that, geographically, the Liberal Party of 1906 was a good deal more broadly based than was the Labour Party of 1945. Apart from the Universities, there was no category of seats in 1906 in which the Liberal Party could not secure substantial representation. But the same claim could not be made for the Labour Party in 1945. As an illustration of this point an analysis is given of a special category of seats—the seaside resorts—in which left-wing candidates might be expected to do badly. In 1906 there were thirteen seats which fell within this category. The Liberals won eight of them. By 1945 there were eighteen such seats. But the Labour Party won only one of them, and that—Great Yarmouth—might almost be regarded as more a fishing town than a resort. In part, this difference may be due to the greater importance which the hotel and boarding-house trade had assumed by 1945 and to the franchise changes of 1918 which gave votes to the many elderly widows and spinsters who live in these towns. Nevertheless the difference between the two results is striking.

Appendix B

Seats where the party which won in the general election of 1906 was defeated in that of January 1910

Government to Opposition

Bath (two members)
Bedford
Berkshire, North or
   Abingdon
Berkshire, South or
   Newbury
Boston
Brighton (two members)
Buckinghamshire, South or
   Wycombe
Burnley
Buteshire
Camberwell, Peckham
Cambridge

Cambridgeshire, East or
   Newmarket
Chelsea
Cheshire, Wirral
Cheshire, Eddisbury
Cheshire, Knutsford
Chester
Christchurch
Colchester
Coventry
Cumberland, Cockermouth
Cumberland, Egremont
Denbigh District
Devonport (two members)

Dorset, North
Dorset, South
Essex, North or Saffron Walden
Essex, North-East or Harwich
Essex, East or Maldon
Essex, South-East
Exeter
Fulham
Glasgow, Central
Gloucester
Gloucestershire, East or Cirencester
Greenwich
Hackney, North
Hampshire, New Forest
Hampshire, Isle of Wight
Herefordshire, North or Leominster
Herefordshire, South or Ross
Hertfordshire, North or Hitchin
Hertfordshire, West or Watford
Huntingdonshire, South or Huntingdon
Huntingdonshire, North or Ramsey
Kensington, North

Kent, North-East or Dartford
Kent, South-West or Tonbridge
Kent, North-West or Faversham
Kidderminster
Kirkcudbrightshire
Lambeth, North
Lambeth, Brixton
Lancashire, South-West or South-port
Lincolnshire, East Lindsey or Louth
Lincolnshire, North Kesteven or Sleaford
Liverpool, Abercromby
Middlesex, Enfield
Middlesex, Harrow
Middlesex, Brentford
Norfolk, Mid-
Northamptonshire, South
Nottingham, East
Nottinghamshire, Bassetlaw
Oxfordshire, North or Banbury
Oxfordshire, Mid- or Woodstock
Oxfordshire, South or Henley
Paddington, North

Penryn and Falmouth

Perthshire, West

Portsmouth (two members)

Preston

Radnorshire

Renfrewshire, East

Rochester

St. Pancras, South

Somerset, Wells

Somerset, East

Somerset, Bridgwater

Southwark, West

Staffordshire, Leek

Staffordshire, West

Stalybridge

Suffolk, North or Lowestoft

Suffolk, North-West or
  Stow-market

Suffolk, South or Sudbury

Suffolk, South-East or
  Wood-bridge

Surrey, North-West or
  Chertsey

Surrey, South-West or
  Guildford

Surrey, South-East or
  Reigate

Sussex, North or East
  Grinstead

Sussex, South or
  Eastbourne

Tower Hamlets, Mile End

Tower Hamlets, Bow and
  Bromley

Walsall

Warwick and Leamington

Warwickshire, South-West
  or Stratford-on-Avon

Warwickshire, South-East
  or Rugby

Wednesbury

West Bromwich

Westmorland, North or
  Appleby

Westmorland, South or
  Kendal

Whitehaven

Wiltshire, North or
  Cricklade

Wiltshire, North-West or
  Chippenham

Wiltshire, East or Devizes

Wiltshire, South or Wilton

Wolverhampton, South

Worcestershire, Mid- or
  Droit-wich

Yorkshire, North Riding,
  Richmond

Yorkshire, West Riding,
  Ripon

Antrim, North

Tyrone, South

Sunderland (to *Independent Tariff Reform)*
Chatham *(from Labour)*
Finsbury, Central *(from Labour)*
Manchester, South-West *(from Labour)*
Nottingham, South *(from Labour)*
Northamptonshire, North *(from Labour)*

Preston *(from Labour)*
Sunderland (second seat) *(from labour)*
Wolverhampton, West *(from Labour)*
Woolwich *(from Labour)*
Tyrone, Mid- *(from Nationalist)*

Opposition to Government

Ayrshire, North
Blackburn
Darlington
Durham, South-East
Grimsby
Lanarkshire, Govan
Lanarkshire, North-West

Lancashire, North-East, Darvven
St. Andrews
Shoreditch
Stockton-on-Tees
Wick
Wigan *(to Labour)*

Changes Within Government Parties

Liberal to Labour
Derbyshire, North-East
Derbyshire, Mid-
Manchester, East
Sheffield, Attercliffe
Staffordshire, North-West

Labour to Liberal
Derby
Middlesbrough
Northumberland, Wansbeck

*Nationalist to Independent
Nationalist*
Cork, Mid-
Cork, North
Cork, North-East

Cork, West
Louth
Mayo, South
Monaghan, South
Westmeath, North

Net Changes

Liberals minus 108
Labour minus 6
Nationalists minus 8
Independent Nationalists plus 8
Government minus 115

Unionists plus 114
Independent Tariff Reform plus 1
Opposition plus 115

Appendix C

Seats which changed hands between the two 1910 elections

Government to Opposition

Ashton-under-Lyme
Birkenhead
Cardiff District
Cheshire, Altrincham
Cornwall, Bodmin
Cumberland, Eskdale
Darlington
Derbyshire, High Peak
Devon, Tavistock
Devon, Torquay
Devon, Ashburton
Dudley
Grimsby
Islington, North
King's Lynn *(from Independent Free Trade)*

Lancashire, Darwen
Lancashire, Newton *(from Labour)*
Leicestershire, Melton
Liverpool, Exchange
Montgomery District
Plymouth (two seats)
St. Andrews District
St. Helen's *(from Labour)*
St. Pancras, West
Salford, South
Warrington
Wigan *(from Labour)*

Opposition to Government

Bedford
Burnley
Camberwell, Peckham
Cambridgeshire,
   Newmarket
Cheltenham
Coventry
Cumberland, Cockermouth
Essex, Saffron Walden
Exeter
Kent, Dartford
Kirkaidbrightshire
Lincolnshire, Louth
Manchester, South-West
Oxfordshire, Banbury
Radnorshire
Rochester

Southwark, West
Staffordshire, Leek
Suffolk, Lowestoft
Sunderland (two seats) *(one
   Labour gain)*
Tower Hamlets, Mile End
Tower Hamlets, Stepney
Tower Hamlets, Bow and
   Bromley *(Labour gain)*
Tyrone, Mid- *(Nationalist
   gain)*
Wakefield
Whitehaven *(Labour gain)*
Wiltshire, Cricklade
Woolwich *(Labour gain)*
Dublin County *(Nationalist
   gain)*

Change Within Government Parties

Liberal to Labour
Fifeshire, West
NET CHANGES
Liberals minus 3
Labour plus 2

Nationalists plus 2
Government plus 1
Unionists minus 1
Opposition minus 1

Appendix D

Sources of passages quoted in the text

Chapter I

a J. A. Spender: *The Life of the Rt. Hon. Sir Henry Campbell-Bannerman*, vol. II, p. 191.

b ibid., p. 193.

c Leading article, December 11, 1905.

d Leading article, December 9, 1905.

e Leading article, December 23, 1905.

f *Parliamentary Debates, Commons*, Fifth Series, vol. 468, col. 174.

Chapter II

a Disraeli: *Sybil, or The Two Nations*, p. 26.

b Lord Edmund Fitzmaurice: *Life of the Second Earl Granville*, vol. II, p. 16.

c Memorandum to the Queen, dated April 7, 1894, quoted in the Marquess of Crewe's *Lord Rosebery*, vol. II, pp. 451–4.

d Emily Allyn: *Lords versus Commons*, p. 144.

e   *Parliamentary Debates, Lords*, Third Series, vol. 149, col. 1771.

f   Sir Robert Peel: *Private Papers*, vol. II, p. 224.

g   Letter to Lord Caernarvon, dated February 20, 1872, quoted in Lady G. Cecil's *Life of Robert, Marquess of Salisbury*, vol. II, p. 25.

h   Memorandum to the Queen, dated April 7, 1894, quoted in full in Crewe, *op. cit.*, vol. II, pp. 451–4.

i   *Crewe, op. cit.*, vol. II, p. 463.

Chapter III

a   Spender: *The Life of the Rt. Hon. Sir Henry Campbell-Bannerman*, vol. II, p. 270.

b   Memorandum quoted in Lord Newton's *Lord Lansdowne, a Biography*, p. 353.

c   ibid., 354–5.

d   Spender, *op. cit.*, vol. II, p. 277.

e   *Parliamentary Debates, Commons*, Fourth Series, vol. 162, col. 545.

f   *Parliamentary Debates, Commons*, Fourth Series, vol. 162, cols 522–3.

g   *Parliamentary Debates, Commons*, Fourth Series, vol. 167, cols. 1739–46.

h   Spender, *op. cit.*, vol. II, p. 312.

i   *Harry Jones: Liberalism and the House of Lords*, p. 110.

j   Spender, *op. cit.*, p. 313.

k   *Parliamentary Debates, Lords*, Fourth Series, vol. 166, cols. 703–4.

l   *Parliamentary Debates, Lords*, Fourth Series, vol. 173, col. 1235.

m   Spender, *op. cit.*, vol. II, p. 350.

n   ibid., pp. 353–5.

o   *Parliamentary Debates, Commons,* Fourth Series, vol. 176, col. 1507.

p   *Parliamentary Debates, Commons,* Fourth Series, vol. 176, cols. 929–30.

q   Spender, *op. cit.,* vol. II, pp. 367–8.

r   *Emily Allyn: Lords* v. *Commons,* p. 177.

s   *Spender, op. cit.,* vol. II, p. 377.

t   Dugdale: *Arthur James Balfour,* vol. II, p. 29.

u   Newton, *op. cit.,* pp. 367–8.

v   ibid., pp. 368–9.

Chapter IV

a   Thomson: *David Lloyd George, the Official Biography,* p. 178.

b   ibid., p. 182.

c   *Annual Register* for 1909, p. 6.

d   Thomson, *op. cit.,* p. 183.

e   Oxford and Asquith: *Fifty Years of Parliament,* vol. II, p. 69.

f   Quoted in Trevelyan's *Grey of Fallodon,* p. 170.

g   *Annual Register* for 1909, p. 145.

h   Margot Asquith: *Autobiography,* vol. II, p. 124.

i   Sir Charles Petrie: *The Life and Letters of the Rt. Hon. Sir Austen Chamberlain,* vol. I, pp. 228–9.

j   Margot Asquith, *op. cit.,* vol. II, p. 122.

k   P. rie, *op. cit.,* vol. I, p. 228.

l   *Annual Register* for 1909, p. 106.

m   *The Times,* July 31, 1909.

n   Emily Allyn: *Lords versus Commons,* p. 180.

o   *Annual Register* for 1909, p. 186.

Chapter V

a   *Annual Register* for 1909, p. 192.

b   Oxford and Asquith: *Fifty Years of Parliament*, vol. II, p. 73.

c   Newton: *Lord Lansdowne, a Biography*, p. 380.

d   *Annual Register* for 1909, p. 221.

e   *The Times*, October 11, 1909.

f   Newton, *op. cit.*, p. 376.

g   Letter to Lord Lansdowne, dated October 8, quoted in Newton, *op. cit.*, p. 377.

h   Birkenhead: *Frederick Edwin, Earl of Birkenhead*, vol. I, p. 198.

i   *Parliamentary Debates, Commons*, Fifth Series, vol. 12, cols. 2122, 2123.

j   Askwith: *Lord James of Hereford*, p. 300.

k   *Parliamentary Debates, Lords*, Fourth Series, vol. 4, col. 1039.

l   *Parliamentary Debates, Lords*, Fourth Series, vol. 4, cols. 1038, 1042.

m   J. Hugh Edwards: *David Lloyd George*, vol. I, p. 321.

n   Dugdale: *Arthur James Balfour*, vol. II, p. 42.

o   Fitzroy: *Memoirs*, vol. I, p. 389.

Chapter VI

a   Spender and Asquith: *Life of Lord Oxford and Asquith*, vol. I, p. 261.

b   ibid., vol. I, pp. 268–9.

c   J. H. Edwards: *David Lloyd George*, vol. I, p. 323.

d   *Annual Register* for 1910, p. 4.

e   Ensor: *England, 1870–1914*, p. 418.

f   *Annual Register* for 1909, p. 269.

g   ibid., p. 268.

h   *Annual Register* for 1910, p. 11.

i   *Petrie: Life and Letters of Sir Austen Chamberlain*, vol. I, p. 237.

j   *Annual Register* for 1910, p. 6.

k   ibid., p. 13.

l   Petrie, *op. cit.*, vol. I, p. 241.

Chapter VII

a   Spender and Asquith: *Life of Lord Oxford and Asquith*, vol. I, p. 268.

b   Memorandum quoted in full in Spender and Asquith, *op. cit.*, pp. 261–2.

c   *Parliamentary Debates, Commons*, Fifth Series, vol. 14, cols. 55–6.

d   Spender and Asquith, *op. cit.*, vol. I, p. 273.

e   *Annual Register* for 1910, p. 25.

f   ibid., p. 56.

g   Quoted in Maurice's *Haldane, 1856–1913*, pp. 260–1.

h   Margot Asquith: *Autobiography*, vol. II, p. 131.

i   Spender and Asquith, *op. cit.*, vol. I, p. 271.

j   *Parliamentary Debates, Commons*, Fifth Series, vol. 16, col. 1548.

k   Quoted in Spender and Asquith, *op. cit.*, vol. I, p. 278.

Chapter VIII

a   Newton: *Lord Lansdowne*, p. 363.

b   ibid., p. 385.

c   ibid., p. 386.

d   *Parliamentary Debates, Lords*, Fifth Series, vol. 5, cols. 167–8.

e   Newton, *op. cit.*, p. 392.

f   Petrie; *The Life and Letters of Sir Austen Chamberlain*, vol. I, p. 251.

g   Oxford and Asquith: *Fifty Years of Parliament*, pp. 86–8.

h   Nicolson: *King George V*, p. 131.

Chapter IX

a   Spender and Asquith: *Life of Lord Oxford and Asquith*, vol. I, p. 285.

b   *Parliamentary Debates, Commons*, Fifth Series, vol. 19, col. 2529.

c   Newton: *Lord Lansdowne*, p. 401.

d   Nicolson: *King George V*, p. 132.

e   Petrie: *Life and Letters of Sir Austen Chamberlain*, vol. I, pp. 256–7.

f   Spender and Asquith, *op. cit.*, vol. I, p. 289.

g   Newton, *op. cit.*, p. 398.

h   Ensor: *England, 1870–1914*, p. 423.

i   Newton, *op. cit.*, p. 400.

j   Spender and Asquith, *op. cit.*, vol. I, p. 289.

jjj   Nicolson, *op. cit.*, p. 133.

k   Dugdale: *Arthur James Balfour*, vol. 11, p. 45.

l   Spender and Asquith, *op. cit.*, vol. I, p. 290.

m   Petrie, *op. cit.*, vol. I, p. 254.

n   ibid., p. 255.

o   Spender and Asquith, *op. cit.*, vol. I, p. 291.

p   Letter to his wife, quoted in Spender and Asquith, *op. cit.*, vol. I, p. 291.

q   Newton, *op. cit.*, p. 401.

r   Ensor, *op. cit.*, pp. 423–4.

s   Birkenhead: *Frederick Edwin, Earl of Birkenhead*, vol. I, p. 205.

t   Petrie, *op. cit.*, vol. I, p. 256.

u   Margot Asquith: *Autobiography*, vol. II, p. 144.

v   Petrie, *op. cit.*, vol. I, p. 254.

w   Birkenhead, *op. cit.*, vol. I, p. 203.

x Spender and Asquith, *op. cit.*, vol. I, p. 287.

y Nicolson, *op. cit.*, p. 131.

z Petrie, *op. cit.*, vol. I, pp. 257–8.

aa Lloyd George: *War Memoirs*, vol. I, p. 36.

bb ibid., vol. I, p. 37.

cc *Journals and Letters of Reginald, Viscount Esher*, vol. III, p. 30.

dd Dugdale, *op. cit.*, vol. II, p. 55.

ee ibid., vol. II, p. 56.

ff Birkenhead, *op. cit.*, vol. I, p. 205.

gg ibid., p. 207.

hh ibid., p. 206.

ii Petrie, *op. cit.*, vol. I, p. 258.

jj Lloyd George, *op. cit.*, vol. I, p. 36.

kk Spender and Asquith, *op. cit.*, vol. I, p. 287.

ll Margot Asquith, *op. cit.*, vol. II, p. 143.

Chapter X

a Nicolson: *King George V*, p. 134.

b ibid., p. 133.

c ibid., p. 130.

d ibid., p. 134.

e ibid.

f Spender and Asquith: *Life of Lord Oxford and Asquith*, vol. I, p. 297.

g Nicolson, *op. cit.*, p. 137.

h ibid., pp. 137–8.

i ibid., p. 135.

j ibid., p. 129n.

k ibid., p. 138.

l ibid., p. 129*n*.

m   Newton: *Lord Lansdowne*, p. 408.

n   Margot Asquith: *Autobiography*, vol. II, p. 145.

o   Esher: *Journals and Letters*, vol. III, p. 36.

p   ibid., vol. III, p. 65.

q   Nicolson, *op. cit.*, p. 138.

r   Fitzroy: *Memoirs*, vol. II, p. 423.

s   Esher, *op. cit.*, vol. III, p. 34.

t   Nicolson, *op. cit.*, p. 133.

u   Newton, *op. cit.*, p. 410.

v   *Parliamentary Debates, Lords*, Fifth Series, vol. 6, col. 746.

w   Esher, *op. cit.*, vol. III, p. 33.

x   Newton, *op. cit.*, p. 405.

y   *Annual Register* for 1910, p. 238.

z   ibid., p. 238.

aa   ibid., p. 254.

bb   ibid.

cc   Spender and Asquith, *op. cit.*, vol. I, p. 299.

dd   Petrie: *Life and Letters of Sir Austen Chamberlain*, vol. I, p. 261.

ee   *Annual Register* for 1910, p. 252.

ff   Petrie, *op. cit.*, vol. I, p. 269 and p. 272.

gg   Ensor: *England, 1870–1914*, p. 426.

hh   ibid., p. 427.

Chapter XI

a   Spender and Asquith: *Life of Lord Oxford and Asquith*, vol. I, p. 302.

b   Esher: *Journals and Letters*, vol. III, pp. 41–4.

c   Spender and Asquith, *op. cit.*, vol. I, pp. 305–6.

d   Newton: *Lord Lansdowne*, pp. 410–11.

e   ibid., p. 411.

f *Parliamentary Debates, Commons*, Fifth Series, vol. 22, cols. 567–70.

g *Annual Register* for 1911, p. 39.

h ibid., p. 39.

i ibid., p. 104.

j Newton, *op. cit.*, p. 415.

k *Parliamentary Debates, Lords*, Fifth Series, vol. 8, col. 670.

l *Parliamentary Debates, Commons*, Fifth Series, vol. 25, col. 1694.

m ibid., Fifth Series, vol. 25, cols. 1772, 1774.

n *Annual Register* for 1911, p. 145.

o ibid., p. 151.

Chapter XII

a Spender and Asquith: *Life of Lord Oxford and Asquith*, vol. I, p. 310.

b Nicolson: *King George V*, pp. 152–3.

c Ronaldshay: *The Life of Lord Curzon*, vol. III, p. 56.

d Nicolson, *op. cit.*, p. 152.

e Dugdale: *Arthur James Balfour*, vol. II, p. 48.

f Wilson-Fox: *Earl of Halsbury*, p. 232.

g Newton: *Lord Lansdowne*, p. 419.

h Wilson-Fox, *op. cit.*, pp. 234–5.

i Quoted in Spender and Asquith, *op. cit.*, vol. I, pp. 312–13.

j Newton, *op. cit.*, pp. 422–3.

k ibid., p. 423.

l Biggs-Davison: *George Wyndham*, p. 208.

m Quoted in Dugdale, *op. cit.*, vol. II, pp. 50–1.

n Wilson-Fox, *op. cit.*, pp. 245–6.

o Newton, *op. cit.*, p. 425.

p ibid., p. 426.

q   Petrie: *Life and Letters of Sir Austen Chamberlain*, vol. I, p. 283.

r   Ronaldshay, *op. cit.*, vol. III, p. 57.

s   Margot Asquith: *Autobiography*, vol. I, p. 148.

t   *Parliamentary Debates, Commons*, Fifth Series, vol. 28, cols. 1482, 1483.

u   Wilson-Fox, *op. cit.*, p. 244.

v   Nicolson, *op. cit.*, p. 153.

w   Blunt: *My Diaries 1888–1914*, pp. 770–1.

x   Wilson-Fox, *op. cit.*, p. 235.

y   *Parliamentary Debates, Lords*, Fifth Series, vol. 9, col. 888.

z   Wilson-Fox, *op. cit.*, p. 250.

aa   Quoted in Petrie, *op. cit.*, vol. I, p. 279.

bb   ibid., vol. I, p. 281.

cc   Wilson-Fox, *op. cit.*, p. 258.

dd   Dugdale, *op. cit.*, vol. II, p. 61.

Chapter XIII

a   Wilson-Fox: *Earl of Halsbury*, pp. 266–7.

b   *Parliamentary Debates, Commons*, Fifth Series, vol. 29, col. 817.

c   Fitzroy: *Memoirs*, vol. II, pp. 457–8.

d   *Parliamentary Debates, Lords*, Fifth Series, vol. 9, col. 836.

e   Spender and Asquith: *Life of Lord Oxford and Asquith*, vol. I, p. 323.

f   Wilson-Fox, *op. cit.*, pp. 258–9.

g   *Parliamentary Debates, Commons*, Fifth Series, vol. 29, col. 981.

h   Spender and Asquith, *op. cit.*, vol. I, pp. 326–7.

i   Fitzroy, *op. cit.*, vol. II, pp. 458–9.

j   *Parliamentary Debates, Lords*, Fifth Series, vol. 9, col. 934.

k   ibid., Fifth Series, vol. 9, col. 950.

l   Nicolson: *King George V*, p. 154.

m   Morley: *Recollections*, vol. II, p. 351.

n   *Parliamentary Debates, Lords*, Fifth Series, vol. 9, col. 1000

o   ibid., Fifth Series, vol. 9, cols. 1037–8.

p   Wilson-Fox, *op. cit.*, p. 275.

q   *Parliamentary Debates, Lords*, Fifth Series, vol. 9, col. 1062.

r   ibid., Fifth Series, vol. 9, col. 1070.

s   Margot Asquith: *Autobiography*, vol. II, p. 154.

t   Quoted by Nicolson, *op. cit.*, p. 135.

u   Esher: *Letters and Journals*, vol. III, p. 57.

Chapter XVI

a   Spender and Asquith: *Life of Lord Oxford and Asquith*, vol. I, p. 351.

b   Ullswater: *A Speaker's Commentary*, vol. II, p. 103.

c   Jennings: *Parliament*, p. 402.

d   Cmd. 7380, p. 3.

Acknowledgements

The author wishes to acknowledge with thanks the permission of the following individuals and publishers to quote from the books listed:

The Life of Sir Henry Campbell-Bannerman, by J. A. Spender: the owners of the copyright and Messrs. Hodder and Stoughton.

Life of Lord Oxford and Asquith, by J. A. Spender and Cyril Asquith: Lord Asquith of Bishopstone: Mr. Stephen Spender and Hutchinson & Co. (Publishers), Ltd.

Arthur James Balfour, by Blanche E. C. Dugdale: Lord Balfour and Hutchinson & Co. (Publishers), Ltd.

Fifty Years of Parliament, by Lord Oxford and Asquith: Cassell & Co., Ltd.

The Life and Letters of Sir Austen Chamberlain, by Sir Charles Petrie: the author.

Autobiography, by Margot Asquith: Eyre & Spottiswoode (Publishers), Ltd.

Life of Lord Lansdowne, by Lord Newton: Macmillan & Co., Ltd.

The Life of Lord Halsbury, by A. Wilson-Fox: Chapman & Hall, Ltd.

King George V, by Harold Nicholson: the author.

Life of Lord Rosebery, by Lord Crewe: John Murray (Publishers), Ltd.

My Diaries, by Wilfrid Scawen Blunt: Martin Secker & Warburg, Ltd.

Frederick Edwin, Earl of Birkenhead, by the present Lord Birkenhead: the author.

David Lloyd George, the Official Biography, by Malcolm Thomson: the author.

George Wyndham, by John Biggs-Davison: the author.

Journals and Letters of Reginald, Viscount Esher: the present Lord Esher and Nicholson & Watson, Ltd.

A NOTE ON THE AUTHOR

Elected to Parliament as a Labour member in 1948, Roy Jenkins (B: 1920) served in several major posts in Harold Wilson's First Government and as Home Secretary from 1965–1967. In 1987, Jenkins was elected to succeed Harold Macmillan as Chancellor of the University of Oxford following the latter's death, a position he held until his own death in 2003. Jenkins grew to political maturity during the twilight of a great age of British parliamentary democracy. As much as Churchill, though in quite a different way, Jenkins was from the cradle a creature of the system that nurtured Palmerston and Disraeli, Gladstone, Asquith and Lloyd George.

Made in the USA
Middletown, DE
15 April 2022

64306263R00194